Beating the Traffic

Josephine Butler and Anglican Social Action on Prostitution Today

Edited by Alison Milbank

George Mann Publications

Published by
George Mann Publications
Easton, Winchester,
Hampshire SO21 1ES
01962 779944

A CIP catalogue record for this book
is available from the British Library

ISBN 9780955241543

Back cover: Copy by E H Odell of the crayon portrait by
George Richmond 1851. Courtesy of Liverpool University Library.

George Mann Publications

Contents

A Message from the
Chair the Archbishops' Council's Public Affairs Division

The work of Josephine Butler in campaigning for recognition of the individual worth of women who are caught up in prostitution is an important part of 19th century church history. The challenge that she put to the Church and society was both radical and prophetic.

In these essays each of the authors draws out elements of the story of Josephine Butler and her campaigns. The fact that the issues of the 19th century are still being realised in the 21st century remind the reader that there is no place for complacency.

The realities of prostitution are a challenge to any thinking Christian and if we look to Josephine Butler for inspiration it is possible that we might be energised to take action.

Not the least of which will be to recognise the 'God given character' which she saw in prostitutes. The challenge for today is to be inspired by Josephine's vision to ensure that her message is recovered and interpreted for our own time.

Rt Revd Dr Tom Butler, Bishop of Southwark

Acknowledgements

This project owes its genesis to the Dioceses of Winchester and Newcastle, and to the inspiration of the Venerable John Guille, Archdeacon of Winchester. Those of us who took part in the colloquium at St Deiniol's Library in September 2006 were invited by him, by Jane Fisher, Director of Social Transformation in Winchester Diocese, and by Professor Michael Wheeler, Lay Canon and member of Chapter of Winchester Cathedral. Professor Wheeler chaired our sessions and gave the whole event a sense of coherence and purpose. The Josephine Butler Memorial Trust most generously supported us financially and by taking part themselves in our deliberations. Our thanks go to all those involved in the St Deiniol's conversations, many of whom are not represented here as authors but whose contributions were most helpful.

In the production of this book, our thanks are especially due to the Venerable John Guille for overseeing its gestation, and to George Mann for his kindness and expertise. Sophie Hacker generously gave us use of her painting for the cover design. Among the librarians who have assisted us are those of the Women's Library, Cambridge University Library, Liverpool University Library, The John Rylands Library of Manchester University, St Deiniol's Library and the British Library.

Introduction

Alison Milbank

Writing in 1977, the East End priest and founder of a refuge for prostituted women, Joseph Williamson, called Josephine Butler, 'the forgotten saint', but that is far from the case today.[1] Where once she might have seemed a relic from another age in her battles against the Contagious Diseases Acts and her attempts to prove that girls were being sold into sexual slavery, Butler and her work have taken on a new relevance in the era of globalisation. Now it is easier than ever before to persuade impoverished and desperate people to risk life and the law to travel illegally to countries where they may be exploited, blackmailed, and sold into forms of modern debt-bondage. Prostitution is one of the most successful forms of trafficking today because it carries fewer risks than trade in other illegal goods, such as drugs, arms, or endangered species of animals.[2]

In the year which marked the centenary of Butler's death in 1906, the dioceses of Newcastle and Winchester, with the support of the Josephine Butler Memorial Trust, brought together a range of scholars and activists to discuss the ongoing significance of Josephine Butler in work with women involved in prostitution. The 'Faith in the City' report of 1986 had led the then bishops of Winchester and Newcastle to 'twin' their dioceses, as one way of responding to the north/south divide. Josephine Butler, who was born in what became the Newcastle diocese and spent her later years in the Close at Winchester, was a figure around which the dioceses might explore the current challenge to the churches posed by prostitution and human trafficking. The colloquium at St Deiniol's Library at Hawarden, which was inspired by the Revd John Guille, Archdeacon of Winchester and chaired by Professor Michael Wheeler, Lay Canon of Winchester, included theologians, literary critics and historians, those involved in inner-city ministry, settlements or youth work training, Diocesan Social Responsibility officers, and activists in the field of human trafficking. The essays in this volume represent some of our thinking, and we hope to aid the Anglican Church and other faith groups involved in this complex and difficult area.

Josephine Butler and Prostitution

Josephine Grey was born in 1828 into an upper-class but radical and devout Northumbrian family, who were highly active with Thomas Clarkson in the movement to abolish slavery.[3] Her family had strong links to Moravianism, Methodism and Congregationalism, although they worshipped at their local parish church. Butler herself is impossible to characterise in terms of churchmanship: her spirituality had both catholic and evangelical elements; she told a Roman cardinal that her church had the real presence of Christ in the eucharist, but equally shared the sacrament with Geneva free church people. Her closest colleagues were often Quakers and members of the Salvation Army. As an imaginative child, the young Josephine was quick to imagine the tortures of a slave existence, including the sexual services that female slaves were called upon to perform. A passion against injustice was her family inheritance, as several of the contributors to this volume point out. After her marriage to George Butler, who became an Anglican priest, she moved to Oxford, in which largely masculine society she was brought up against the unfairness of the double standard in sexual relations then prevalent. It was at Oxford that she first took a 'fallen woman' into her home, when she employed a convicted infanticide after her discharge from prison.

At Cheltenham, where George Butler had been appointed as Vice-Principal of Cheltenham College, he and Josephine were the horrified witnesses of the fatal fall of their young daughter Eva from the banisters, and this trauma led Josephine Butler towards solidarity with the wretched. After arriving in Liverpool, she sought out the company of women in Brownlow Hill Workhouse, and so began her involvement with prostituted women.[4] She would take those too sick to be given places in existing refuges into her own home, and founded enlightened communities for the fit and able.

At the same time Butler became involved in attempts to gain access for women to higher education, leading the North of England Council for Promoting the Higher Education of Women, which sought to raise the status and training of governesses and schoolmistresses. She was also involved in presenting the petition for access to university examinations at Cambridge, and in agitating through The Married Women's Property Committee for women to be allowed to own property and earn money in their own right. Later, she would argue that women needed the suffrage if they were to achieve social and professional equality.

As a result of the public prominence into which all this political work had brought her, Josephine Butler was approached to lead the Ladies' National Association for the Repeal of the Contagious Diseases Acts. A series of Acts, beginning in 1864, sought to limit the spread of venereal disease among the army and navy by forcible registration and internal examination of women in towns with regiments nearby or in naval ports. If found to have such a disease, the women were detained in lock hospitals for three months, a period which was later extended to nine months. A group of influential doctors and others sought both to extend the Acts to all areas, and to move towards a licensing system for legalised brothels.[5] This battle to have the Acts repealed was the 'Great Crusade' of Butler's life, and it took until 1883 to have the offensive elements of coercion removed from the legislation; the Acts themselves were not fully repealed until 1886.

This campaign drew together all the threads of Butler's interests: her practical care of prostituted women and desire to give them self-respect and dignity and the comfort of a real home; her public work to raise the educational reach and ensure the independence of working women. It also spoke to her abolitionist approach to political issues, which for Butler, as for so many in Britain and America, had a religious basis. She named her daughter Evangeline after the heroine of Harriet Beecher Stowe's abolitionist tale, *Uncle Tom's Cabin* (1852), and her son, Augustine, after Eva's martyred father in the same novel. Stowe's Eva is a child who makes strong friendships with the enslaved and opposes their enslavement but who also seeks their conversion as an essential element in their human flourishing. Butler too spoke of Jesus to the women she made friends with, not so much to bring them to repentance as to reveal to them their value in God's eyes. For Butler, forcible examination and detention was a form of slavery, which, moreover, turned women of all sorts into the fixed identifiable status of prostitute. Not only was repeal of the Acts a matter of simple justice and human rights, it was also a religious crusade, to restore the Divine image in oppressed womanhood.

If Butler deserves the title 'saint', one reason is for her courageous endurance of the loss of caste and reputation and the opprobrium that her stance and its public nature earned her. She became a social pariah, was publicly vilified in the press, and received a number of death threats. Her husband lost any chance of the clerical preferment that his intellect and vision deserved, but he supported his wife unreservedly. Butler describes some of her adventures in *Personal Reminiscences of a Great Crusade* (1896), which included dealing with mob violence on a number of occasions. Butler was a brilliant campaigner: using by-elections to put up candidates on the repeal ticket, marshalling petitions of the great and good, travelling the country to speak to working people's groups. She was, by all accounts a charismatic speaker, deriving her power from a combination of evangelical fervour and incisive marshalling of facts. Above all, her own potent faith and obvious love for the women affected by the Acts spoke for her, even in the dryly masculine atmosphere of the Royal Commission of 1870-71, to which she gave evidence. She was not fully prepared on that occasion for the substantiation required for her assertions, but learnt quickly, so that later affidavits to the police or government were carefully put together.

It was as a result of her repeal work that Butler became aware of the situation on the Continent, in countries such as France, Italy and Switzerland, where equivalents to the Contagious Diseases Acts were one arm of State legislation of prostitution. Butler visited hosts of European brothels (as she also did in Britain), as well as the notorious St Lazare prison in Paris, which housed women who had not registered as prostitutes, or who resisted examination. Her experience in Paris was so traumatic that she rarely spoke of it. Women under this regulatory system, Butler discovered, were treated as if they were not human at all, but mere objects. Butler became involved in a European movement for repeal, the British, Continental and General Federation, founded in 1875, and which sought 'the abolition of female slavery and the elevation of public morality among men'.[6]

One aspect of the Continental legalised system that horrified Butler was the prevalence of child prostitution, despite its ostensible illegality. Not only was the St Lazare full of very young girls, but Butler visited an institution for hundreds of former child prostitutes, most of whom were aged from five to eleven years. Furthermore, the low age of consent in Britain – twelve years – compared to the Continent made British girls a saleable commodity abroad, and Butler and her allies obtained evidence of what would now be called human trafficking. According to Jordan's biography, Butler nursed a number of girls rescued and brought back to Britain in her own home.[7] In 1880 Butler became involved in a complex trial against Belgian brothel owners and certain police officials for trafficking offences. Following on from this successful prosecution, Butler expected stronger legislation in Britain to prevent such abuses, including raising the age of consent, but it was not forthcoming. She therefore joined forces with William Stead, the editor of the somewhat inflammatory *Pall Mall Gazette*, to prove the existence of the trade in children by sending a former procuress, Rebecca Jowett, with Stead to buy a young girl and take her abroad, where they found her a proper job as a housekeeper. The experiment was successful, and Stead published lurid accounts of the transaction in a series of articles in his newspaper under the headline, 'The Maiden Tribute of Modern Babylon'. They had all the incendiary effect of stories about paedophiles today and set public opinion aflame. Unfortunately, the publicity caused the embarrassed parents to claim that their child had been abducted, and a charge was laid against Stead and Jowett, both of whom were sent to prison. The associated publicity did, however, serve the cause of raising the age of consent, which became sixteen years in 1895.

After the repeal of the Contagious Diseases Acts, Butler turned her attention to the British Empire, having discovered that they were still being used against women in the colonies, causing in India, for example, a number of suicides. Butler found it much more difficult to attract sympathy for Indian rather than white slavery, and became very angry at the double element of oppression involved – both men over women and colonial oppressor over the native subject. Butler herself was unable to travel to India both because of her own precarious health but especially that of her husband. The two women whom she sent to gain evidence, Dr Kate Bushnell and Mrs Elizabeth Andrews, brought home a wealth of detailed testimony to the existence of forcible examination and official British State provision of prostitutes for particular regiments, many of whom were widows, sold to the British by their husbands' families; a number of them were children. Registration and examination of prostitutes in India was officially ended in 1895.[8]

Towards the end of her life, Butler often found herself at odds from her fellow workers, partly because some sought to ally what she saw as an abolitionist and liberatory movement with temperance and 'social purity' alone, without the emphasis on the dignity and empowerment of the enslaved women. She also became estranged from some more socially radical elements when she failed to oppose the Boer War. Most radicals saw the conflict as an act of imperial aggression but Butler, whose son Charles had worked in South Africa, was highly aware of the racist ideology and practice of the Boers, and it was on the grounds of anti-slavery that she took her stand in the book, *Native Races and the War*, in 1900. It caused her to be shunned by her own supporters.

After the death of George Butler in 1890, Josephine Butler lived in a series of lodgings where, in typically energetic Victorian fashion, she kept up a voluminous correspondence with the various organisations and workers of the Abolitionist cause. She was, however, in great and continual pain from a whole series of ailments, although still holding on with great delight, to life itself. She died peacefully, in the presence of her nurse and landlady, on 30 December, 1906, and was buried at Kirknewton.

Even from this brief sketch of the main external events of Butler's life, her importance for us today is clear. She sought to address a great social wrong – the enslavement of women in prostitution – at a time when it was regarded as a necessary evil for the health of the masculine population. Many Christian people – including for a long time, the convocations of Canterbury and York – supported the Contagious Diseases Acts as means of prevention of disease. At the same time Butler made a complete distinction between women involved in prostitution and the system itself. Christians today similarly have to deal with a society that tacitly accepts prostitution, and somehow proclaim a different and non-objectified vision of sexual relations based on love and commitment. Faced with prostitution, they have to find a way to hate the institution and yet love those involved in it.

Part 1: Theological Reflection and Practice

The papers in this volume are attempts to think through the moral praxis demanded of those who would work with or think about prostitution. Although the reader will learn a great deal incidentally about Butler's practical engagement, the focus is much more on her rationale and principles, and their utility or limitations. Essays in the first part of the volume deal with Butler herself. Jane Jordan, in the first chapter of this book, 'Josephine Butler and the Moral Reclaimability of Prostitutes', shows how different Butler's approach was from the punitive attitude of many religious rescue workers of her day, such as Revd John Armstrong, and the Church Penitentiary Association he founded. Hearteningly, Jordan suggests that Butler might have drawn inspiration from the Tractarian Felicia Skene, whose work with the poor and prostituted in Oxford involved love not judgement, and sought to show solidarity with fallen women, rather than the distance promoted by the CPA. Butler went one step further than Skene in actually using women who had been involved in prostitution as leaders in the work of reclamation, such as Rebecca Jowett, who moved from being a procuress to rescuing other women and girls.

Rod Garner in 'Truth Before Everything' examines the basis of Butler's sense of prophetic authority and her inner integrity, comparing it to John Henry Newman's distinction between 'notional' and 'real' assent. He demonstrates how Butler's concept of truth was based on her personal experience of God and her mystical awareness of His presence, from which she drew her sense of truth as a mode of life. Garner is careful to discriminate Butler's attentive waiting upon God from a fundamentalist position: she was always open to fresh understanding as she sought to operate a 'moral praxis' of faith. He does, however, suggest a limitation in Butler's position that those working in pioneer ministries today might heed, in her private and individual approach to belief and action, which did not make full use of the community of faith and the resources of tradition.

David Scott's paper is in some sense a pendant to Rod Garner, in that he also examines the heart of Butler's springs of action in her mystical apprehension of God and what he calls, quoting Timothy Radcliffe, her 'cell of self-knowledge'. Butler wrote a pioneering biography of St Catherine of Siena in 1878, and Scott shows how the life of this female contemplative and visionary, who as simply a Tuscan peasant woman, spoke with prophetic force to the Pope and kings, bears upon that of Butler herself. In her biography writing, Scott sees Butler engaged upon the attention to tradition and the community of the faithful that Garner believes is lacking in Butler's understanding of truth. Ironically, however, Butler chose as her subject a woman who, although she sought the right to wear the Dominican habit, was very much an individualist, operating like Butler from her own self-authenticating visionary authority.

Hester Jones similarly is attentive to the relation between Butler's 'still voice of silence' and her prophetic self-understanding. She explores moments in Butler's writing which bring others' suffering into her experience of contemplative prayer, where barriers between self and others, masculine public and private feminine spheres can be blurred and reshaped as communion. Butler's prophetic vision, for Jones, lies in the 'liminal moments' in which she holds victim and oppressor together in the fullness of the Divine presence. Again the question of the relation of self to others is foregrounded, with Jones emphasising the concept of 'independence' in Butler, which is the result of dependence on God in what Butler calls 'soul leisure', and which results in a prophetic mode of relationality.

My own contribution, 'Josephine Butler's Apocalyptyic Vision of the Prostitute and Modern Debates on Prostitution', begins the turn in the book towards the present day. I delineate a strong apocalypticism in Butler's writing and belief in the imminence of the second coming of Christ, and argue that it allows Butler to understand the prostituted woman, in her enslavement, as a sign of the need for liberation and Divine justice for all humanity. Equally, however, in her liberation from prostitution, she acts as a sign and a foretaste of God's kingdom breaking into the world. I go on to argue that in contemporary debates between feminist abolitionists who see prostitution and trafficking as forms of oppression, and libertarians who argue that one should empower sex workers and remove the stigma of prostitution, Butler offers a different way that both empowers and liberates, and treats prostituted women as equally victims and agents.

In 'Religious Motivation and the Abuse of Women', Ann Loades explores a difficult ethical area: the ability of women to protect themselves and their children from domestic abuse. She examines Butler's own life to discern how she came to have the confidence to question men's rights over women's bodies, and to move the fight for equality before the law from the middle-class sphere of educational opportunities to outcast women involved in prostitution. Loades attends to the examples of physical violence meted out to this latter group, about which Butler protested vigorously. Loades, however, criticises Butler for too easily, from the position of her own egalitarian marriage, stressing the self-sacrificial nature of female love and its Christ-like character. In this way, Loades argues, female qualities can be used to entrap women in abusive situations.

Part 2: Butler's Legacy

The latter part of the book is concerned with Butler's relevance to today's problems and challenges. With Kenneth Leech's paper we reach the modern and the practical, with a discussion of how Anglicans, including Ken Leech himself, have responded to prostitution in the East End of London, particularly in the area around Cable Street in the docklands. He describes the growing globalisation of the organisation of prostitution, and interestingly, the way in which models of good practice and influence also circulate globally, so that he ends by describing the 'Rahab's Sisters' project that evolved in Oregan, USA, after exchanges between British and American priests and lay-workers through the Marigold Project. This international sharing of ideas and resources looks back to Butler's own International Federation a century before.

Janet Batsleer examines contemporary debates in 'Sex Work and the Politics of Rescue,' moving from presenting some of the facts, as far as they are known, about prostitution in Britain today, to how a 'situated engagement' with sex work might go beyond the 'first aid' of dealing with sex workers' welfare, or the social control that merely seeks through ASBO's (Anti-Social Behaviour Orders) and other means, to clear prostitution out of public sight. She examines how prostituted women themselves evolve certain ethical codes, as well as a mental dissociation that makes it possible to do the work and survive. Batsleer suggests a reworking of this distancing from the self in terms of a space of wonder, whereby the 'other' woman is seen in enchanted form as surprising and positive in her alterity; it is a way of imagining a new relation between the self and the other.

Finally, Carrie Pemberton, director of Churches Alert to Sexual Trafficking Across Europe (CHASTE), responds in the present to Butler's abolitionist approach to prostitution as a mode of enslavement. She outlines the contemporary situation in which sexual trafficking is a growing trade, and suggests how Butler's belief in state intervention might be of service today, taking Swedish government action as an example. Pemberton's is an appropriate essay to end our volume, because her work of research, activism and public communication is so similar to that of Butler herself.

There are various ways of reading this series of essays. For the Church historian, we offer original research on a fascinating and influential social reformer and her place in the religious life of the nineteenth century. For the theologian, Butler's deep engagement with Christology and apocalyptic is explored and shown to be quite original. For those involved in urban mission and social responsibility, Butler offers a way to relate prayer and practice, and to reflect theologically upon experience in a way that is not driven by the primacy of the secular.

Despite the very different approaches present in this collection, they offer a surprisingly unified picture of a religious anthropology: a vision of the human person as theologically understood. The subjectivity which emerges from these pages is very far from the atomised individual of contemporary capitalism and, I would argue, equally from the secular humanist conception of the self as an end in itself. Instead, a very rich and complex image of Christ is discerned through attention to the Divine creation of the human person as embodied in relationality. Our independence and individuality are asserted through our participation in the Divine, where we find our true self – 'your life is hidden with Christ in God' as Paul puts it in Colossians 3.3. Butler always spoke to that hidden deified self when she addressed outcast women. She was fond of quoting the story of Mary Magdalene's meeting with Christ in John 20, in which she recognises the risen Christ when he calls her by name. The resurrection establishes a subjectivity of both incorporation and individuality, which can only be experienced through identification with Christ.

Equally, in our need for liberation we are all *solidaire*, as Butler put it, deliberately using the language of the Paris Communes. A Christian anthropology has to hold together the Divine image that we all share, and the fact that we have all marred it: the reality is the former, so that the Christian, like Butler, has to learn to 'elicit the God-given character' from those we encounter, as from ourselves. If there is anything we have to learn from Butler in the violence, greediness and environmental crisis of our own day, it is that combination of fierceness and gentleness that David Scott alludes to in Butler: fierceness and utter opposition to evil wherever it is found; but hope and recognition of the Divine in the human self.

'There is no evil in the world so great that God cannot raise up to meet it a corresponding beauty and glory that will blaze it out of countenance.'[9]

Endnotes

[1] Joseph Williamson, *Josephine Butler. The Forgotten Saint* (Leighton Buzzard: The Faith Press, 1977). I am grateful to the late Father Joe for sending me a copy of this book, and thus introducing me to her work.
[2] See the examples from Thailand in Siriporn Skrobanek, Nataya Boonpakdee and Chutima Jantateero, *The Traffic in Women: Human Realities of the International Sex Trade* (London and New York: Zed Books, 1997), p. 98.
[3] The biographical sketch here is indebted primarily to Jane Jordan's modern biography, *Josephine Butler* (London: John Murray, 2001), and Butler's own *Personal Reminiscences of a Great Crusade* (London: Horace Marshall, 1910), which was first published in 1896.
[4] Terminology used for women involved in prostitution is somewhat loaded. 'Prostituted woman' seeks to avoid a fixed identification of someone by this role; 'sex worker' seeks to normalise prostitution as a mode of employment and undergird a rights perspective; 'prostitute' was the term in use in Butler's day when 'whore' or 'woman of the streets' were alternatives. The reader will find a range of terms in play in the essays, with 'prostitute' sometimes unavoidable but never meant to imply disrespect.
[5] See Jane Jordan, *Josephine Butler*, pp. 106-26; Glen Petrie, *A Singular Iniquity: The Campaigns of Josephine Butler* (New York: Viking, 1971).
[6] Jordan, *Butler*, p. 165.
[7] Jordan, *Butler*, p. 192.
[8] See Jordan, *Butler*, pp. 236-49. Petrie, *Singular Iniquity*, pp. 226-37.
[9] Josephine Butler, quoted in Williamson, *The Forgotten Saint*, p. 96.

Josephine Butler and the Moral Reclaimability of Prostitutes

Jane Jordan

Dr Jane Jordan is a Senior Lecturer in the English Department at Kingston University where she teaches nineteenth century literature. Jane's biography, Josephine Butler, *was published in 2001 and was featured on Woman's Hour and the BBC2 programme 'Scandalous Women'. Jane is co-editor of the five-volume collection of Butler's writings,* Josephine Butler and the Prostitution Campaigns *(2003), and her essay on Butler's biographical sketches of prostitutes has recently been published in* Sex, Gender and Religion: Josephine Butler Revisited *(2006). Jane's biography* Kitty O'Shea; An Irish Affair, *a study of Katharine O'Shea, mistress of the Irish leader, Charles Stewart Parnell, and his secret intermediary with the British Government, came out in 2005. Jane is currently writing a biography of the Victorian popular novelist, Ouida. Jane's approach is therefore that of the biographer, and one who has done extensive research on Butler's private and unpublished papers and correspondence. In this essay she breaks new ground by suggesting for the first time a female Anglican inspiration for Butler's rescue work, and she demonstrates how Butler developed her own 'church' of women who, themselves rescued, would reach out to other women.*

∾

S ince her death on 30 December 1906, Josephine Butler has received the highest honour given by the Anglican Church to a Christian woman. At first, the date of her death, but most recently the date of her baptism, 30 May, has been commemorated in the Church Calendar. Visual representations of Butler have also been incorporated into the actual fabric of the Church: she is memorialised in the stained glass windows of the Lady Chapel in Liverpool's Anglican Cathedral (consecrated in 1924), and also appears in the new East Window of St Olave's Church in London which was largely reconstructed after bombing in the Second World War. Now, in order to mark the centenary of her death, in 2006, the Parish Church of St Mary's, Kirknewton, where Butler is buried, has commissioned its own commemorative stained glass window and sculpture. The 'canonisation' of Josephine Butler by the Church of England in the hundred years since her death would appear to be unproblematic. Yet, Butler's own relationship with the Anglican Church in the latter half of the nineteenth century was not an easy one. Both in her private rescue work and her leadership of the LNA, Butler, the wife of a clergyman, either found herself working outside the Church or in opposition to it. Her distancing herself from the Established Church is explained in part by the nature of her religious upbringing, as she expressed it to her Quaker friend and LNA colleague, Mary Priestman:

> *I thought everyone knew I am not of the Church of England & never was. I go to the Church once a Sunday out of a feeling of loyalty to my husband – that is all. I was brought up a Wesleyan, but my father was allied with the Free Church of Scotland, & my mother was a Moravian. I imbibed from childhood the widest ideas of vital Christianity, only it was Christianity. I have not much sympathy with the Church.[1]*

As a small child, Butler was taken each Sunday to the Methodist Meeting-House used by the tenants and workers on her father's Milfield estate in Northumberland. Then, when an Irvingite Church was established at nearby Barmoor (the Irvingites were followers of a Revivalist group formed in 1832 by Edward Irving and Henry Drummond, who believed in the imminent Second Coming of Christ), the Greys' governess became a convert and Josephine went with her to hear the prophesyings of Irving's followers. The Greys appear to have been unreservedly sympathetic towards this new movement (John Grey she describes elsewhere as 'a *free* Churchman of wide sympathies'), and welcomed the visits of local convert, Mr Sitwell of Barmoor Castle, who mesmerised young Josephine with his talk 'of a heaven at hand on earth', although she would later reflect that 'the simple Methodist worship was always dearer to us'.[2] When she was older, the whole family 'trudged dutifully every Sunday' to the Parish Church of St Andrew's, Corbridge, two miles from their new home at Dilston, 'where an honest man in the pulpit taught us loyally all that he probably himself knew about God, but whose words did not even touch the fringe of my soul's deep discontent'.[3] A few years before her death, Butler was the subject of bemused scrutiny from a party of non-believers attending the annual Federation conference at Geneva, in September 1899, who asked, 'how is it that [Mrs Butler], a rebel against the superstitions and false conventions which have placed woman in a position in which she has become the victim of much injustice, – she proclaiming openly her revolt against this state of things, yet appears to be a convinced Christian of the evangelical type'? Butler framed her reply in her periodical, *Storm-Bell*, explaining that she had 'a very great respect for religious teachers and Christian ministers; but personally, they are *out of account* in regard to my own mental history'.[4]

Butler is referring here to the spiritual crisis she experienced as a young woman oppressed by what she had read and witnessed of human suffering and social injustice. Her father's study of parliamentary reports on the slave trade, her own experience of seeing the 'skeleton limbs' of famine victims in Ireland, and, too, her consciousness of the prejudices of society on the question of sexual inequality, all contributed to what she called her 'travail of soul'.[5] Unwilling to accept 'a faith received at second-hand', Butler began to interpret the Bible independently and to speak directly to God, 'as a person who could answer', spurred to do so by her 'desire to know God and my relation to him'.[6] It was through her autonomous reading of the scriptures that Butler came to regard Christ's treatment of fallen women as the 'keynote' upon which the world had so far failed to 'tune its voice'.[7] She was convinced that 'a single act of His towards a single individual was designed to be the type, for all ages, of the acts required of every Christian in every similar case'; not once, but three times, she argued, the Gospels record that Christ made an emphatic distinction between the sin, which was to be condemned, and the fallen woman who was to be forgiven and restored 'to her lost position among the honest and the pure'.[8] In her prayers, Butler represented fallen women and prostitutes as 'the victims also & slaves of lust… poor women who are driven as sheep to the slaughter into the slave market of London'.[9] In the first of many papers she published on the subject of 'The Moral Reclaimability of Prostitutes' (May 1870), Butler gave further emphasis to her sympathetic stance towards fallen women by turning the sexual double standard on its head. 'It would have been easier for me, and more in my line', she told her audience, 'to read a paper before two or three hundred prostitutes on "the reclaimability of profligate men"': such women readily acknowledged their wrong-doing, according to Butler, but they had 'piercing questions' regarding the outwardly respectable middle class men, 'grey-haired fathers of families', who used them and persuaded them that prostitution was a necessity (as one prostitute said to her, 'Surely such men are very cruel to say so, for they know well enough that when once we begin this life we dare not think of God ever again').[10] Yet not until 1888 did the Church of England re-examine the commandment against adultery and thereby condemn the sexual double standard in terms Butler would have approved. At the Pan Anglican Synod held that year, it was pronounced that the Church 'bestows more censure upon the man, who by reason of his strength is better able to subdue vicious propensities than the woman'.[11]

By her own account she was a nominal Anglican at best, and in recent years attempts have been made to situate more precisely Butler's spirituality, and in doing so to understand the motivations for her feminism and her vocational work through her affiliation with a particular denomination. Eileen Janes Yeo acknowledges how difficult a task this is, since Butler and so many prominent nineteenth century feminists 'seem almost promiscuous in the way that they borrowed from whatever Christian tradition suited their purposes'.[12] Most recently identified by Helen Mathers as an Evangelical, it is generally accepted that Butler 'held loosely to denominational ties', and that the position she took up as an outsider liberated and empowered her.[13] My own concern here is to consider the precise context within which Butler's faith and her feminism were forged during her brief years in Oxford, when Tractarianism was at its height, for she would later realise that her early married life in Oxford was her 'seed time' of which her missionary work amongst fallen women and prostitutes in Liverpool was 'a kind of harvest'.[14] Hitherto, biographical accounts of Butler's vocation, my own included, have accepted the broad outline given by Butler herself in her *Recollections of George Butler* (1892), and confirmed in her surviving personal correspondence: that it was the 'sore heart wound' of her five-year-old daughter Eva's accidental death that prepared her to visit and minister to prostitutes at the Brownlow Hill Workhouse in Liverpool, some of them mere children like Eva, 'being cruelly murdered', as she put it; and that at that time her 'sole wish was to plunge into the heart of some human misery, and to say (as I now knew I could) to afflicted people, "I understand. I, too, have suffered"'.[15]

There is, however, a context for understanding the direction of Butler's subsequent devotion to the moral reclaimability of prostitutes which has been neglected, a context provided by the involvement of the Anglican Church in this work. It is as necessary to discuss the existing religious models which Butler rejected as it is to consider those practitioners who had a lasting influence upon her own methods.

Butler published the results of her own research into the history of efforts made by the Anglican Church to rescue fallen women in her early article, 'Lovers of the Lost' (*Contemporary Review*, 1870). Since the Reformation, so she writes, she could find evidence of apostles of the lost only in the Roman Catholic Church: 'when we ask what recognition of their duty to the Magdalene has been given by... our own, we find, till comparatively recent years, a blank'.[16] She is here referring to the efforts made by the Oxford Movement in the establishment of Anglican Church Penitentiaries for the purpose of reforming and reclaiming fallen women. This was at the very time that the Butlers were living in Oxford at the beginning of their married life. Leading Tractarians acknowledged the Church's past methods of rescue and conversion had been relatively unsuccessful, and that it had failed in its duty to this class of penitents. A Church Penitentiary Association was founded in the spring of 1852 by the Vicar of Tidenham in Gloucestershire, the Revd John (later Bishop) Armstrong, who in 1848 announced his ambitious plans for a central organisation to coordinate efforts, and to provide funds and practical advice, to Houses of Mercy which he envisaged growing up in each and every diocese of the country. These would be headed by Wardens (unmarried clergymen with a vocation for rescue work), and administered by Anglican Sisterhoods (instead of salaried matrons, as had previously been the case). Armstrong conceived of a network of refuges in towns and cities from which suitable cases could be sent on to penitentiaries in the countryside where inmates would receive a lengthy course of theological instruction and practical training before being sent to 'some colony under clerical control' in order to begin a new life.[17] The initial £800 raised by his 1849 Appeal was divided between two new Houses of Mercy which opened that year, at Clewer,[18] near Windsor, and Wantage in Berkshire, and a third which opened in 1851 at Bussage, in Armstrong's own diocese.

Armstrong was motivated by his compassion for 'the deep misery of this class of sufferers, and the injustice their case met with', and from the pulpit he preached on the subject of the sexual double standard, which judged male adultery a 'venial' sin, but female sexual transgressions 'unpardonable', reminding his congregation that 'in the eyes of God the guilt of all is equal'.[19] However, despite his wish to establish a system that offered greater compassion to fallen women seeking refuge, Armstrong was clear that discipline must come first.[20] His initial conception of Houses of Mercy (so described in his 1849 Appeal) had, by the time of the founding of the CPA in 1852, been amended to Houses of Penitence.[21] At the heart of the process of reclamation was a formalised confession made by the penitent ('who', noted Armstrong, 'ought all to have been excommunicated') to a member of the clergy, for only 'he is empowered to pronounce, in the name of God, the absolution and remission of sins'.[22] Indeed, the Revd T. T. Carter of Clewer insisted that the penitentiary chaplain's *sole* contact with individual penitents was to hear confession.[23] Once absolution had been formally granted by the chaplain, penitents were permitted to receive the Holy Communion: in fact, it became the practice to allow penitents to receive the sacrament at the end of their first year's training and preparation. On no account were penitents to speak to the Sisters of their sinful lives: Armstrong called for the observance of this 'very stringent rule' in order to protect the Sisters, almost all of whom were likely to be single women.[24] Even though he was advised that many of the applicants would not be penitents 'in any real and saving sense, but merely weary [and] disgusted with the hopeless misery of their plight',[25] Armstrong was convinced that the formal testifying to past sins, the granting of absolution, and the receiving of the sacrament, would not only be of service to the individual penitent, but would 'reviv[e] the Church's rule of confession for burdened consciences', and thus perpetuate the work of the Oxford Movement, which was to revive the power of the Anglican Church in Society.[26]

It is evident that, at the time, Josephine Butler took an interest in the formation of the Church Penitentiary Association (the CPA). It is with admiration that she later refers to 'good Bishop Armstrong's' second appeal, published in 1851, in which he reproaches the Church for not having done enough to 'go after the lost sheep in the wilderness', and she had read Revd T. T. Carter's biography of Armstrong, published in 1857, a year after Armstrong's death.[27] Yet in Butler's own rescue work, she appears to have been deeply influenced by the theory and practice of her contemporary Felicia Skene (1821-99) (whose missionary work lay with female prisoners in Oxford), and who was one of the most outspoken critics of the CPA.[28] Skene was the aunt of Josephine's young Oxford friend, Zoe Skene, who in 1855 married Revd William Thomson, fellow and tutor of Queen's College, Oxford, and later Archbishop of York (1862-90). Thomson assisted his wife's aunt in her rescue work, and, like his friend George Butler, Thomson was very much a moderate in the Tractarian controversy.[29]

Felicia Skene worshipped at the parish church of St Thomas the Martyr in Becket Street, a short walk from St Giles, where George Butler briefly served as curate from 1854-56. St Thomas's, which lay in a neighbourhood of Oxford 'abounding in houses of ill-fame and in every kind of wickedness',[30] had been transformed by the Reverend Thomas Chamberlain (1810-1892), very much a Tractarian clergyman. In fact, the church was at the forefront of the Oxford Movement: leading members of the movement, such as Dr Pusey, preached there, daily services were revived, and, too, the wearing of Eucharistic vestments. In 1847 Chamberlain founded an Anglican Sisterhood attached to the church, led by his cousin, Marian Hughes (the first woman to be professed by Dr Pusey, in 1841), and it was to this sisterhood that Chamberlain attempted to guide Skene, hoping that in time she would superintend it. Skene declined the offer, and went her independent way, preferring to work out her principles 'gradually and experimentally'.[31] As her biographer E. C. Rickards has commented, 'It was a true instinct that led her firmly to refuse... nature had marked her out as a free lance. She must be allowed to choose her own time and methods, often most unconventional'.[32]

Skene was first called to work as a nurse, indeed, to superintend nursing, at the time of the two cholera outbreaks in Oxford (1849 and 1854). This experience, which took her into some of the poorest and most squalid areas of the city, led her to begin visiting the Spinning House attached to the Old County Gaol in Oxford which was reserved for female prisoners.[33] She quickly recognised the need for an open-all-hours refuge for such women and girls on their release from prison, and from that time on began the practice of keeping her own street door open all night. She continued her prison visiting for more than 40 years, and she recorded her experiences in many published articles. Although Skene was, in these early days, an orthodox Anglican, fully committed to the principles of the Oxford Movement, and the author of theological tracts (even publishing a defence of formalised confession in 1854),[34] her personal experience of working with female offenders led her to question the principles of the newly formed CPA. She objected to those penitentiaries which required a certificate of perfect health from applicants ('By that rule ninety-nine out of a hundred are struck from the list of possible recipients of the charity').[35] And she was highly critical of the wasting of funds on the provision of expensively furnished, 'not to say luxurious', penitentiary chapels, and extensive domestic quarters for the Sisters themselves: 'And what is the result? ...where one would wish to gather hundreds of these unhappy women, we find that there is space for eight, twelve, fifteen, twenty, or thirty penitents only!'.[36]

Skene's methodology also departs in many ways from the recommendations of the CPA. Her guide to rescue work, *Penitentiaries and Reformatories*, was published in 1865, one year before Josephine

Butler gained permission to visit women detained in the Bridewell at the Brownlow Hill Workhouse.[37] In her pamphlet, Skene offers a number of clear and simple guidelines that are strikingly similar to those adopted by the Butlers. Bearing in mind the character of the majority of admissions, she advised that penitence was to be taught, not expected. The class of women who sought refuge at such institutions were for the large part prostituted at a very young age, 'totally dead to all sense of right', and 'entirely ignorant of religious truth'. It was, she said, a great error to require women and girls 'unconscious of their own degradation' to exhibit signs of penitence as a prerequisite to their admittance, and then to subject them to a 'system of conventual rule and severe religious observance, which the best-disposed novice that ever sought to be trained as a nun would find hard to bear!'[38] Skene's advice was for prayers and religious instruction to be kept simple, and rules to a minimum; and there was to be no place for punishment. Above all, Skene took love, and not discipline, as her watchword, and she followed none but Christ's example, which was to 'save the lost, to reform the erring, to raise the fallen by means of love alone, in all gentleness, meekness, and tenderest compassion'.[39] Crucially, Skene exhorted Sisters not to 'keep these unhappy women at a distance, in order to teach them the heinousness of their sin and cast difference between the pure and the fallen' (which was precisely the recommendation of Bishop Armstrong).[40] Rather, they should try to work on the feelings of outcast women and to represent themselves as *fellow* sinners.

It is curious that in her writings Butler makes no mention of Skene's influence, although one should acknowledge that she is quite reticent in speaking publicly of her rescue methods.[41] To date, I have been unable to locate any documentary evidence to link Butler and Skene, yet it is inconceivable that Butler was unaware of the particular nature of Skene's vocation. Their life's work intersects at two key points. Butler dates the beginning of her own rescue work to a case in Oxford (where the Butlers lived from 1852-56). On learning of the situation of a young woman then in Newgate Prison, where she was serving a sentence for the crime of infanticide (her lover having perjured himself and deserted her), Butler's impulse was to travel to London to visit the woman in prison, and, like Skene, to speak 'of the God who saw the injustice done, and who cared for her'.[42] It was George Butler who suggested that they should write to the chaplain at Newgate to request that the woman come to their house as a domestic servant once she had completed her term of sentence. Skene's 1865 pamphlet, *Penitentiaries and Reformatories*, has already been mentioned. In 1866, the very year that Butler's missionary work began in Liverpool, Skene published her novel *Hidden Depths: A Story of a Cruel Wrong*, which describes the consequences of the seduction of Annie Brook, an ignorant child of sixteen, by a man of the world.[43] When, towards the end of the novel, an attempt is made to provide refuge for Annie at a Church Penitentiary, the character Mr Thorold voices Skene's own uncompromising criticisms of the Houses of Penitence established by the CPA, as rehearsed in her earlier pamphlet. Thorold despairs of their 'fatal error of dealing with those unhappy girls, as if they were, what they are called – *penitents*; whereas not one in a hundred has even such knowledge of God... as would enable them to understand what penitence means', and he declaims against the '*unfortunate* idea, that, instead of working on their affections', the exemplary ladies who have charge over them, seek to 'teach them the difference between the holy and the fallen by treating them with distance and coldness, and by rigorously demanding, and enforcing by penalties, the highest respect to themselves as their superiors'.[44]

As might be expected, the Church's attempt to reform Annie Brook is an utter failure, and Annie's stay in a penitentiary is brief. Although, initially, she baulks at one of the rules of admission – a written promise that she will agree to stay for a period of two years – the girl is persuaded to sign, but she runs away when she learns that her punishment for failing to observe one of the set periods of silence is a term of solitary confinement on a diet of bread and water. Skene's point, made through Thorold, is that the CPA prioritised its rigorous system of reclamation over the character and experience of individual women: 'I cannot tell you the vexation with which I hear, whenever a new penitentiary is about to be commenced, that a lady from one of the other refuges has been sent to teach the persons engaged to work in it the "proper" system of management, so that each one is firmly planted in the mistakes of its predecessors'.[45]

The principles upon which Josephine Butler based her own work of reclamation were a sound repudiation of those adopted by the CPA. From the first, Butler intended her Liverpool House of Rest to admit that class of women and girls who would have been turned away from existing Church Penitentiaries as too sick, too old, or too morally hopeless. Her choice of name is significant: to have called her Home a House of Mercy would have been to suggest that moral erring was all on the side of the Magdalenes, while a 'House of Penitence' was anathema to Butler. She says that she took the name from a House of Rest she had heard of in Brighton: it was implicitly a non-judgemental rest that she offered the poor and weary. As Butler explained to her widowed sister, Fanny, who moved to Liverpool to help in the work, 'My desire is, if God will let me, to gather a little handful of dying penitents, to speak peace & hope to those who have perhaps never had a chance of being good & may never have known what true love is'.[46] She never wavered from this central tenet, and reflected that in a vast city like Liverpool there was no provision for the sick and dying: 'when the girls fall ill or into lingering consumption [the refuges] cannot keep them'.[47] Jane Cragg, matron of the Benediction House in Liverpool, just a street away from the Butlers' house, at 56 South Hill, told her that her House of Rest was 'just what she has dreamed of for years, as she says it is so heartbreaking to leave them out to die in the streets or workhouse when they begin to spit blood and cough'.[48] Cragg, whose refuge could house upwards of 40 young women, frequently passed on incurable cases to Butler. In this she was consistent, too. When, some fifteen years later, Butler established a new House of Rest in Winchester, she described the venture as a 'shelter for poor girls and young women who were recognised failures, morally and physically… judged for one reason or another not quite suitable for other homes or refuges'.[49]

Physically fit women whose age was against them, since it was perceived that they had had time to become hardened to an immoral life, were also discriminated against. In the words of Rebecca Jarrett, the best known rescue case associated with Josephine Butler, in 'those day[s] if you was over 25 year[s] of age no one would take you in[.] Here I was about 36 or 38 it was no use I was too old to be reclaimed (sic)'.[50] At the Bridewell in Liverpool, Butler found herself approached by women older even than Rebecca, middle-aged and elderly women whom she vowed not to exclude ('Often they are the best *not* the worst'), and she was affected by the plea of one old woman who begged her: 'Please dear lady, am I too old for you to care for me, or for me to be sent to any Institution? I wd go anywhere & obey you in all things'.[51]

Butler's anger at the injustice which would have been meted out to the true penitents who sought her out is exemplified in the case of the prostitute Ellen Weald, who in February 1867 appeared at the Butlers' doorstep having sold up her apartment and all her fine possessions: 'I have come to put myself in your hands', she told Butler, 'to bear any penalty you like, and to go to any Penitentiary you like'.[52] On one occasion, Butler called at Ellen's temporary lodgings on some errand and found her on her knees, 'her white arms raised above her head in an attitude of entreaty... "I wish to speak to you, Madam", she said... "I want to know – can I ever be – pardon me, Madam, can I ever be *holy?*"'. This was a woman who had received little or no moral or religious education as a girl, and who was not even '"convinced of sin" in a wholly orthodox way', yet during her brief time at the Butlers' house, she said that she had 'seen into a new world; *holiness is the most beautiful thing I ever saw: I never saw anything like it before'*. Butler assured her that not only was holiness possible for Ellen, 'but I added, *"thereunto are ye called!"'*.[53] Because Ellen was in good health, and willing to enter a penitentiary, Butler made an initial inquiry at Clewer,[54] but since Clewer was full, she applied to the chaplain at a refuge in Birmingham, who hesitated to admit Ellen on account of her age – at 30, she was, he feared, 'too old to reform, but I'll give her a trial however unsteady she may be'. Butler was incensed ('such a *hard* letter'), and argued that if God could grant repentance to 'the grey-haired fathers of families and the churchgoing religious merchants who have kept her for their private prostitute', he would surely do so to 'poor Ellen, who has had so few advantages and who left her sins at the *first call*'.[55]

Although Butler frequently made use of repeal literature to promote the reclamation of prostitutes, she is far more expansive upon the question of her methods in her private correspondence. Like Felicia

Skene she shunned the rigid structures imposed upon the inmates of larger institutions, and described the single Protestant Penitentiary in Liverpool as 'prison-like in character'.[56] Her guiding principle, which, one feels, must have been taken directly from Skene, was 'that there is only one power wh[ich] can begat true repentance - namely *Love*'.[57] As far as discipline went, she assured Eva's godmother Mrs Myers (who was involved in rescue work in Cheltenham), 'I am *quite* sure about love & gentleness being the chief power'.[58] It was Mrs Glayn, a Headmistress in Manchester, who made Butler re-think her own role at the House of Rest, for she seems to have foreseen her work to lie in the recruitment of Magdalenes from Brownlow Hill, and to 'leave the whole working of [her little hospital] in abler hands'. Glayn recognised Butler's special talents and advised her that, on the contrary, she must attend her patients daily, 'for it may be that no one could do exactly your part of the work. Whenever we see that we are *loved* by wretched & guilty people we must consider that we have a gift from God which must be used for Him'.[59] By early February 1867, Butler had secured two temporary rooms nearby, 'where I could put 6 or 8 patients'; in the meantime, she began looking for a house to rent, again near at hand, 'so that I cd spend a good part of each day there & come & go'.[60]

The speed with which she went about her independent mission was extraordinary. By the last week of February, Butler had got hold of an unoccupied house (annual rent, £250) which she fitted up as a little hospital. At this very time, she was notified that the workhouse committee had decided to withdraw a donation, of 50 beds and a grant of £200, which they had proposed to make in support of her efforts. Butler remained convinced that as many as two hundred women were ready to follow her, yet her own House of Rest could take no more than thirteen. Undeterred, within ten days she had found another property, which was to serve as a temporary lodge and needlework room for those women seeking employment (she was able to offer them 6d. a day); on Good Friday, the 'Industrial Home', as it was known (which eventually housed an envelope factory), was officially blessed by George Butler.

From what we know of Butler's own religious upbringing it is no surprise that she insisted that the religious instruction provided in her House of Rest must be 'very wide & simple & unsectarian'.[61] Instruction, such as it was, was provided both by George and Josephine. Butler describes her practice of reading aloud a short Catechism to give her patients 'a simple cheery hope in Christ our Saviour'.[62] One of her concerns at Brownlow Hill was that a single chaplain was provided to minister to 4,000 inmates, one quarter of whom were in the hospital ward or infirmary, 'so that their souls really cannot be attended to'.[63] From her private correspondence of the time it is evident that concern for their 'souls' was Butler's overriding preoccupation. Although her motivations were compassionate (ensuring that consumptive girls and women could die in the privacy and comfort of a home) as well as practical (offering domestic or industrial training to those women fit enough to begin a new life), Butler explained to her sister Fanny, 'you know it is really for their *souls* that I wish to do it'.[64] Jane Cragg was convinced by what she saw that Butler's patients were 'assured of the love of God & to feel that the Good Shepherd had really found them', and delighted her by referring to her patients as Mrs Butler's 'little flock'.[65]

Unlike those penitentiaries founded under the auspices of the CPA, it was never Butler's practice to make penance a prerequisite to admission: as Alison Milbank expresses it, 'recognising the economic basis of prostitution, Butler saw no need for penance on the part of her guests'.[66] In her eyes, prostitutes were more sinned against than sinners, doubly the victims of economic exploitation and of the sexual double standard – another position she shared with Felicia Skene, and, apparently, Bishop Armstrong, although the penitentiaries he helped to found were not operated in a manner consistent with this view. In one of the two brief accounts she gives of her visits to the Bridewell at the Brownlow Hill Workshouse, Butler describes how she dropped to her knees to the level of the oakum pickers, most of whom were seated on the damp brick floor, and said to them, 'Courage, my darlings, don't despair. I have good news for you. You are women, and a woman is always a beautiful thing. You have been dragged deep in the mud, but still you are women. God calls to you... I dare to prophesy good for you, and happiness even in this life'. Anticipating the moral objections of her reader, Butler continues, 'Did I speak to them of their sins? Did I preach that "the wages of sin is death"? Never! What am I, – a sinner, - that I should presume to tell them that they were sinners?'.[67]

Aside from their governing principle of encouraging repentance through the administering of love and compassion alone, Butler and her husband shared the conviction that confession to a *human* agency need play no part in the reclamation of fallen women. Of her very first Magdalene, Mary Lomax, who died in their home in March 1867, Butler was firm that 'We said nothing to her about her past, or about *sin*. It was not our habit to do so'.[68] In fact, it was the case that Mary, like many of the girls, did feel drawn to confide her history to Butler. However, it was not penitence in the conventional sense that led to Mary's conversion, but the agency of love that offered her a new life, such that a week or so before Mary's death, Butler could report that 'she is so *clean* taken out of all memory of sin even that one feels as if talking to a being of angelic purity… I am not exaggerating'.[69] The theme which resonates through the Communion Service which George Butler used at the inauguration of the Industrial Home is one of *divine* forgiveness and absolution. In his explication of the first lesson, a reading from Isaiah 55, George asked his congregation to forsake their sins before God alone: 'He will abundantly pardon – not as man, i.e. grudgingly, remembering our sins – but fully & completely'. In the handwritten notes of George's, which survive, he makes the distinction between confession before God and confession to himself or to Josephine quite explicit: 'We do not wish to pry into the secrets of your past lives'.[70]

In her published and unpublished records of her rescue work, Butler often alludes to the role of her husband, an ordained minister, in saying prayers over the dying or administering the last sacrament to patients they received in their own home or at the House of Rest. In her *Recollections of George Butler*, however, she admits that 'his character continued to be essentially that of a layman. He never had a cure of souls'.[71] Josephine Butler evidently did. In the absence of her husband, or the workhouse chaplain, Butler is just as likely to take upon herself the role of granting absolution to dying Magdalenes – absolution, that is, without having heard a formalised confession. She recalls how, on one of her first visits to the workhouse infirmary, she was moved to say to one dying patient, '"Woman, thy sins are forgiven thee", & I just spoke the name of Jesus again & again. She looked at me, poor skeleton, with deep sunk eyes *burning*… & gasped *"I believe it"*.[72]

This episode is recounted in greater detail in Butler's late article 'A Word to Christian Sceptics' (*Storm-Bell*, November 1898). She describes how, just as she was about to enter the large hospital ward, she met the workhouse chaplain about to leave, 'his hands pressed upon his ears, in order to shut out the sound of a torrent of blasphemy and coarse abuse hurled at him by one of the inmates, to whom he had spoken as his conscience had prompted him, and under a sincere sense of duty'.[73] Butler herself instinctively walked towards the bed of the woman, from whom he had turned away, and whom she describes as 'hideous to look at... who had lived the worst of lives, descending lower and lower'. Her ribs kicked in by the man she lived with, she was now dying fast, and in agony. As she stood by the bedside, Butler asked herself, 'Was it possible for anyone to love such a creature? Could she inspire any feeling but one of disgust? Yes, the Lord loved her, - loved her still, and it was possible for one who loved him, to love the wretch whom *He* loved'.[74]

> *I do not recollect what I said to her, but it was love which spoke. She gazed at me in astonishment[...] She took my hand and held it with a death-grip. She became silent, – gentle. Tears welled from the eyes which had been gleaming with fury. The poor soul had been full to the brim of revenge and bitterness against man, against fate, against God. But now she saw something new and strange. She heard that she was loved; she believed it, and was transformed.*

The contrast between the reaction of the representative of the Church of England and Butler's own independent and sometimes unorthodox methods is nowhere better encapsulated than in this episode. The workhouse chaplain who turns his back on the dying woman, his hands over his ears, symbolises effectively the practice of the Anglican Church which was to sort those women begging admittance to a penitentiary into those it judged truly penitent, prepared to confess their shame and guilt, and those it judged irredeemable - a moral distinction never attempted by Butler herself. Butler's concluding words are directed to the 'Christian Sceptics' of her title. She says that in such cases she has often been asked, 'but had [the Magdalene] any clear perception of her own sinfulness? Did she understand, etc.?', to which Butler replied that she did not know: 'I only know that love conquered, and that he who inspired the love which brought the message of *his* love to the shipwrecked soul, knew what he was doing and does not leave his work incomplete'.[75]

Another episode she later published is the story of the death of a girl Butler calls 'Emma', who died in lodgings in Liverpool on the night of 14 October 1872 (she was put in lodgings because the Butlers' house was then full).[76] About half an hour before Emma's death, George Butler administered the sacrament, which Josephine said she would share: 'she and I, poor sinners as we were, and rejoice together in the words, "This is My blood which was shed for *you*"'.[77] However, the text of George Butler's solemn 'little service', attended also by Emma's landlady, does not survive. Indeed, much of Emma's narrative, one of five brief biographical sketches of prostitutes which Butler published in periodicals associated with the repeal movement, is given over to Butler's own words of consolation and absolution. Emma had not wished to receive the sacrament, 'of which Mr Butler had spoken to her', until she had made a full confession of her past, not to George, but to Josephine. Three weeks before Emma's death, Josephine recalled that she 'heard the whole sad story, and then persuaded her to get rid of the whole burden of her sins at once, and to cast it all on Christ. I taught her some of the most comforting of the promises of God:- "Thy sins and thine iniquities I will remember no more"'.[78] Repeatedly, on this and subsequent visits leading up to the night of her death, Butler assures Emma of salvation.

It is clear, too, that she had told Emma the story (which Emma half remembers and has to be prompted by Butler) of Mary Magdalene's having been honoured as the first person to whom the resurrected Christ appeared. From Emma's story we learn that Butler did not simply speak to her dying Magdalenes of Christ's love, but of Christ's promise of liberation, a liberation at once spiritual and earthly. I have never shared the reservations expressed by some commentators that Butler's rescue work, 'although caring and protective, was also hierarchical and custodial', and 'sanctioned an authority relationship between older middle-class women and young working women'.[79]

What Emma's story reveals to us is that Butler disseminated her feminist interpretations of the Scriptures by sharing them with her largely working class 'flock'. Mary Lomax's story further provides evidence that Butler also communicated her feminist analysis of the *causes* of prostitution. In a private family letter Butler says of Mary that she '*can* grasp the whole sad subject of prostitution like a *man*, calmly, & philosophically, & yet with the deep indignant tenderness of a Christian'.[80]

Butler's renown as a rescue worker led to her being asked to head the Ladies' National Association for the repeal of the Contagious Diseases Acts. Her personal knowledge of outcast girls and women gave authenticity to her political campaigning, and of course she would continue to visit and minister to this class of women, now on the police register, known familiarly as 'Government Women', taking evidence from those detained in Lock Hospitals wherever possible. When, after fifteen years' experience of running her Liverpool House of Rest, the Butlers moved to Winchester, where George was appointed Canon of the Cathedral, Butler's first concern was to establish a new refuge there, although she was now compelled to hire a matron because her parliamentary work in London became so demanding at this time. The situation was all the more pressing since Winchester was a garrison town under the jurisdiction of the Acts, legislation largely welcomed by citizens and churchmen alike for its clearing the streets of disorderly behaviour. It was, though, a town in which the Salvation Army already had a strong footing; rescue work amongst prostitutes was already established. And it was due to the Salvation Army's influence that Butler's own rescue methods took on their most socially radical aspect.

While the CPA had envisaged offering permanent residency to those penitents, in the words of Bishop Armstrong, 'too unstable to preserve themselves in the slippery places of the world',[81] and considered that such women might carry out domestic duties at the penitentiary so as to pay their way, the Salvation Army supported the active missionary work of their own converts, whom they encouraged to revisit local drinking houses and brothels in order to preach redemption and proselytise on behalf of the SA. It was their 'principle of sending class to class' that Butler now embraced.[82] Rebecca Jarrett, former prostitute and procuress, rescued by Florence Booth at her Whitechapel refuge, was sent down to Butler's Winchester House of Rest (or House of Healing, as it had been described to Jarrett), in order for her to recover her health (Jarrett was a recovering alcoholic, she had a chronic lung complaint, and a diseased hip). When her patient was stronger, Butler suggested to Jarrett, who wished for an active life, that she might help local rescue efforts in Winchester and Portsmouth by going into the streets and recruiting women herself. Jarrett's mission was so successful that Butler set her up in a separate house in the town, Hope Cottage, a refuge for healthy girls who wished to begin new lives.

Jarrett had weekly conferences with the Butlers at the Cathedral Close and had support, too, from SA officers who would drop in for tea, but aside from this she was effectively given exclusive responsibility for the souls under her care. For Butler, the success of Jarrett's mission was a revelation: 'We may have to confess that our old rescue methods are ineffectual', she confided to Florence Booth, and asked whether, 'instead of spending years in reforming case after case inside our Homes, may we not be led of God in the power of His spirit to send forth the saved-lost ones in bands to save others'? She conceived of whole armies of women like Jarrett, who 'might go out into the streets & gather in such a full & blessed harvest of those poor little girls. These are bold thoughts, dear Mrs Booth; & 99 Christian workers in a hundred would probably cry out that it is impossible, or that it would be a very unsafe experiment...'.[83] Such sentiments could not have been further from Bishop Armstrong's concern to place penitents under the exclusive supervision of 'gentlewomen... of the upper ranks'.[84] Most touching, to my mind, is Butler's choice of phrase in describing Rebecca Jarrett's 'full & blessed harvest'. It was, after all, her own divine gift of harvesting souls for which she had thanked God in 1867. What her Winchester experience demonstrates is that Butler did not rigidly apply the principles she herself had formed. She could adapt: with fifteen years behind her of deep and varied experience in the moral reclamation of prostitutes, Josephine Butler sought the interests of individual girls and women first and never attempted to 'fix them for a rule of life'.[85]

Endnotes

[1] Women's Library, Josephine Butler Collection, Josephine E. Butler to Mary Priestman, 17 January 1883.

[2] Liverpool University Library, Josephine Butler Collection, JB 1/1 1906/10/07 (I), Josephine E. Butler to Fanny Forsaith; ibid., JB 1/1 1902/03/16, Josephine E. Butler to Maurice Gregory.

[3] Josephine E. Butler, 'Emancipation As I Learned It', *Storm-Bell*, January 1900, p. 258.

[4] Ibid., p. 254 (emphasis added).

[5] Josephine E. Butler, *Our Christianity Tested by the Irish Question* (London: T. Fisher Unwin, 1887), p. 44; WL, Typescript draft speech by Josephine E. Butler for the Jubilee Conference of the Federation, 1905.

[6] WL, Josephine Butler Collection, Josephine E. Butler to Professor Benjamin Jowett, n.d. [c. 1860-70].

[7] Josephine E. Butler, 'The Lovers of the Lost', reprinted in Jane Jordan and Ingrid Sharp, eds., *Josephine Butler and the Prostitution Campaigns: Diseases of the Body Politic*, 5 vols (London: Routledge, 2003), I, p. 96.

[8] Ibid., p. 95, p. 100.

[9] Northumberland Record Office, ZBU.E3/A2, Josephine E. Butler, 'Private Thoughts 1856-1865', p. 37.

[10] Josephine E. Butler, 'The Moral Reclaimability of Prostitutes', reprinted in Jordan and Sharp, eds., *Josephine Butler and the Prostitution Campaigns*, I, p. 123.

[11] WL, Josephine Butler Collection, Revd George Butler, 'Progress of the Abolitionist Cause in the Anglican Church', speech given at the annual Federation Conference held at Copenhagen, August 1888.

[12] Eileen Janes Yeo, 'Protestant Feminists and Catholic Saints in Victorian Britain', in Eileen Janes Yeo, ed., *Radical Femininity: Women's Self-representation in the Public Sphere* (Manchester: Manchester University Press, 1988), p. 136.

[13] See Helen Mathers, 'The Evangelical Spirituality of a Victorian Feminist: Josephine Butler 1828-1906', *Journal of Ecclesiastical History*, 52, no.2 (April 2001), pp. 282-312. The quotation here is taken from Alison Milbank, 'Josephine Butler: Christianity, Feminism and Social Action', in Jim Obelkevich, Lyndal Roper and Raphael Samuels, eds., *Disciplines of Faith: Studies in Religion, Politics and Patriarchy* (London: Routledge & Kegan Paul Ltd, 1987), p. 155.

[14] Josephine E. Butler to Edith Leupold, 8 March 1867, reprinted in Jordan and Sharp, eds., *Josephine Butler and the Prostitution Campaigns*, I, p. 83. Although, throughout the early 1850's, Butler desired to do practical good in society, she was physically depleted through giving birth to her four children in quick succession, and says of herself 'I was so weak & useless… & could *do* nothing except pray', ibid.

[15] The first two quotations are taken from LUL, Josephine Butler Collection, JB 1/4/1, Undated Statement to Sons; the last is from Josephine E. Butler, *Recollections of George Butler* (Bristol: J.W.Arrowsmith, 1892), p. 183. See Jane Jordan, *Josephine Butler* (London: John Murray, 2001), pp. 66-71, for Butler's strong sense of connection between the death of her daughter and her work with fallen women and girls in Liverpool.

[16] Reprinted in Jordan and Sharp, eds., *Josephine Butler and the Prostitution Campaigns*, I, p. 103.

[17] Revd Armstrong to Mr Ford, 8 September 1848, reprinted in Revd T. T. Carter, *A Memoir of John Armstrong* (Oxford & London: John Henry and James Parker, 1857), p. 210.

[18] In September 1849, a Mrs Marquita Tennant, the Spanish widow of an English clergyman, established a refuge for prostitutes close to Clewer Church, Windsor, a garrison town which attracted a great deal of prostitution. Within three years, Tennant was forced through ill health to give up the management of the project, which was then overseen by the Tractarian vicar of Clewer, T. T. Carter. A purpose-built house, House of Mercy, was founded, as was an Anglican Sisterhood, the Community of St John the Baptist, led by Harriet Monsell, which took over the rescue and reclamation of penitents.

[19] Carter, *A Memoir of John Armstrong*, p. 195, p. 198.

[20] While he very sensibly recommended that the Constitution of the Penitentiary should be subject to review after a trial period of two years, Armstrong was nonetheless anxious to 'get discipline well fixed before the whole house was full', ibid., p. 211.

[21] See Carter, *A Memoir of John Armstrong*, p. 240-1.

[22] Ibid., p. 231, p. 232.

[23] See J. F. M. Carter, *Life and Work of Rev T. T. Carter* (London: Longman, Green & Co, 1911), p. 97.

[24] Carter, *A Memoir of John Armstrong*, p. 221. There is evidence that in the early stages of development some church leaders needed to be persuaded of the efficacy of leaving fallen women and prostitutes under the supervision of Anglican Sisterhoods. See, for example, Revd T. T. Carter's tract, published one year after his own foundation of the Community of St John the Baptist, otherwise known as the Clewer Sisters, 'Is it well to institute Sisterhoods in the Church of England for the care of female penitents?' (1853). In his original appeal, Armstrong seeks to reassure those women wishing to enter a Sisterhood that they would in no degree 'be harmed or pained by knowledge of evil… not the faintest allusion to former life must be allowed to pass between the matrons and the penitents; such silence… would serve to heighten in the penitents the sense of their sin, by representing it as something too dark to be spoken of, except in the most solemn way to the chaplains, the pastors of the guilty flock', 'An Appeal for the Formation of a Church Penitentiary', in Revd T. T. Carter, ed., *Essays on Church Penitentiaries by John Armstrong* (London: John Henry & James Parker, 1858), pp. 125-6.

[25] Quoted in Carter, *A Memoir of John Armstrong*, p. 233.

[26] Ibid., p. 230.

[27] Butler quotes from Armstrong's writings dating from 'eighteen years ago' in her article 'Lovers of the Lost' (1870), reprinted in Jordan and Sharp, eds., *Josephine Butler and the Prostitution Campaigns*, I, p. 97; in this article she also quotes from T. T. Carter's, *A Memoir of John Armstrong*, ibid., I, p. 101.

[28] Anne Summers, in her study *Female Lives, Moral States* (Newbury: Threshold Press, 2000), notes that Skene was, like Butler, working independently with female offenders, yet she does not pursue the connection, p. 51. Felicia Skene's house in Oxford, 34 St Michael's Street, was commemorated with an Oxford Blue Plaque in 2002. I am indebted to former Lord Mayor of Oxford, and member of the Oxfordshire Blue Plaque Board, Ann Spokes Symonds, for suggesting the likely influence of Felicia Skene upon Josephine Butler's rescue work.

[29] In 1861 Thomson responded to the Tractarian enterprise, *Essays and Reviews*, with his own *Aids to Faith*.

[30] E. C. Rickards, *Felicia Skene of Oxford: A Memoir* (London: John Murray, 1902), p. 88. Felicia Skene's house in Oxford, 34 St Michael's Street, was commemorated with an Oxford Blue Plaque in 2002.

[31] Ibid., p. 142.

[32] Ibid., p. 94.

[33] Once a separate building, the Spinning House, which Skene visited for over twenty years, was eventually merged with the Old City Gaol which Skene visited from 1878 to her death and recorded these later cases in her prison diary (see Ch.15, 'Prison Diary and Letters', Rickards, *Felicia Skene of Oxford*, pp. 208-224).

[34] Felicia Skene, *The Ministry of Consolation: A Guide to Confession for the Use of Members of the Church of England* (London, 1854).

[35] Felicia Skene, *Penitentiaries and Reformatories* (1865) (Whitefish, Montana: Kessinger Publishing, 2004), p.7.

[36] Skene, *Penitentiaries and Reformatories*, pp. 6-7. The purpose built House of Mercy at Wantage, for example, provided accommodation for eight sisters but only 30 penitents and cost £2,600 to build and furnish. The Community of St John the Baptist at Clewer, one of the most fashionable and aristocratic of sisterhoods, paid out £2,500 for land on which to build and a further '£6,500 for the erection of the imposing buildings', Mumm, *Stolen Daughters, Virgin Mothers*, p. 90.

[37] A second edition of Skene's pamphlet was published by the Edinburgh publishers Douglas & Edmonston in 1866.

[38] Skene, *Penitentiaries and Reformatories*, p. 9.

[39] Ibid., p.14.

[40] Ibid., p.11.

[41] Butler is perhaps most expansive about the setting up of her House of Rest in her biography of her husband, but even here she says 'I do not want to make a long story of this', *Recollections of George Butler*, p.184.

[42] Ibid., p. 97. When giving evidence before the Royal Commission (December 1870-May 1871), Butler said that her work with fallen women began at Oxford, PRO, 'Report from the Royal Commission on the Administration and Operation of the Contagious Diseases Acts 1866-69 (1871)', PP, 1871 (C.408-I), XIX, Q.12,842.

[43] Skene's novel was first published in two volumes by the Edinburgh publishing house, Edmonston & Douglas, who had issued her pamphlet the previous year. The novel was later reprinted in a cheap single-volume edition at the time of Butler's own investigations into child prostitution, in particular the trade in under-age virgins, the results of which were exposed in W. T. Stead's sensational series of articles, 'The Maiden Tribute to Modern Babylon', in his paper, the *Pall Mall Gazette*, 6-10 July 1886.

[44] Felicia Skene, with an introduction by W.Shepherd Allen, MP, *Hidden Depths: A Story of a Cruel Wrong* (London: Hodder & Stoughton, 1886), p. 167.

[45] Ibid., p. 168.

[46] WL, Josephine Butler Collection, Josephine E. Butler to Fanny Smyttan, 12 February 1867.

[47] Ibid.

[48] Ibid.

[49] Butler, *Recollections of George Butler*, p. 402.

[50] SA, Rebecca Jarrett Papers, 'Rebecca Jarrett', p. 4, typed transcript of one of the autobiographical fragments written by Jarrett when she was in her eighties. Jarrett also bemoaned the fact that '41 years ago there was not a Home in London to help a woman to get over the drink'; however, at the conclusion of the eight supplementary sheets attached to this typescript, Jarrett notes that since she joined the Salvation Army in the early 1880s, 'I have seen opened Homes for women over 25 and thank God a lot is doing well', p. 8.

[51] WL, Josephine Butler Collection, Josephine E. Butler to Mrs Myers, 26 February [1867].

[52] Ibid.

[53] Under the pseudonym 'Laura', Ellen Weald's history is recounted by Butler in the last of her five biographical sketches of former prostitutes, 'The Dark Side of English Life. Illustrated in a Series of True Stories. By Mrs Josephine E. Butler: No.V – Laura', *Methodist Protest*, May 1877, pp. 51-52.

[54] While Butler's intention to send Ellen to the Anglican sisterhood at Clewer may at first appear inconsistent, she was perhaps sensitive to Ellen's superior upbringing ('a little coarseness may do harm. She is so keenly alive to it', WL, Josephine Butler Collection, Josephine E. Butler to 'My dear A[lan Raper]', n.d.). Clewer, like many other Church Penitentiaries, not only provided separate accommodation for middle-class and working-class penitents, but would have offered Ellen specialist training in 'the higher levels of domestic service or nursing', see Mumm, *Stolen Daughters, Virgin Mothers*, pp. 103-105.

[55] WL, Josephine Butler Collection, Josephine E. Butler to 'My dear A[lan Raper]', n.d.

[56] Ibid., Josephine E. Butler to Fanny Smyttan, 27 February 1867.

[57] LUL, JB 1/1 1905/04/)) (I), Josephine E. Butler to Fanny Forsaith, Secretary of the British Committee of the British, Continental & General Federation for the Abolition of Regulation. The very same advice is given in Skene's novel, *Hidden Depths*: 'If you can win her personal love to yourself, you will have done a great deal towards her ultimate rescue; for where the love of God does not exist, human affection is the only other impulse that can work for good within the soul... It is often allowed to serve as a guide to the higher, purer love, and it can at least accomplish what haughtiness and severity could never effect', p. 168.

[58] WL, Josephine Butler Collection, Josephine E. Butler to Mrs Myers, 26 February [1867].

[59] The visit to Manchester is recounted in ibid.

[60] Ibid., Josephine E. Butler to Fanny Smyttan, 12 February 1867.

[61] Ibid., Josephine E. Butler to Mrs Myers, 26 February [1867].

[62] Ibid., Josephine E. Butler to Fanny Smyttan, 12 February 1867.

[63] Ibid.

[64] Ibid.

[65] Ibid.

[66] Alison Milbank, 'Josephine Butler: Christianity, Feminism and Social Action', p. 158.

[67] Josephine E. Butler, 'Memories', *Storm-Bell*, June 1900, reprinted in Jordan and Sharp, eds., *Josephine Butler and the Prostitution Campaigns*, I, p. 291, p. 292. Butler gives another account of her first visit to the oakum sheds in *Recollections of George Butler*, p. 184.

[68] LUL, JB 1/1 1905/04/00, Josephine E. Butler to Fanny Forsaith.

[69] Josephine E. Butler to Edith Leupold, 8 March 1867, reprinted in Jordan and Sharp, eds., *Josephine Butler and the Prostitution Campaigns*, I, p. 84.

[70] LUL, JB 1/4/3 Order of Service, Revd George Butler, 'Prayers at the Opening of the Industrial Home', n.d. [Good Friday, 1867].

[71] Butler, *Recollections of George Butler*, p. 63.

[72] WL, Josephine Butler Collection, Josephine E. Butler to Fanny Smyttan, 12 February 1867.

[73] Josephine E. Butler, 'A Word to Christian Sceptics', reprinted in Jordan and Sharp, eds., *Josephine Butler and the Prostitution Campaigns*, I, pp. 286.

[74] Ibid., I, p. 287.

[75] Ibid., I, p. 207.

[76] Like Felicia Skene, Butler always found temporary lodgings for women she couldn't place immediately at her House of Rest.

[77] Josephine E. Butler, 'The Dark Side of English Life. Illustrated in a series of true stories. No. IV Emma', *Methodist Protest*, April 1877, p. 40. The five sketches were published in the *Methodist Protest* in consecutive months, from January to May 1877. The first three also appeared in the *National League Journal*, in March, April and June of that year.

[78] Ibid., p. 39.

[79] Judith R.Walkowitz, *Prostitution and Victorian Society: Women, Class and the State* (1980) (Cambridge: Cambridge University Press, 1994), p. 117. Even Walkowitz acknowledges that at other times, Butler 'approached prostitutes on a more egalitarian basis', as 'sisters' rather than 'daughters', ibid.

[80] Josephine E. Butler to Edith Leupold, 8 March 1867, reprinted in Jordan and Sharp, eds., *Josephine Butler and the Prostitution Campaigns*, I, p. 84.

[81] Armstrong, 'An Appeal for the Formation of a Church Penitentiary', p. 126.

[82] Josephine E. Butler to Florence Booth, 26 March 1885, reprinted in Jordan and Sharp, eds., *Josephine Butler and the Prostitution Campaigns*, IV, p. 109.

[83] Josephine E. Butler to Florence Booth, 26 March 1885, reprinted in ibid., IV, p. 109.

[84] Armstrong, 'An Appeal for the Formation of a Church Penitentiary', p. 123.

[85] Skene, *Hidden Depths*, p. 167.

2

Truth Before Everything

Rod Garner

Rod Garner is an Anglican priest, writer and theologian. He is currently Vicar of Holy Trinity, Southport, Theological Consultant to the Diocese of Liverpool and Hon. Canon (Designate) of Liverpool Cathedral. A Mancunian by birth he was ordained in 1978. Since then he has worked in urban communities combining the work of parish ministry with a varied remit as a theological educator. He has a research interest in the contemporary city and funding from the Josephine Butler Trust assisted his doctoral studies at the University of Manchester. His Ph.D led to the publication of Facing the City: Urban Mission in the 21st Century *(2004). He has written and contributed to several other books and is currently working on a short study guide on Josephine Butler that will bring her to a wider audience. Outside of urban ministry he retains a passion for philosophical theology and preaching. He is a Fellow of the College of Preachers and an Inspector of Theological Colleges and Courses for the House of Bishops. Rod's background in urban mission undergirds his examination here of Butler's conception of truth as relational, and he is not afraid to challenge the attenuated character of certain aspects of Butler's 'grammar of faith' as a warning to those engaged in ministry today.*

Only by the most absolute assertion of the uttermost truth, without qualification or compromise can a nation be waked to conscience of that truth or strengthened for duty.[1]

In 1897 Josephine Butler once again felt the hand of Providence on her shoulder. The 'just and holy cause' to which she had devoted so much of her life - the repeal of the Contagious Diseases Acts

- appeared under threat following the publication in *The Times* of a letter written by Lady Henry Somerset. In summary, it contained six proposals for the reimposition of legislation in India that Josephine regarded as even more repressive and unjust than the original CD Acts. It also raised the spectre of the State regulating in precise detail 'a disgusting and deadly vice', 'a vice which is the scourge of the world, the curse of the nations'.[2] She felt constrained to speak out: titled ladies had no right to canvas recommendations crucially affecting the lives of poor women mired in prostitution in a distant part of the British Empire, and no compromise could be made with an evil principle that bore the hallmark of Satan. Writing in a personal capacity and without the knowledge of even her most intimate friends, Josephine penned a robust response in the form of a pamphlet, *Truth before Everything*, printed in July 1897 and running to 9,000 copies. The pamphlet can be read variously as a call to arms, a restatement of guiding principles, a denunciation of wickedness in high places and a demand for justice. In what she clearly saw as an apocalyptic context, where no quarter could be given, a battle had to be waged not just against Government proposals and the misguided sentiments of men and women of rank but the legions of 'unclean spirits' pitted against the Divine light. In style and tone, the pamphlet is combative and uncompromising and its twenty four pages reflect a formidable resoluteness and a very practical intelligence.[3]

From the family devotions of her childhood[4] and her reading of the Bible, Josephine realised that sin could darken the mind of a nation as well as individuals, and that only by the unequivocal assertion of truth could a race or society recover 'from a species of moral atrophy - from a paralysis of the sense of justice'.[5] Given what we know of her dislike of self-importance and outward show[6], she would have been embarrassed by any comparison with other luminaries of the Christian faith. Nevertheless, it is possible to see in her stance intimations of Bunyan's Mr Valiant for Truth, Luther's impassioned 'Here I stand, I can do no other' and, nearer our own times, Solzhenitsyn's 'One Word of Truth' acceptance speech at the Nobel Prize ceremony in 1970.[7] Not once but many times, and frequently in the face of powerful and hostile opposition, Josephine made what Nadine Gordimer, writing from the context of apartheid in South Africa, has described as the 'essential gesture'.[8] Her speeches and writings would often contain the declaration of Abolitionist, William Lloyd Garrison (1805-79) to the extent that it became a personal mantra: 'I will be as harsh as truth, and as uncompromising as justice. I am in earnest - I will not equivocate - and I will be heard'.[9]

The sentence will appear dogmatic perhaps even unpleasantly authoritarian to a contemporary culture predicated on moral relativism, a suspicion of higher or metaphysical truths and an understandable fear of religious fanaticism. Writing in *The New York Times* recently, Arthur Schlesinger Jr draws attention to the messianic consciousness rooted in the mind of America that can easily mutate into obsession. He quotes with approval the definition of a fanatic cited by Mr. Dooley, the Irish bar tender created by Finley Peter Dunne: 'a fanatic does what he thinks th'Lord wud do if He only knew th'facts in th'case.'[10] The point about Josephine however is that she was a moralist, not a self-righteous, obsessive prig and, like Iris Murdoch, a century later, preferred the 'hard idea of truth to the facile notion of sincerity'.[11] The interesting and significant question here relates to Josephine's understanding of truth. What did the concept mean to her - both in relation to its nature and sources - and how did she arrive at the truth when issues of great principle were at stake? A further question also presents itself when we consider the increasing attention being paid by the Government to the role of faith communities in promoting urban regeneration and community relations. In a post 9/11 world where rigid theologies, understandings and practices are frequently seen as sources of conflict, are Josephine's methods, approach and world view still tenable in the area of Christian social action where the quote 'exclusivity or superiority of one interpretation of truth over the other',[12] threatens the pursuit of social justice and human well-being?

If we take these questions in order, it is clear from Josephine's own writings that her understanding of truth arises out of her intense religious faith, derived from a knowledge of God and an allegiance to the person and teachings of Christ. Introducing a collection of essays entitled *Woman's Work and Woman's Culture* in 1869 she wrote:

Once more I venture to say I appeal to Christ, and to Him alone,
as the fountain-head of those essential and eternal truths
which it is our duty and our wisdom to apply to all the changing
circumstances of human society. Believing as I do that He is Very
God, and that He was, in human form, the Exponent of the mind
of God to the world, I hold that His authority must be higher than
that of any man or society of men by whom the Truth which we
receive - so far as we receive Truth from men at all - can only
be transmitted. I believe all His acts to have had a supreme and
everlasting significance.[13]

The introduction makes clear that a relational truth underpins her personal creed. The truth which guided her and to which she appealed was not derived from churches, creeds or catechisms but 'direct from God'.[14] This was to engage her personality at the deepest level of existence, and in Christ she saw the love and compassion of God that she appropriated as an inward reality. If she had been moved by the example of the saints and martyrs of the early Christian centuries, she had little real allegiance to the established Church, choosing instead from her early years the solitary way of the pilgrim soul in search of the truth which would sustain her through life. From the beginning she had pressing questions on her mind that clerics could not answer, and above all she desired intimacy with God. To both tasks she devoted much prayer and long periods of solitude and to each she brought a formidable determination. In her mind and heart Josephine came to experience God and Christ as distinct but identical sources of the divine spark that animated her life, her thirst for social justice and her extraordinary compassion for the wretched and destitute. Her grandson and biographer wrote:

One might, with all reverence, put it like this. There was first
a belief in God, amounting to an absolute knowledge of His
existence; secondly, an equally firm conviction that Christ was
God; and, thirdly, a very clear understanding of the Holy Spirit.
Then, what was so impressive in her worship of the first two
Persons of the Trinity was their coalescence in her mind. For there
will be noticed in some of the phrases of these later letters what

can only be called an interchangeability of the Father and Son. And that was more wonderful because it was instinctive, not cultivated. She loved them both, not separately, nor equally, but as One. It is difficult to analyse further this tremendous endowment. There seems no need. It was so very simple. She knew God.[15]

This last remark is particularly revealing. The sceptical mind will question how Josephine knew that she knew God and will argue for different interpretations of her experience. For Josephine however, such experience was primary and self-authenticating and existed prior to the scientific or philosophical difficulties concerning how what she claimed to know was possible or how it could be explained. She knew with the philosopher and theologian Pascal that 'the heart has its reasons that reason knows nothing of'[16] and that religious faith cannot be reduced to powers of the intellect alone in its pursuit of the truth. She also knew that the act of commitment to what she described as 'deep, difficult holy work'[17] necessarily entailed risk and therefore the possibility of criticism or error. Although Protestant by temperament and broad association and indifferent to matters of religious dogma, she would have concurred with John Henry Newman in two important respects. The social reforms she so ardently desired could never be achieved by needless equivocation or the religious timidity that lacked the courage to counter the fashionable objections of her times to strong assertions of faith. She never heard Newman preach but his Oxford sermons on faith, reason and commitment reflect her stance and disposition towards these matters. Newman observes:

> *We are so constituted that if we insist upon being as sure as is conceivable in every step of our course, we must be content to creep along the ground, and can never soar. If we are intended for great ends we are called to great hazards.*[18]

On another occasion he writes:

> *Yet a faith which generously apprehends Eternal truth [...] is far better than that cold, sceptical, critical tone of mind, which has no sense of an overruling, ever present Providence, no desire to approach its God, but sits at home waiting for the fearful*

clearness of his visible coming, whom it might seek and find in due measure amid the twilight of the present world.[19]

We can hear the audible 'Amen' on Josephine's lips, but this should not be taken as proof that her knowledge of God or her belief in providence came easily to her. She was no stranger to spiritual crises and the truth she upheld had to withstand the deepest questioning on account of the undeserved misery and injustices she saw all around her. We shall return to her remonstrations with God a little later as a means of demonstrating the integrity that she brought to her quest for truth. At this point we can note that when the love of God the Father seemed remote or distant, it was to his Son that Josephine turned. In her own love for the outcast and poor, she recognised the compassion of Christ and it was to his character and commands that she gladly gave her complete obedience. In both she found an authoritative truth that could not be denied, even when his teachings were severe. Her stance is a compelling example of Newman's celebrated distinction between notional and real assent to be found in his classic essay on the nature and justification of faith.[20] The attitudes and convictions that drove her on evidenced an assent that was indubitably real and centred on the 'Saviour of the world and the poor multitudes who need that Christ'.[21]

The propositional truths ostensibly contained in liturgy, creeds and doctrines made no impact on Josephine. To introduce another distinction, it was the truth of Jesus rather than the truth about him that captivated her. Such truth did not emerge as the conclusion of sustained investigation or an intellectual argument and nor was it something that simply, so to speak, occurred to her. It was a truth that in the words of Psalm 100, had endured from 'generation to generation', and represented a form of personal acquaintance that constituted a vital store of moral knowledge. She was driven by the lure of the Incarnation and saw in the self-giving of Christ a profound significance. She grasped that logic alone could not do justice to, still less explain the One to whom the New Testament bore witness. The life and death of Christ had to be contemplated morally, had to be seen as in themselves acts of moral self-denial that had the power to inspire and encourage others to self sacrifice.[22] In his obedience and readiness to bear appalling burdens there was to be seen a beauty and pathos to which love could be the only response:

My God, I love thee; not because
I hope for heaven thereby,
nor yet because who love thee not
are lost eternally.
Thou, O Lord Jesus, thou didst me
upon the cross embrace;
for me didst bear the nails and spear,
and manifold disgrace,

And griefs and torments numberless,
and sweat of agony;
yea, death itself; and all for me
who was thine enemy.
Then why, O blessed Jesus Christ,
should I not love thee well,
not for the sake of winning heaven,
nor any fear of hell;

not with the hope of gaining aught,
not seeking a reward;
but as thyself hast loved me,
O ever loving Lord!
So would I love thee, dearest Lord,
and in thy praise will sing,
solely because thou art my God
and my most loving King.[23]

The words are not Josephine's but we are not mistaken in supposing that they reflect her moral and religious sentiments. In loving the example and brokenness of her Lord she also loved the Father who suffered in his Son. She had long prepared her heart for the reception of this truth that was to shape the moral praxis that defined her mission. And in this way she was to point not just to the importance of Christology for the rendering of practical service to the marginalised but also to the prayer and quietness that were for her the concomitants of religious truth-seeking expressed in terms of a performative discipline. As a sometimes impatient and zealous reformer, Josephine nevertheless possessed an inner life that was sufficiently schooled in humility to persuade her of the necessity of waiting and paying attention in order to discern the will of God.[24] It is impossible to understand her motivation and methods if this central fact about her is not grasped. She did not presume knowledge of the divine will and her moral resoluteness is misunderstood if it is taken (wrongly) as evidence of privileged knowledge of the purposes of the Almighty.[25] In a letter written after a period of illness she acknowledged the absolute necessity of silence in a world overburdened with excessive noise and the vapid prayers of well-meaning Christians that contributed to the overall din.[26]

The letter reflected the hard won peace of her old age that transcended the agitation of her early years when her praying, as we noted earlier, entailed much wrestling with God arising from a deep discontent with the world's ills. Aged only seventeen she would runaway into the woods close by her home and cry aloud to God to ameliorate the injustices and cruelties she saw around her. She would shriek to God to come and deliver.[27] What we can infer from this incident is the deep sense of social injustice that she had imbibed from her father. In later life she would identify with the prophets of old:

> *Justice, justice is what we with them desire. Our hearts cry out for justice, our souls are a thirst for justice. Like the Hebrew prophet of old we are sometimes constrained to exclaim 'Justice has fallen in the streets'.*[28]

Her cry for justice arose not just from her moral anguish at the state of things but also her need to understand the ways of God. She was not afraid to engage in the task of theodicy - of how she could continue to believe and trust in a good and loving God when innocent suffering was so prevalent. In the face of this challenge she was prepared to ask the searching questions that brought moral integrity to her believing and also took issue with the prevailing assumptions of her time concerning women's faith in general:

> *I think there prevails among clever men who do not know intimately the hearts of many women, an idea that women generally accept Christianity without a thought or a difficulty;*

*that they are in a measure instinctively pious, and that religion
is rather an indulgence of the feelings with them, than anything
else [...] For myself I can say that to be guided by feeling
would be simply dangerous; that I am obliged to give feeling
a subordinate place, and to be guided by a stern sense of right
throughout a life which involves daily and hourly self denial.
I believe there are few honest women knowing anything of
religion, who would not confess the same.*[29]

Josephine cultivated a tutored moral sense that was not content
to trust to feeling alone when God's truth was at stake. It would be
too much to claim that, like Augustine, she thought in questions but
there was about her a mental restlessness and energy that led her
mind to refashion what it found theologically inadequate. This was
not simply intellectual curiosity on her part but stemmed from her love
of truth and her frustration with those who failed to provide answers
or guidance. It was not just the established position of the Church of
England or its creeds that kept her at arm's length from its embrace: it
was also its inability to provide the help or illumination she required as
she grappled with the mystery of the 'strange man on the cross', who
was also for her the agent of God's truth in a world where his goodness
and power were open to question. She needed a Church that could
engage with her concerns, that saw truth as something more than a
convenience or tidy formulation. In this she was to be disappointed
but the more important fact remains. Thinking and questioning for
Josephine constituted a moral activity: clarity of thought mattered
because religion was the deepest form of life, and her engagement
with God and the issues of her day required an educated heart and a
passionate mind. Quite probably she saw the doctrinal assumptions of
the Church as morally inferior to her own highest beliefs and standards.
No less likely, she would have agreed with Simone Weil that we are
to prefer truth to Christ himself and that if we follow truth we cannot
go very far without falling back into his arms.[30] Josephine knew along
with the Psalmist that the Lord had 'set her feet in a large room' (Ps.
31.8). The basis of her conviction about him therefore had to be spread
as widely as her thought would range.[31]

This principle extended beyond the specifically theological: in her writings and campaigns her impassioned prose was strengthened by her grasp of the subject, the range of her knowledge, her attention to detail and the forensic skill she employed to expose the moral and logical inadequacies of her opponents' arguments. That she so often saw through the specious and the spurious when faced with hypocritical or dishonest proposals was in part due to her moral gravitas - the strenuousness that informed her reading of the human condition and her belief that everything was ultimately judged from a perspective that was not of this world.[32] And to this we must add the quality of her intellect. This she employed not in order to dazzle or impress others - a facet of her Oxford years that she found deeply depressing in its learned men - but to advance her arguments, to make sense of the mass of publications and statistics she had to analyse and the complex constitutional procedures that had to be negotiated. In the sixteen year campaign to repeal the Contagious Diseases Acts, over nine hundred public meetings were organised and five hundred and twenty books and pamphlets on prostitution were published.[33] Josephine read voraciously and immersed herself in these nuanced and complex issues, always conscious that in her conversation with God and the lesser intelligence of men '... every faculty of the mind and emotion of the soul is called to its highest exercise'.[34] It is not surprising therefore to learn that she was held in such high regard by her husband George.Writing to a friend late in life, she recalled in her letter that 'from my earliest married life, my dear husband used to say, if there was any difficult problem or crisis before the world "I must ask my dear wife, she is such a politician"'.[35]

This accolade was accorded to her with no irony intended: it reflected her realism concerning the complexities of the world, her understanding of politics as 'the art of the possible' and her unyielding conviction that her cause would not fail even when the politics surrounding her campaign work became mean, protracted and occasionally vicious. Truth was on her side and like Wilberforce before her she was 'God's politician'.

How serviceable is this kind of belief today in a global urban culture characterised by competing truth claims? In what Zygmunt Bauman has described as our increasingly 'liquid' world[36] where religions once isolated from each other now inhabit the same street or are looking at each other over the same wall, does Josephine's single-minded approach to truth-seeking appear anachronistic or even dangerous? If the utility of faith communities is increasingly being acknowledged by the Government in relation to social inclusion and community cohesion, it is no less true, as a recent report of the Joseph Rowntree Foundation makes clear, that such communities also have had the potential to produce 'tribal social networks that excluded others, perpetuated stereotypes, punished deviants, created stagnation and isolation and inhibited knowledge'.[37] In America where the Bush administration channelled £1.25 billion to faith-based charities in 2005 for social services provision there is also unease in some quarters that funding is being used to spread religion rather than the alleviation of poverty or need.[38]

Even when it is conceded that Josephine possessed a fervent disposition that did not easily tolerate other points of view when the truth was in danger of being lost or compromised, a truth that in part derived from her private, direct access to God, she has no place in the pantheon of contemporary religious fundamentalism. Her mind in certain respects at least was open to fresh disclosures; she had an innate capacity for learning new things, incorporating into her world view what was held to be shocking by less supple or searching religious minds. Scientific controversies, for example, even when they called into question the religious account of human origins were not for her 'the Enemies of God'; in her view 'they have helped us to a revelation of a wider universe, a larger purpose and a greater God than we had before realised'.[39] She was however less charitably disposed to doctrinal controversies and in this instance, unlike Newman, she would have found the idea of dying for a dogma unnecessary and odd. She grasped, intuitively perhaps, that at the beginning of it all there was at the heart of the Christian religion not an idea, not a philosophy but a moral praxis made singular in time and space in Jesus. It was this truth rather than the minutiae of later theories and doctrines that claimed her allegiance but also exposed a weakness in her stance that will be examined shortly. If Josephine was intolerant, it was primarily in relation to tyranny, oppression and injustice. Her strongest language in *Truth Before Everything* is employed against human duplicity, the lack of sympathy of one human heart for another and the easy accommodation of the world to the principles of self-interest and opportunism. She was genuinely counter-cultural, ready whenever necessary to embrace a principled pragmatism if this meant the hungry being fed and the poor protected, but never prepared to sacrifice the truth she had learned from Christ in order to serve the interests of the State. In a very singular way she stood as a sign of contradiction to worldly powers, prepared when necessary, in a memorable phrase of St Benedict, to move from the 'desert to the market place' and back again. By embracing this principle of oscillation she remained open to the truth of the Son of God who beckoned her to share in life's sorrows and sadness. That this came about was due to her attitude of attentive waiting and deep engagement with God that liberated her truest self, purified her motives and made her available to care for others.

In the vastly changed context of today with its shifting networks and complex relations, it is still necessary however to ask whether Josephine's confessional stance and grammar of faith constitute a good model for social action in relation to the required openness to Otherness that lies at the heart of dialogue, partnership and the religious requirement in all three monotheistic faiths to work for the common good. To what extent does her Christianity, and therefore her truth, define itself, 'on the one hand against other positions and, on the other, with respect to other positions'?[40] Graham Ward provides an example of what this might look like on the ground:

> *I live with my Jewish neighbour, I eat with my Muslim friend,*
> *I listen with the Quaker who sits and listens with me, and I*
> *slowly learn about the religions of South Asia [...] I can and do*
> *remain a Christian, but my body is continually mapped onto*
> *other bodies [...] We must necessarily make judgments with*
> *regards to all sorts of things and we must, with equal necessity,*
> *confess our ignorance. We must suspend our judgment about*
> *those who pursue love, mercy, justice and righteousness in other*
> *practices and in other communities with other liturgies and*

symbolic exchanges. We must sink ourselves deeper into our own traditions, meditating upon the grammar of faith we live [...] and not be afraid that others do things differently [...] in the urban spaces we share and produce [...] The real questions about the relation of different faith communities and traditions only emerge as we learn to live together without fear'.[41]

The passage calls for the tact and courtesy that may lead to a more comprehensive awareness of the activity of God beyond familiar boundaries along with what Mary Warnock has described as a 'continuum of imagination'[42] that, so to speak, realigns our vision of Christ for this time and no other. Josephine by nature, upbringing and her capacity for hard thought went a long way towards fulfilling these requirements and it is possible to imagine her responding positively to the complexity that defines contemporary urban culture. There is however an important caveat to be lodged at this point that has to do with the interesting and suggestive phrase, 'grammar of faith', that has featured in the previous paragraphs.

If I may digress for a moment, I have recently reviewed a slim volume of stories and articles on urban mission,[43] representing thirty eight contributions from practitioners across the denominations sharing a costly 'commitment to God's kingdom in the city'.[44] The book contains impressive evidence of a huge amount of energy, courage and imagination being expended in the name of Christ in the inner cities and outer estates. All can be seen as examples of Josephine's own commitment to the poor of her day. But there is something else that binds her to these testimonies that has to do with their palpable impatience with ecclesiastical structures and tired formulations that impede the work of true discipleship. 'We unlock the Bible in our own way', remarks one contributor and 'sit lightly to Christology, doctrines of the atonement, sacraments, baptism and so forth'.[45] Josephine employed the same kind of attenuated theological template to remarkable effect. It is also true that the demanding crucible of the urban does require risk, innovation and a readiness to experiment in relation to what will actually work in any given context. But no less true however, urban practitioners must also ensure that their purposeful action and prayer are both informed by the wider resources of ecclesial wisdom, tradition and experience that contribute to constructive theological understanding and, crucially, shape Christian identity. Otherwise urban mission can easily become a matter of personal taste, untutored theological sloganising or a potentially dangerous religious enclave defined by sharp boundaries and a fierce assertion of distinctiveness in relation to the wider community. Furthermore its grammar of faith will appear thin and meagre. There is obvious merit in a faith that is centred on the relational and saving truth of Christ. But when it fails to be informed by the wider communal and propositional dimensions of Christian believing that bring about a greater degree of coherence and integrity to its truth and vision, and, still less, by the wisdom and practices of other faith traditions, there are legitimate grounds for concern.

Josephine was not sectarian in her thinking and was never slow to engage with groups or societies with whom she shared a common cause. But her grammar of faith was undoubtedly a private and personal affair which 'tended to reduce - almost to nullify - those aids to a good life which average practising Christians cultivate'.[46] John Wesley had pointed out a century earlier that there was no such thing as a solitary Christian, but Josephine refuted this claim by staying close to her experience of God and his revelation in Jesus. This was her truth - the source of her 'truth before everything'. We are entitled to ask however whether her truth might have been enhanced and deepened by a greater willingness to view worship and liturgy as more than private opportunities for 'uninterrupted contemplation',[47] and Christian doctrine as a necessary corrective to highly subjective versions of faith that can become dysfunctional because they have no appreciation of religious roots, or the centrality of corporate faith in relation to Christian formation.

The question is important for two reasons. For some time now religious belief has been marked by an exaggerated individualism that reduces believing to an interior and personal activity that is widespread in the churches and beyond. Authenticity is accorded to a personal credo in preference to a body of assumptions inherited and held in common and a rootless individualism assumes centre stage grounded in private opinion and preference. The weakness of this position in relation to the human search for truth and meaning that characterised Josephine's life is the failure to recognise that a fuller understanding of truth always requires the fruits of others' labours that are able to augment, stimulate and regulate individual exploration. This is not indoctrination but rather the frank admission that the truth by definition can never be the sole prerogative of any one individual. Aristotle is our teacher here:

> *The investigation of the truth is in one way hard, in another easy [...] no one is able to obtain the truth adequately, while on the other hand we do not collectively fail but everyone says something true about the nature of things, and while individually we contribute little or nothing to the truth, by the union of all a considerable amount is amassed.* [48]

We shall never know whether Josephine's husband as a teacher of classics shared this insight with her as they studied together in their lodgings on quiet Oxford evenings. What we can say at this point is that the fundamental simplicity and conviction that she brought to the love of God manifested in Jesus (and we recall that both owed much to hard thought and prayer) bypassed what the Church had to offer her as itself a seeker after truth and a community of truthfulness. And this rejection on the part of one who placed 'truth before everything' may be regarded as a presumptuous act that effectively denied her access to a corporate framework of knowledge within which she may have reached a more authentic level of faith and understanding, and therefore a more gracious apprehension of the truth. Notwithstanding the intellectual defects and moral laxities of the Church to which she gave her tenuous allegiance and the undoubted integrity of her own prophetic insight concerning social injustice, her stance would have been strengthened by the recognition that truth is always two-eyed and is a matter of 'holding together the two poles of a dialectic, rather than opposing the parts played by the individual and the community'.[49]

The relevance of this to our own context is obvious. We need the humility to recognise that our truth seeking is necessarily a provisional and communal task. Truth is always in some sense an inherited affair. For the great majority of believers there is no solitary religious sphere and we learn to the end of our days from the accumulated wisdom and experience of others, within and beyond the churches. As faiths are increasingly exposed to each other as religions in the contested and potentially fractious arena of the urban and as fundamentalism reasserts itself across the world with a new and terrifying ferocity, the need for dialogue and the investigation of our respective religious foundations has never been greater. In her own day Josephine dug for the truth: the requirement today is that we dig more widely.

Endnotes

[1] Words spoken by Wendell Philips at the grave of Lloyd Garrison, as quoted in Josephine Butler, *Truth Before Everything* (Liverpool. Pewtree and Co., 1897), p. 1.
[2] Cited in letter of resignation from the Purity Department of the World's Women's Christian Temperance Union (WWCTU) 27 Sept. 1897.
[3] 'You won't think I am a visionary or dreamer. I never was that. I am too practical, and always wanting work rather than contemplation.' Quoted by A.S.G. Butler, *Portrait of Josephine Butler* (London: Faber & Faber, 1954), p. 177.
[4] Josephine's father, John Grey assembled his family and household for an act of worship at the end of each day. See F. Moberly Bell, *Josephine Butler* (London: Constable 1962), p. 17.
[5] Butler, *Truth before Everything*, p. 9.
[6] 'I absolutely decline to write my own life. I hate the very appearance of egotism, and I feel almost a disgust of speaking of myself.' Part of letter to the Misses Priestman, 4 February 1891, quoted by Jane Jordan, *Josephine Butler*, p. 260.
[7] The title is part of a Russian proverb, 'One word of truth outweighs the whole world'.
[8] Cited by F. Keane in his autobiography, *All of These People* (London: Harper 2005), p. 25.
[9] Jordan, *Butler*, p. 116.
[10] A. Schlesinger, Jr., 'Forgetting Reinhold Niebuhr', *The New York Times*, September 18, 2005.
[11] Cited by A. S. Byatt in her *Passions of the Mind: Selected Writings* (London: Chatto and Windus, 1992), p. 72.
[12] O. McTernan, *Violence in God's Name*, (London: Darton, Longman & Todd, 2003), p. 148.
[13] Cited by Butler, *Portrait of Josephine Butler*, p. 47.
[14] Butler, *Portrait of Josephine Butler*, p. 46.
[15] Butler, *Portrait of Josephine Butler*, p. 174.
[16] Blaise Pascal, *Pensées*, ed. Louis Lafuma (Paris: Editions du Seuil, 1962), série II, no. 423 (277), p. 180: 'le coeur a ses raisons que la raison connait point'.
[17] Cited in *Celebrating The Saints*, compiled by R. Atwell (Canterbury Press , 1998), p. 171.
[18] John Henry Newman, *Sermons, chiefly on the theory of religious belief, preached before the University of Oxford* (London: Rivington, 2nd edition 1844), p. 208.
[19] Newman, *Sermons*, p. 213.
[20] John Henry Newman, *Essay in Aid of a Grammar of Assent*, ed. I.T. Ker, (Oxford: Clarendon Press, 1985).
[21] Butler, *Portrait of Josphine Butler*, p. 170.
[22] The same line of thought is evident in C. Gore, *The Incarnation of the Son of God* (London: John Murray, 1891), p. 110.
[23] 'O Deus, ego amo te, ' translated by Edward Caswall, in *The English Hymnal* ed. Percy Dearmer et al (London: Oxford University Press, 1906), no. 80, p. 66.

[24] Writing on this theme Simone Weil comments: 'We do not obtain the most precious gifts by going in search of them but by waiting for them. Man cannot discover them by his own powers and if he sets out to seek for them he will find in their place counterfeits of which he will be unable to discern the falsity. Attention consists of suspending our thought, leaving it detached, empty and ready to be penetrated by the object, it means holding in our minds, within reach of this thought, but on a lower level and not in contact with it, the diverse knowledge we have acquired which we are forced to make use of. Above all our thought should be empty, waiting, not seeking anything, but ready to receive in its naked truth the object which is to penetrate it'. See her *Waiting on God* (London: Collins Fontana 7th edition, 1973), pp. 72-73.

[25] In this respect she would certainly have been aware of Lincoln's memorable words to the American nation in his inaugural address: 'The Almighty has his own purposes.' See A.Schlesinger Jr. *New York Times* 18 Sept 2005.

[26] Butler, *Portrait of Josephine Butler*, p. 178.

[27] Butler, *Portrait of Josephine Butler*, p. 180.

[28] *Truth Before Everything*, p. 9.

[29] Jordan, *Butler*, p. 44.

[30] Cited by R. Harries, 'Religion and Science – Old Enemies or New Friends' in *Modern Believing*, 47, no. 1 (January 2006), pp. 22-27, p. 26.

[31] Austin Farrer comments 'Faith perishes if it is walled in or confined. If it is anywhere it must be everywhere, like God himself: if God is in your life, he is all things for he is God'. See his *A Celebration of Faith* (London: Hodder & Stoughton, 1990), p. 60.

[32] Josephine's world view – particularly the relation between the temporal and the infinite can be seen in the thinking of Reinhold Niebuhr: 'The combination of moral resoluteness about the immediate issues with a religious awareness of another dimension of meaning and judgement, must be regarded as almost a perfect model of the difficult but not impossible task of remaining loyal and responsible towards the moral treasures of a free society on the one hand, while yet having some religious vantage point over the struggle.' Cited by A. Schleringer Jr, *New York Times*, 18 September, 2005.

[33] P. Hollis , *Women in Public: A Woman's Movement 1850-1900* (London: Allen & Unwin 1979), p. 199.

[34] Jordan, *Butler*, p. 43.

[35] Ibid.

[36] Z. Bauman, *Identity* (Cambridge: Polity Press 2004), p. 82.

[37] Extract from Church Times review, 17 March 2006, *Faith as Social Capital; Connecting or Dividing?* , eds. R. Furbey, A. Dinham, R. Farnell, D. Finnerson, G. Wilkinson, C. Howarth, D. Hussain, S. Palmer (Cambridge: Polity Press, 2006).

[38] See *The Guardian*, 11 March 2006, p.17. 'Some of these organisations do good work, but for some of them their first goal is winning a new soul to convert and that type of activity should always be funded with private dollars'. Rob Boston, 'Americans United for Separation of Church and State'.

[39] Jordan, *Butler*, p. 40.

[40] Graham Ward, *Cities of God*, (London: Routledge, 2000), p. 257.

[41] Ward, *Cities*, pp. 257-58.

[42] Mary Warnock, 'Imagination - Aesthetic and Religious', *Theology*, LXXX, November 1980, no. 696, pp. 403-09, p. 404.

[43] *Urban Church : A Practitioner's Resource Book*, eds. M. Eastman & S. Latham (London: SPCK, 2004).

[44] Eastman and Latham, *Urban Church*, p. ix.

[45] Eastman and Latham, *Urban Church*, p. 21.

[46] Butler, *Portrait of Josphine Butler*, p. 166.

[47] Butler, *Portrait of Josephine Butler*, p. 166.

[48] Aristotle, *The Metaphysics*, ed. Hugh Lawson-Tancred (Harmondsworth: Penguin, 1998), p. 43.

[49] *Believing in the Church: The Corporate Nature of Faith*. The Doctrine Commission of the Church of England (London: SPCK, 1981), p. 61.

Josephine Butler and St. Catherine of Siena

David Scott

David Scott was a parish priest in Cumbria for eleven years, and since 1991 has been Rector of St Lawrence and St Swithun in Winchester. He won the Sunday Times/BBC national poetry competition in 1978, and in 1986 was awarded the Geoffrey Faber Memorial Prize for his first book of poems, A Quiet Gathering *(1984). His second collection,* Playing for England *(1989) was a Poetry Book Society Recommendation. His most recent collection,* Piecing Together *was published in 2005. In examining the nature of the relation between Butler and the medieval saint, David is drawn to the way in which each woman unites mystical apprehension of the Divine with intense engagement with the world. He also reveals Butler to be a pioneer of a scientific approach to religious experience.*

I n April 2000 'a letter to the Dominican Order' was published to celebrate the naming of St Catherine of Siena as one of the Patrons of Europe. Timothy Radcliffe who was Master of the Dominicans at the time wrote the letter, which was entitled, 'St Catherine of Siena (1347-80) Patroness of Europe'. The century before Radcliffe's letter, in 1878, Horace Marshall and Son, London, published the first edition of Josephine Butler's biography of Catherine of Siena.

To start this paper with Timothy Radcliffe brings us right into the place where the energy of St Catherine emerged from a deep contemplative faith. 'Catherine worked on two seemingly contradictory levels, a public level and a private level. She walked with Popes and had their ear on the international policy making, but she also cultivated what she called 'a cell of self-knowledge'. [1] Josephine Butler also worked on the dynamic forged by those apparent opposites, which is the reason why she was so fascinated by St Catherine herself. Josephine Butler wrote a good deal, much of it in the cause of women's rights. She wanted to give back to abused women their own original divine identity, their dignity, and a space to regroup and flourish. In Catherine of Siena, Josephine Butler found someone who shared a similar 'spirituality' which was based both on private prayer and public action.

Timothy Radcliffe offers insight into the point of stability for Catherine, which enabled her to marry her inner and outer selves:

> *Catherine of Siena offers a liberating answer to the contemporary quest for identity. It takes us far away from a false identity based on status, wealth and power. For at the heart of our being is the God whose love sustains us in being. This is the place of contemplative prayer, where one meets God who delights in loving and forgiving, and whose own goodness we taste. Here we discover the secret of Catherine's peace and her dynamism, her confidence and her humility. This is what made this young woman, with little formal education a great preacher. This is what gave her the freedom to speak and to listen. This is what gave her the courage to dive in and address the great issues of her time.* [2]

The purpose of this essay is to open up an aspect of Butler's writing which may be unfamiliar to some, and also to go some way to rescue her reputation as a biographer and a 'spiritual writer' in the light of the critical essay by Pat Starkey, 'Saints, Virgins and Family Members: Exemplary Biographies? Josephine Butler as Biographer', in which she accuses Butler both of an uncritical attitude to her subject, and also of subsuming Catherine to her own personal agenda. There is no doubt that Butler's biography of Catherine of Siena is hagiographical, and that she uses material written in the fourteenth century to account for Catherine's canonisation. However, the purpose of Butler's book is threefold. First, to tell the story of Catherine's life as clearly and vividly as she could, given the range of her sources. Then secondly, to use that story to draw examples of the way God enters the lives of certain people in profound ways for the benefit of the Church; and thirdly, to allow Butler to live through some of her own experiences and feelings by means of the account of someone who lived under similar pressures and through similar crises.

To call that third process 'self-making' as Starkey does, and to accuse Butler of putting herself 'centre-stage' is a gloss on her biography of Catherine of Siena that can hardly be substantiated.[3] When Starkey says, 'even in the lives of the saints, her heroes and heroines are shown to share her preoccupations', she is saying little more than that many people living on the same planet travel the same paths at different historical times, but inevitably share similar feelings about it. To say that Butler 'ceased to be merely the author who pointed out the exemplary nature of her subjects' actions and herself became both narrator *and subject*' is, in the case of this biography of Catherine of Siena, quite misleading.[4] Biographers obviously choose subjects because of the empathy they feel towards the subject, but that does not mean that in every case and on every topic the biographer gets in the way of their subject. On the contrary, it could be that the subject illuminates aspects of the biographer's character as it may well do the reader's, and that surely is one great purpose of literature.

To take just one particular example, Starkey writes: 'In all three saints' lives (Butler wrote lives of St Agnes, and Pastor Oberlin, as well as St Catherine of Siena), Josephine uses traditional hagiographical format, for example by demonstrating their juvenile piety.'[5] 'Juvenile piety', if you want to put this common phenomenon in such 'loaded' words, is a natural spiritual phenomenon. It is a human reality. Why criticise it or belittle it? To outlaw a 'traditional hagiographical format', if that indeed was the reality, an experience of sanctity, of the divine indwelling in human character, to be cynical about that, is no task of a biographer of a religious subject.

In the light of Starkey's essay, I have attempted to convey a sense of Butler's book and her portrait of Catherine's early spiritual life, not as a 'self-making' but as a process of self understanding that illuminates the experiences of both biographer and her subject. The bulk of *Catherine of Siena* is taken up with the political and historical aspects of the Papacy in which Catherine played a major role. Unfortunately it has been impossible in this essay to cover the whole of the book, and consequently the early spiritual journey, through conversion and the dark night to the vision of Christ will have to suffice as evidence of Butler's ability to enter into the heart and mind of her subject, which may well have struck deep chords with her own journey, but not, as Starkey assumes, and I contest, to the extent of 'self making'.

Josephine's biography of Catherine of Siena was written in something of a lull in her campaigning work between 1876 and 1878. The 1870's were lean years for the repeal movement. Her son Charles had been sent to Clifton College in 1874, but was ordered home after suffering from fainting fits. This caused the headmaster, Percival, to 'blow up' poor Charlie and caused Josephine to write, 'Percival *hates* me and it seems he let it out in his anger – what can you expect of a man who loves the *Acts*.'[6] She took Charlie to recuperate in the Lake District and also had some continental holidays too, which included a conference at Geneva at which she delivered sterling addresses to the Hygiene Section of the Conference and denounced the forcible examination of women.

In this period Josephine was able to devote considerably more time than usual to writing. In 1876 she had published *The Hour before the Dawn*, which was an attack on the sexual double standard and a plea for understanding for the prostitute, about whom she challenged the reader with the words, 'what was her life and what was yours?'[7] If sexual double standards were not controversial enough, Butler entered another world of religious controversy with her biography of St Catherine of Siena. Material on the lives of Saints had become a controversial issue in the nineteenth century, dividing Reformed and Catholic traditions. During 1848 Newman and F.W. Faber became closely involved in a controversy over Faber's translation of some lives of saints. In October 1848 Newman wrote to Faber declaring his anxiety over 'a row blowing up'.[8] Newman expressed reservations about Faber's decision to publish the life of St Rose of Lima. Some old Catholics criticised the series because it concentrated on Italian, French and Spanish saints, and because many of the lives contained extravagant accounts of miracles and austerities, and some revealed scandals in Catholic countries. Eventually the series was approved, and publication was resumed. In 1844, four years prior to Newman's reservations on St Rose, his own Life of St Stephen Harding, albeit an English Cistercian monk, had been published. The writings of the Oxford Movement had paved the way for a greater understanding of the place of the Saints in English devotion, and works such as Baring Gould's *Lives of the Saints* (1872), and Butler's own biography of St Catherine of Siena in 1878, passed into circulation without very much public scandal.

What is so interesting about the biography of Catherine of Siena is that it predates the considerable amount of material in English which began to emerge from 1890 onwards, both more generally on the subject of mysticism, and more particularly on Catherine of Siena. These are some of the landmark publications of the period: 1878, Josephine Butler's biography of Catherine; 1881, E. B. Pusey quoting Catherine in his *Spiritual Letters*; 1887, A. T. Drane's *The History of Catherine of Siena and her Companions*; 1896, *Dialogue of the Seraphic Virgin*, translated by Algar Thorold; 1899, Dean Inge's Bampton Lectures *Of Christian Mysticism*; 1902, Dom Cuthbert Butler of Downside begins his *Western Mysticism*, published 1922; 1902, William James, *Varieties of Religious Experience*; 1905, *Letters of Catherine of Siena* by Vida Scudder; 1907, Edmund Gardner's Biography of St Catherine; 1909, Rufus Jones of Harvard, *Studies in Mystical Religion*, quoting Gardner's biography on Catherine; 1910, Gardner's reprint of a 1521 treatise including Catherine's *Cell of Self-Knowledge*; 1911, Evelyn Underhill's *Mysticism*. That brings us to 33 years after Butler's biography, which is some indication of how much the book was a pioneer work in the area of mysticism.

The question then arises, just what material did Butler have to work on? There were of course works in Italian, and we presume it was these she studied, both for background, such as Muratori's *Annali d'Italia* of 1743-49, Villani's *Istorie*, and in French, Sismondi's *L'Histoire des Républiques Italiennes*. J. A. Symonds' *Siena and St Catherine* was available to her, as was Nicholas Tommasin's, *The Spirit and the Works of St Catherine* (1860), and Raimundo of Capua's *Life of St Catherine*, which was available in translation in an American edition. Butler was fluent in both French and Italian, and had, with her husband, assisted Dante Gabriel Rossetti with his translations for *The Early Italian Poets* (1861).[9]

St Catherine lived from 1347-1380. For much of this time the Pope was resident at Avignon. Pope Clement V had requested the seat of the papacy should move to France in 1305. Siena was one of the many walled cities that had a fiercely independent existence in fourteenth-century Italy. Butler points out how, in this period,

> *Many of the old-fashioned virtues had disappeared, and revolting vices prevailed, especially in the courts and palaces of princes, both lay and ecclesiastical. Base intrigues were the order of the day and the only recognised means of earthly success. The aristocracy set an example of every crime, and the grossest debauchery reigned in their palaces and castles. Poison and the knife were daily revealed too in the struggle to hold their own against rivals. Troops of assassins were retained in their pay, and a complete protection was granted to brigands in return for the services they rendered to their lordly employers.* [10]

The church of the time came in for a great deal of criticism too. 'No sight could have been more sad, more indecent, it may be said, for a Christian soul to contemplate than the sight that the Christian then presented in the persons of the prominent representatives.' The major factor for a study of Catherine of Siena, in relation to the Church was the position of the Papacy. Pope Clement V had removed the seat of the Papacy to Avignon. Six Popes after him continued to live in this voluntary exile, far from their duties and their people.

> *The voluntary exile of the Pope, and his neglect of the interests of his subjects, had a most melancholy effect upon the faith, the morals and the politics of the Church. The corruption of the prelates, the dishonourable and scandalous lives of the young cardinals, and the universal licence of the city were so notorious to all Europe that Avignon received the name of the 'Western Babylon'* [11].

Butler may have been quoting Sismondi here word for word but it suited her thesis and gave her a template for her thoughts about the moral state of late-nineteenth century England.

Into this 'Western Babylon' of fourteenth-century Siena was born a remarkable woman who later was acknowledged as a saint. One of Catherine's great political achievements, setting aside for a moment her spiritual heritage, was to help restore, almost single-handed, the Papacy back to Rome. 'It was Catherine', wrote Butler, 'the wool dyer's daughter who first dared to address to the Pope at Avignon letters full of severe truth, setting forth to him the miseries of his Italian subjects, the evils of his non-residence and the gross cruelty of his unworthy legates: it was she who prevailed in her endeavour to bring back the Sovereign Pontiff to his country, and to awaken him to a sense of his responsibilities towards his torn and distracted folk.'[12]

Biography is unlikely ever to be a pure science. Some link with the subject attracts the biographer and the story is written with that inspiration behind it. The way in which the private devotional life and the public, political church life of Catherine of Siena were united to make her a powerful political force was an attractive mix for Butler, and throughout the biography it is possible to sense Butler's own life-story finding resonances in Catherine's. The connections begin even at the early stages of Catherine's life. Catherine felt set apart by God from an early age, and she needed to get away from the city and be alone. Josephine Butler, similarly liked nothing better than to ride in the countryside of her native Northumberland, and in writing of Catherine's childhood, it is possible to sense a bond. 'As soon as Catherine could walk [...] she contracted a habit of wondering from home; a habit which developed in her maturer age, and which became the subject of some inward questioning of her own heart'.[13]

These long solitary walks of Catherine 'showed her love for nature, the birds and beasts and flowers. Every man, woman and child was to her a friend, a dear fellow creature to be greeted without reserve, to be confronted, consoled, congratulated, pleaded with or gently rebuked as one beloved of the common Father and redeemed by the precious blood of Christ'.[14] Butler writes about the similarities in the religious nature of certain children through the ages, particularly in regard to the abandonment of the home, and a setting off, who knows where, for the sake of Christ. Particularly interesting is the comparison that Butler makes between Catherine and Theresa of Avila, and in her quoting the work of J. A. Froude (1818-1894). Froude was a great friend from university days of her husband George. Froude had a stormy time, ending in the loss of his Christian faith, much to the sorrow of his friends. Froude's psychological study of Theresa of Avila contained a record of the famous journey of the child Theresa who set out determined to be a martyr for Christ. Theresa left home 'without asking leave, or saying a word to anyone, they started, and had crossed a bridge when an uncle encountered them', writes Froude, 'and took them home. The martyrdom project coming to an end they (Theresa and her brother) thought of turning hermits and built themselves cells in the garden; but here the mechanics failed them; the roofs fell in and they lost heart'.[15] As we read Butler on Catherine of Siena we get to know Butler herself more deeply. The connection between the two can be seen most clearly in the twin inspirations for their lives: religion and politics. The political life followed the real religious upsurge within both. We have begun to see the seeds of Catherine's religious life, but the full force of her spiritual commitment takes a significant step forward as she secures for herself a space for private prayer. Before Catherine's 'cell of self-knowledge' became a reality, a simpler and more tangible cell was set aside for her to pray and commune with God. There was a considerable sorrow in the Benincasa family over the fact that Catherine did not want to marry in the conventional sense, but wanted to be betrothed to Christ. 'He who has united my soul to his, has all the riches of heaven and earth and he can provide for and protect me'.[16] This commitment had its tangible symbol in the setting up of a small cell or room, which became Catherine's sanctuary, and the place where she could commune with God.

Here she devoted herself to prayer and to the study of the will of God. For three years she scarcely quitted this cell. She put forth during these years the strength of an athlete in her wrestlings with heaven, determined first to know her Saviour and her own heart, and then to do and bear in this world whatever he should ordain for her [...] These years were a stern and energetic preparation for the combats of the future life.[17]

Although Butler certainly had many similar inward feelings about God as Catherine did, in her family life she went far from the path of monastic celibacy. Her life was to include bringing up a human family, and as wife to George and soul mate in his varied ministries through the years, and to share in all the joys and trials that family commitment brought. This included the tragic incident of the death of her daughter Eva in 1864. This death, which must have been to a certain extent a death to part of herself, may be comparable to Catherine's death to self and a growing openness to the will of God in spiritual growth and commitment to a 'stern and energetic preparation for the combats of her future life'.[187]

Butler speaks with feeling when she describes Catherine's struggle with physical tiredness and the desire for sleep. '[Catherine] confided to her friend and biographer Raymond, the victory over sleep had cost her more than any other, and that she had undergone inexpressible conflicts in triumphing over the natural desire for repose. Such conquests over self have never been absent in the lives of the saints'.[19]

Catherine took on the mantle and the rule of life of the Dominicans. She became an associate, and took the title of Brethren and Sisters of the Militia of Jesus Christ. She wore the black and white habit of the Dominican. In the biography, Butler adds a significant note at this point: 'What life, (Catherine) thought, could be so blessed as this? What mission so sacred as this carrying the lamp of truth from city to city? Who so happy as these messengers, disencumbered of all worldly ties, and ready for all the martyrdom of life as well as for death?' And then she adds this: 'But she was a woman!'[20]

It is at this point in the biography that Butler comes to the very heart of the spiritual springs of human action, and Butler sets aside a page to explain and in a sense to fight the cause of the inner life as the power house, the engine room, the spark that generates a life of commitment, service and action for the love of God and for the needs of the people in the society of the day. We can tell how much it is a personal testament, as well as part of the biography. Butler uses some interesting language to do with 'spirituality', very much the language of the day, in which 'science' was taking a leading part in the religious debates. She writes as a prelude to the manifesto, 'The science of which Catherine was a devotee is, let it be remembered, pre-eminently an experimental science. For many, however, if it is needless that I should speak thus; nor will I attempt any explanation or apology for the manner in which our saint constantly speaks of that which the natural eyes hath not seen, nor the ear heard, but which God has in all times revealed to them that persistently seek him'.[21]

Then follows a most interesting section about prayer:

Those who have any experience of real prayer know full well that in the pause of the soul before God after it has uttered its complaint, made known its desires, or sought guidance in perplexity, there comes the clearer vision of duty, and the still small voice of guidance is heard, rectifying the judgement, strengthening the resolve, and consoling the spirit; they know that their influence, external to us and yet within us, gently and forcibly moves us, deals with us, speaks with us, in fine. Prayer cannot be truly called communion, if the only voice heard be the voice of the pleader. Be still, be silent, then, dear reader, if you are disposed to object. If you have not yet heard the voice of God speaking within you, it is because you have not pleaded enough with him; it is because you have not yet considered or acted in the matter in a truly scientific manner.[22]

In the 1870's this is an unfamiliar voice in the literature of spirituality. There is a unique blending of Methodism, 'You have not yet pleaded enough with him'; the Quaker, 'the voice of God speaking within you'; and something else sounding rather modern, 'acting in a truly *scientific* manner'. It is intriguing to imagine that Butler may well here have been influenced by the teaching of her husband George. George was concerned to elevate some of the then minor subjects such as Geography as subjects for serious study in the University. The beginnings of a cross fertilisation between science and religion, and between practical and contemplative spiritualities, may well have been another of Josephine Butler's contributions to the Church of her day.

Writing the biography of Catherine of Siena in 1876-78 at a time when the Contagious Diseases Act had been in operation for a decade, and six years before its repeal, Butler must have been wondering if her campaigning was ever to have any effect and reap its reward. As well as being a time of comparative lull, it was probably also feeling like a low point of the campaign. Butler had written her passage in the biography about Catherine's 'dark night of the soul' but an even deeper darkness was about to be described. Butler spends a considerable time charting these stages. We have heard something of the 'dark night' but Catherine, writes Butler, 'was to pass through one of those bitter conflicts, the very memory of which is pain to those who have endured them'.[23]

> *Catherine was assailed by the most humiliating temptations and by exciting phantoms of the imagination, which haunted her sleeping and waking. She saw in her dreams impure orgies, wherein men and women seemed to invite her by words and gestures to join with them; she was tormented inwardly, her eyes, her ears, her soul, seemed to be defiled. She endured combats too horrible to relate. All the passion of her young southern blood seemed to rise up in a fierce rebellion against her own resolution and the ruggedness of the way of the cross.'* [24]

It seems appropriate here to repeat the famous passage from the writings of Henry Scott Holland concerning Josephine Butler, when he saw a glimpse of her through a carriage window at the height of the campaign to repeal the Contagious Diseases Act.

> *About twenty eight years ago, in passing up Holborn, a face looked at me out of a hurrying hansom, which arrested and frightened me. It was framed on pure and noble and beautiful lines: but it was smitten, and bitten into, as by some East wind, that blighted it into a grey sadness. It had seen that which took all colour and joy out of it. I felt as the children who saw Dante pass as a shadow through the sunny square: and whispered 'He has been in Hell'. The face had a look, I thought, of recognition before it had swiftly gone: and, after I had recovered my memory, I knew that it was Josephine Butler. A day or two later, a message reached me from her, to warn me that a tremendous storm was about to break, and that all the friends of the Cause must be prepared for the emergency [...] and then, I knew that I had seen, that day in Holborn, Mrs. Butler in the thick of that terrible work that she has undertaken for God. She was passing through her*

*martyrdom. The splendid beauty of her face, so spiritual in its high
and clear outlines, bore the mark of that death upon it to which
she stood daily and hourly committed. There was no hell on earth
into which she would not willingly travel, if, by sacrifice of herself,
she could reach a hand of help to those poor children whom
nothing short of such sacrifice could touch. The sorrow of it passed
into her being. She had the look of the world's grim tragedy in her
eyes. She had dared to take the measure of the black infamy of
sin: and the terrible knowledge had left its cruel mark upon the
soul of strange and singular purity.* [25]

Returning to Butler's own description of the trials of Catherine,
which we left at the point of the most humiliating temptations, we
discover another direction from which temptation fired its arrows, and
that was in the direction of enticing her to settle down to the joys and
satisfactions of a life concerned only with human love. Butler writes:

*The woman's heart within [Catherine] was beating fresh and
warm: she was young, her soul was full of music and of poetic
imaginations. Who more fitted by nature than she to realise the
highest and sweetest of human love? It was the era of romance,
the age of the troubadours. She had heard many a fair tale of
love; the noblest of earthly lovers seemed to woo her; the vision
stood near her, and looked in her eyes; his exquisite human
pleadings broke in upon the songs of angels, and extinguished
the voice of her heart's spouse. When she slept, exhausted, she
dreamed herself in the midst of a sweet home – her own; she
seemed to clasp in her arms the little infant which lay upon her
breast; and waking, the woman's heart within her was well
nigh broken. Her little room was filled with a strange mingling of
heavenly and earthly music. The love-songs of the troubadours
interrupted the strains of the Magnificat and the penitential
psalms. She had hours of agonising hesitation of will. Wise and
practical counsellors seemed to advise her: 'why be so rash to
choose a life in which you cannot persevere? Why extinguish
within you the holy impulses of nature, which God has implanted
within you? Many among the saints were married [...] but the*

celestial wooer prevailed. The love of loves was again more
perfectly manifested to her, the agony was over, and she fell at
the feet of Jesus. [26]

Butler is concerned to pinpoint the sense of destiny and calling in
Catherine of Siena, as if, again, it clarified something in her own life,
and which explained her own trials within her calling. In the essentially
lonely commitment to the cause of women caught up in prostitution,
misunderstood by many, vilified and scorned, Butler found in Catherine
a soul-mate, both a woman, and a dedicated person, and one of
complete purity of motive. A telling passage reveals this connection in
the biography:

I do not find that there entered into Catherine's thoughts
the smallest idea of merit or of reward in renouncing earthly
joys and human ties. The most careful search through all her
utterances, written or spoken, fails to reveal a single word
claiming to herself and merit. Her dying words give the key
to the faith or the philosophy which she embraced from her
childhood, 'Yes, Lord, thou callest me, I come to thee; I go to
thee, not on account of my merits, but solely on account of thy
mercy, and that mercy I have implored in the name, O Jesus, of
thy precious blood'. [27]

Butler reflects on Paul's words, that Catherine was ready to be
'accursed from Christ for her brethren's sake'. Writing in the lull of
1876-1878 Butler was not yet to know the continuing uphill struggle
that was to be so much part of the next five to six years. She was not at
the time to know how much of what she wrote of Catherine was to be
reflected in her own struggle. Butler writes vividly, no doubt copying
the sources, but invests the account with a true foreboding of her own
'dark night of the soul':

A still darker period arrived, in which her sufferings were
such as almost to deprive her of her reason. Diabolical beings
seemed to pursue her with screams inviting her to take part in
their abominations [...] her soul was plunged into a profound
melancholy, all the strength to continue in prayer seemed about

to forsake her [...] she cast herself at the feet of God, determined not to murmur, but patiently to await his return and help. Her little room at the Fullonica seemed to be infested with these impure spirits [...] the evil spirit seemed still to taunt her, saying, 'poor miserable creature, thou canst never pass thy whole life in this state; we will torment thee to death, unless thou dost obey us.'[28]

Then follows one of the most famous incidents in the life of Catherine. She had fallen to the very pit of despair and says, 'Be it so, I have chosen suffering for Christ's sake, and I am willing, if need be to endure this till death.' This total abandonment and commitment is the moment when she is lifted up by God and is described in these words by her biographer:

Immediately on pronouncing this determination, a great light seemed to descend from above, filling the place where she kneeled with heavenly brightness. The devils left her, and One better than the angels came and ministered to her. The Lord Jesus himself drew nigh to her, and conversed with her of her trial and her victory.[29]

The final piece of dialogue concludes this section of the book. The inward spiritual strength of Catherine is secure, and it enabled her to turn outwards towards the world in faith and courage: 'But Catherine, like St Anthony, said to the Lord, "Where wast thou when my heart was so tormented?" "I was in the midst of thy heart," he replied...it is not thy trouble that pleaseth me, but the *will* that has supported that trouble courageously"'.[30]

Those words, 'the will that supports the trouble courageously', could be something of a motto for the spiritual life of Josephine Butler. We have looked, perhaps rather exhaustively, at those aspects of Catherine of Siena's spirituality that resonated with Josephine's. We have seen their mutual love of the natural world, the desire for solitude in which to listen to God, the inward cell that powered an outward, public life, the image of the cross in times of temptation, and the woman's heart that comes alongside Christ's through love and service.

I would like to conclude with two seeming paradoxical aspects of Josephine's spirituality which defy easy categorisation and point to a character living on the fulcrum of the divine and human worlds. One set of opposites is activity and contemplation, and the second is fierceness and gentleness. Of intense activity throughout her life there seems to have been no end. She says herself that she always wanted work rather than contemplation. She had the ability to inspire others to work for the repeal of The Contagious Diseases Act, because she was herself so passionate about it. Her spirituality had a very strong active side to it. She spoke at rallies across Europe. Work and the activity of the Holy Spirit meshed. She was driven by the need to get justice done. Action had its own momentum.

However, lying behind the action was a full devotional life fed by a theology of the 'Divine Image' impressed on the 'fallen' and the outcasts, even the 'madly sinful'. Scripture passages that particularly moved her were the story of Hagar in Genesis 18, the Magnificat in St Luke's Gospel, where God regarded to lowliness of the handmaiden, and the eschatological passages in Isaiah, Daniel, and Revelation, where she discerned the powerful image of God's glory blazing evil out of countenance and described the New Creation. 'Then shall the mountains bring peace to the people, and the little hills righteousness' (Ps. 72.3).

The rhetoric of the coming of the Redeemer was a powerful influence in her contemplative life, which issued in action when the time needed redeeming. She wrote:

> *The light of day will fall upon all the dark places of the earth,*
> *now full of the habitations of cruelty, and there shall come forth,*
> *at the call of the Deliverer, the thousands and tens of thousands*
> *of the daughters of men now enslaved in all lands to cruelty and*
> *lust [...] but rising in inherent majesty, the Redeemer's Kingdom*
> *will strengthen and extend, wide as the limits of nature's*
> *boundary, far as sin has diffused its poison.*[31]

The other set of opposites that powered Josephine's inspiration was that of fierceness and gentleness. The fierceness was a kind of righteous indignation commonly experienced among social reformers, which welled up within her when she saw injustice at work. She felt the abuse as if it was perpetrated on her. She said it was 'the awful abundance of compassion that made her fierce'.

Set against this fierce compassion was a gentleness that somehow echoed the beauty of her physical presence. An example of this came with that absolutely defining moment of Josephine's life when, in 1864, she held her dead child Eva in her arms. It was that experience which lay at the root of her compassion. She wrote of that experience:

> *The only other transfiguration more beautiful which I ever saw was that sweet look of holy awe and wonder and peace which passed over our darling's face when she died, as if she stood face to face with God. The glory of the mountains recalled that awful sweetness, and calmed my soul. I felt God to be so great and high and calm that the earth's longest agonies are but a moment's pain in comparison with the eternity of glory hereafter. If God made this earth so beautiful what must his heaven be?* [32]

This defining tragedy struck before the full momentum of her campaigning life had begun. Shortly after the Contagious Diseases Acts were repealed, in 1888 towards the end of her life, another experience provides illumination on Josephine's gentleness and vulnerability. Josephine was attending evensong in Winchester Cathedral, where her husband George was a Residentiary Canon. Josephine felt faint:

> *A moment more and I should have dropped. I could scarcely steady my steps, and my sight failed, when suddenly there passed a flash of light, as it seemed, before my eyes, something as white as snow and as soft as an angel's wing; it enveloped me, and I felt myself to be held up by a strong and loving arm, and supported through the nave to the west door, where the cool summer breeze restored me. It was my husband. He was in his own seat near the entrance to the nave, and his quick ear had caught the sound of my footstep. Quite noiselessly he left his seat and took me in his arms, unobserved by anyone. The flash of light (the angel's wing) was the quick movement of the wide sleeve of his fine linen surplice, upon which the sun shone as he drew me towards him.* [33]

I hope I have been able to show in this essay some of the ways in which Josephine Butler took inspiration from a medieval catholic saint, St Catherine of Siena, and by doing so produced one of the most pioneering works of biographical spirituality, in English, in the nineteenth century. Also, though centuries apart in time, their similarity in temperament, both deeply private, and yet both constantly in the public arena, gives some model for contemporary ways of living a Christian life of service and prayer.

Endnotes

[1] Timothy Radcliffe, *I Call You Friends* (London: Continuum, 2001), p. 122.

[2] Radcliffe, *Friends*, p. 122.

[3] Pat Starkey, 'Saints, Virgins and Family Members: Exemplary Biographies? Josephine Butler as Biographer', in *Sex, Gender, Religion: Josephine Butler Revisited*, ed. Jenny Daggers and Diana Neal (New York: 2006), pp. 112-49.

[4] Starkey, 'Saints, Virgins, and Family Members', p. 149.

[5] Starkey, 'Saints, Virgins and Family Members', p. 137.

[6] Quoted in Jordan, *Butler*, p. 178.

[7] Jordan, *Butler*, p. 182.

[8] On the volume, see *Faber: Poet and Priest: Selected Letters by Frederick William Faber from 1833-1863*, ed. Raleigh Addington (Cowbridge and Bridgend, Glamorgan: D. Brown and Sons, 1974), pp. 114-18.

[9] See *Josephine E. Butler: An Autobiographical Memoir*, ed. George and Lucy Johnson (Bristol: J. W. Arrowsmith, 1909), pp. 28-29.

[10] Josephine E. Butler, *Catherine of Siena: A Biography* (London: Dyer Brothers, 1892), p. 10.

[11] Ibid.

[12] Butler, *Catherine of Siena*, p. 11.

[13] Butler, *Catherine of Siena*, p. 22.

[14] Butler, *Catherine of Siena*, p. 23.

[15] Butler, *Catherine of Siena*, p. 25.

[16] Butler, *Catherine of Siena*, p. 30.

[17] Butler, *Catherine of Siena*, p. 31.

[18] Butler, *Catherine of Siena*, p. 32.

[19] Ibid.

[20] Butler, *Catherine of Siena*, p. 34.

[21] Butler, *Catherine of Siena*, pp. 38-39.

[22] Butler, *Catherine of Siena*, p. 39.

[23] Ibid.

[24] Butler, *Catherine of Siena*, p. 40.

[25] Quoted in Moberly Bell, *Josephine Butler*, p. 178.

[26] Butler, *Catherine of Siena*, p. 41.

[27] Butler, *Catherine of Siena*, p. 42.

[28] Butler, *Catherine of Siena*, p. 44.

[29] Ibid.

[30] Ibid.

[31] Butler, *Hour Before the Dawn*, p. 108.

[32] Butler, *Recollections of George Butler*, p. 131.

[33] Butler, *Recollections of George Butler*, cited in Williamson, *The Forgotten Saint*, p. 105.

Josephine Butler
'The Still Voice of Silence': Prophets and Prostitutes

Hester Jones

Hester Jones's approach is that of a literary scholar who attends to the texture of Butler's writing to discern its theological project. As the published work mentioned here indicates, her approach is influenced by her expertise in the area of women's writing. Her doctoral research explored the language of friendship in seventeenth and eighteenth-century writing, particularly that of Alexander Pope, and she has published parts of this work in article form. This feeds into the way in which this article is concerned with how one may encounter the other human person in all her difference through contemplative prayer. More recently, Hester has published on a range of women writers, including Elizabeth Bowen and Emily Dickinson, and a book about Christina and Dante Gabriel Rossetti. She has also co-edited a book of essays on the poet W. S. Graham. At present she is working towards a book about twentieth-century poets and their relation with Christianity. She is currently Lecturer in English at the University of Liverpool. In September 2007 she moves to the University of Bristol as a Senior Lecturer.

❧

As Alison Milbank observes in her trenchant and elegant 1987 essay on Butler, writing about Butler is like entering a 'minefield', so contradictory can she seem. Consequently, writers tend to assume a particular stance and correspondingly often find her wanting in one way or another. Uglow, whose article 'From Sympathy to Theory' Milbank responds to with care, takes a largely secular, historicist and feminist approach. She identifies as weaknesses both Butler's apparent championing of sexual chastity for men and women, and, following Judith Walkowitz's *Prostitution and Victorian Society*, the tension in Butler's writing between 'egalitarian' and 'custodial approaches' to the prostitutes whose life became her focus. That focus has itself also incurred criticism, as a fruitless restriction of time and energy, from earlier critics such as Bell and Petrie.[1]

To some extent, the feminist politicisation of Butler, arising out of Forster's *Significant Sisters* and Boyd's *Three Victorian Women who changed their World*, was a reaction to an earlier approach that tends towards hagiography (Williamson's *Forgotten Saint* is a good example). A little like her contemporary Christina Rossetti, Butler seems, with her attempt to bring political liberalism, feminism and Christianity into harmony, to resist a rounded and fully sympathetic assessment of her value and contribution. For the theorist Uglow, therefore, she was, somewhat severely, a campaigner but 'not a theorist'; to the historian Pat Starkey, she emerges as a poor historian and biographer; even to Alison Milbank, she falls short in not embracing the Christian Socialism current at her time. There is something, perhaps, in Butler's work, a fragmented disjointedness, which evades the defining categories offered by academic criticism.[2]

I suggest, however, that Butler's work explicitly enacts a desire for the reconciliation of polarities. Her work with and for prostitutes – and both prepositions are essential here – epitomises and also illustrates this larger engagement. From one perspective, that of Christian humanism, such a focus has seemed to be a diminishing exercise; from another, the secular feminist, it is compromised by Butler's Christianity and does not go far enough. But Butler passionately resists the demand for fixed allegiance, for acquiescent occupation of one constructed space or another, either the feminised space called 'home', the private sphere, or the masculinised sphere of work and action. Her writing, rather, powerfully challenges constructions which inhibit, limit or narrow the potential of an individual; but she is not I think, as Milbank perhaps implies, narrowly individualist in her failure to engage with the collective. Rather, I argue that in probing at the limits of the binaries she presents, she seeks to find an 'other' space in which both elements may be brought more closely together.

Perhaps surprisingly, this attempt to make pliable the sometimes rigid distinctions of feminine and masculine, private and public, is often addressed by recourse to the term 'independence' and to the role of the 'independent' person. Independence is not equivalent to autonomy in her view; it is relational, and in this sense, I suggest, has much to offer debates current in feminist and theological thinking about the relational nature of feminine selfhood, and, in particular, the revisioned understanding of the theological idea of kenosis (self-emptying), which feminist theologians have fruitfully discussed. More centrally, Butler engages throughout with the idea of prophecy and often assumes the role of prophet in her assumption of what Walter Brueggemann describes as the 'alternative' consciousness of prophecy. Brueggemann maintains in *The Prophetic Imagination* that such figures are called both to 'energize' and to 'criticize' a dominant ideology, whatever it may be; through both 'dismantling' dominant structures and also by offering a vision of hope towards which such a community may move.[3]

Brueggemann suggests, further, that 'to choose between criticizing and energizing is the temptation, respectively, of liberalism and conservatism […] to be called where this dialectic is maintained is an awesome call. And each of us is likely to fall to one side or the other.' Later, he invokes Dorothy Soelle who writes that prophetic criticism 'consists in mobilizing people to their real restless grief and in nurturing them away from "cry hearers" who are inept at listening and indifferent in response.' I suggest that Butler is also concerned to find ways of moving towards a 'response' which is nurturing rather than indifferent; that such a response is achieved momentarily, often within the space of contemplative prayer; and that this space offers an alternative model of reaching out to the model of kenotic dispossession which threatens to endorse rather than challenge differences of power in society.

Furthermore, despite the clear challenges to approaching Butler's work from a feminist perspective, which have already been indicated, there are also surprising parallels between what she attempts to negotiate and contemporary work by feminist theologians and writers. *Swallowing a Fishbone*, for example, focuses around the theological understanding of kenosis, the doctrine that the Christian God absconds from or empties his transcendent omnipotence within the Incarnation. Debate has raged over the extent to which this renunciation goes, whether it is total or temporary, or whether divine transcendence continues to coexist in the person of Christ with his human vulnerability to suffering. As the authors observe, feminist insight makes this doctrine particularly problematic; self-emptying is, perhaps, a divine action to be emulated by those with power, but a dangerous example to set to those without. Feminist thought has responded in various ways, from the desire to step back entirely from such exaltation of abnegation, as exemplified by Daphne Hampson's work, to the perception, expressed by Sarah Coakley, that, as she puts it, abuse of power is always a temptation regardless of situation. By contrast, Coakley offers the experience of contemplative prayer, with its willed acceptance of passivity, as an empowering response to the potential for violation and destructive assertion present in every moment and in every person. The tension between autonomy and loss-in-exchange is extended in attitudes to Christian tradition; for Coakley, continuing to engage with Christian theological tradition, albeit in its often distorting and, from a feminist perspective, destructive forms, offers a route into divine flourishing.[4]

I suggest that Butler was, indeed, offering images of divine kenosis that take account of and begin to acknowledge, at least, the dangers of abasement and condescension present in the Christian account of kenosis. Consequently her writing about herself, about women and about prostitutes, is often marked by a similar pattern, one revolving around the question of how a Christian kenotic response incorporates or deals with what Butler sees as the perpetual presence of power imbalance, whether in gender relations, in larger social patterns or in the self. Further, as does Coakley, I suggest Butler presents the contemplative space as one in which the inequities of power, however they are experienced, may be both acknowledged and resolved. Neither of Uglow's terms, 'custodial' and 'egalitarianism', I think, adequately expresses the pains Butler takes to approach this profound challenge, that of reconciling individual self-interest with the good of others.

Woman's Work and Woman's Culture

Butler's edited collection of essays, *Woman's Work and Woman's Culture*, to which she wrote a characteristically dynamic and impassioned introduction, offers my first example of the engagement to which I refer.[5] The book followed hard on the heels of Mill's *On the Subjection of Women* and shares with it a resounding challenge to a definition of women which depends on their relation to men: both prize a commitment to women's independent being. In an unacknowledged irony, Butler begins by quite fiercely defending the independence of her book from that of Mill's: as Eve followed Adam, so her book follows the earlier by a accident of timing, but remains its own, co-existing with, not dependent on or stolen from, his. What is lost in temporal originality, is however perhaps restored in the opportunity to share the plight of the 'second sex'. 'Where there is monopoly on the one hand, there is loss and waste on the other', inviting the implication that this secondary work is, for all its excellence, impaired and 'wasted' by the former; but 'what shall we say of the broken hearts, deep discouragement and dismay, the deadness of souls';[6] this particular example of 'waste' enables her to write with authority and passion where Mill, for all his monopoly, writes only from a distance. Women, she goes on, are 'not men's rivals but helpers; there is no antagonism that is not injurious to both.' This is a frequent plea, and one which seems to be defending an essentialist and complementary understanding of gender; but what is surprising here is Butler's attack not only on the blind complacency of the masculine sphere, as she presents it, but also on the narrow 'exclusiveness of the domestic hearth', traditionally of course the feminine sphere. Instead, she proposes an 'enlargement of hearts' and an 'opening out and giving forth of the influences of home', a process, one infers, in which the concept of home will lose the associations of tribal or familial 'monopoly' and dare to incorporate in its larger and looser fold, the alien and other, what Kristeva has come to call the 'abject'.[7] Butler identifies the tendency to close ranks within the home as deriving from a 'fear of revolution', a term she uses quite often. Instead, she pleads for an interdependence, an openness to the other where 'each has something to give and to receive', an exchange which, she argues, will make society stronger.

Like her forebears in this area, Mary Astell and, to some extent, Mary Wollstonecraft, Butler finds herself employing a utilitarian defence of such an anti-materialist argument to a troubling degree; she argues, as had Astell in her early defence of women's education, *A Serious Proposal to the Ladies*, that resisting the 'general scramble for husbands' will enhance 'the attractiveness of women' rather than impairing it; again like Astell, she seeks not merely to subvert social and gender imbalance but to promote a perhaps more radical, and therefore more threatening, dissolution of the terms at play, so that both the static 'home' and 'public' spheres, through what she terms a 'communion', become arenas of mutual exchange and transformation. This vision becomes clearer towards the end of the introduction, where Butler declares that, in relation to the 'other', whether woman, the poor or prostitute, both the masculine 'systematic' attempt (legislation, penitentiaries) and feminine 'individualizing' efforts (personal rescue work) fail by virtue of their exclusion of the other. Butler privileges instead, in the repeated phrase, pointedly vague in its reference, 'influence of home elements into the system' and the 'setting free of feminine powers and influences from the constraints of bad education.' Her reference point here is not only freedom, but also 'play', the exertion of an imaginative and visionary capacity, releasing the self from the imposition of mechanical 'rules' operating in larger units.[8]

Recollections of George Butler

In her introduction to this volume of essays, therefore, Butler presents a case for the socially regenerative effect of the playful blurring of boundaries between masculine and feminine worlds, accentuated in contemporary culture and social thinking. This space becomes, in Butler's vision, a redemptive and prophetic testimony to the possibility, not just of the 'home' entering the public sphere, as is sometimes thought, but rather of these mutually exclusive categories accommodating a larger, more fluid and more enlivening form of 'communion'. This focus on the creative play made possible by such an expansion may be seen elsewhere in her writing too. We see such creative dissolution, in particular, in Butler's use of the biographical genre, where, as many have observed, biography seems to be a mask for Butler's own desire to record her own life. Such an apparent desire for the limelight is most clearly demonstrated in her *Recollections of George Butler*, large parts of which were recycled in her own *Autobiographical Memoir*, and whose predominant focus is the author herself and her crusades.[9] In this respect, Butler is of course not the first female writer to use an account of a distinguished husband as an opportunity for dispersed self-writing.[10] But I suggest that this is not entirely the product of egotism veiled as altruism, as Pat Starkey has intimated.[11]

George and Josephine become elements in an opposition that is repeatedly investigated by Butler: the relation between worldly involvement and spiritual calling. The vision she presents is again an interdependent one, in which the 'separate elements' as she called them, of husband and wife cannot easily be separated. In social terms, the couple adopted a conventional dispensation, where George pursued an educational career and his wife bore children and occupied the home. In the terms of the autobiography, however, George assumes a secondary and supportive role, in which his silent withholding from criticism, complaint, or even a desire to uphold any advantage of gender, is remarkable. As I shall go on to show, Butler presents George by implication as a prophetic and exceptional presence, undeterred by worldly competitiveness, rooted in the Word of God and an example of heroic integration, both of practical and spiritual power. The portrayal may indeed by idealising and obscuring by turns, but, as the subjective terms 'recollections' and 'memoir' acknowledge, they are intended as a personal record and vision, not a claim to 'objective' fact. Such a blurring of the outlines of the auto/biographical genre is a feature, once again, of Butler's approach, an aspect of her desire to open out the parameters of the self, the private and the individual – and this fluidity in an understanding of the subject foreshadows more recent definitions of so-called feminist 'auto/biography'.[12]

Josephine Butler recounts a number of vivid and memorable anecdotes, some often quoted by commentators, but on the whole without much consideration of their form or symbolic quality. Within these, other figures, George himself and a range of women are indeed located peripherally, and yet they serve both as clear correlatives for Butler and also as significant others, entirely different from and yet speaking to the self. George is largely a silent but also authoritative presence, a counterbalance in his attributed 'independence' firstly to the narrator's own determined understandings and secondly to the context in which both are placed. One episode occurring during the Butlers' time in Oxford is perceived as formative, and may illustrate this dual operation. Butler describes her memories of this time as 'some very sweet, others grave';[13] and it seems indeed to have provided opportunity for the newly married couple to enjoy many shared pleasures, whether in reading, riding, walking or studying, which in later life were denied through pressure of other commitments; but, as she says, this life at Oxford also 'had its shadow side'.[14] She puts this down to the segregated existence of many academics, deprived of 'intercourse' with other people, and she finds an environmental parallel, attributing this cultural insularity in part to the geography of Oxford, islanded as it was at that time by a 'stagnation of moisture' which gave it a Venetian remoteness from the real. Oxford becomes, in this rendering, a monstrous conflation of the idealised and the abject, stagnant and damp, unreal and yet powerful. She thus concludes, 'a one-sidedness of judgement is apt to be fostered by such circumstances – an exaggeration of the purely masculine judgement on some topics, and a conventual mode of looking at things'. 'Conventual' here targets the corporately disembodied prejudices she encountered: she 'the only woman', 'sat silent […] and listened, sometimes with a sore heart; for these men would speak of things which I had already revolved deeply in my own mind, things of which I was convinced, which I knew, though I had no dialectics at command with which to defend their truth'.[15] Butler, who in the Introduction to *Woman's Work* invokes *Lear,* represents herself here as a kind of Cordelia, whose 'truth' is manifest in pain (the sore heart) and in an awkward silence, a silence which derives both from deficiency (the lack of 'dialectics', as she contemptuously calls the oppositional language of debate from which she felt excluded) but also from something positive, the weight and depth of solitary thinking, 'long revolved in my own mind', as she puts it.[16] The insular stagnancy of Oxford seems here to deny yet also to contribute to the enclosed 'revolvings' of Butler's inward perceiving of 'truth', especially the truth of the inbuilt monopoly of social privilege which, as an educated woman, she enjoys yet cannot use as she would like.

Only a few pages later, at the conclusion to this section, she relates a conversation in which both partners compare the 'axioms of the day' with the sayings of Jesus which 'were, we confessed to one another, revolutionary. George Butler was not afraid of revolution. In this sense he desired it, and we prayed together that a holy revolution might come about'.[17] Inward revolving, in other words, so different from the 'earthly theories' voiced by both academic and ecclesiastical establishments, leads naturally to earthly revolution, the holistic overturning of worldly structures in the living out of spiritual truths. A silence pregnant with revolutionary potential is thus, through George, placed in opposition to the deadly silence achieved through an excess of words, the silence of repression rather than of contemplation.

This opposition is located in particular around a discussion of a 'book by Mrs Gaskell' (her fallen woman novel, *Ruth*, published in 1853) – a book, perhaps too scandalous to be named, and which provoked conclusions Butler regards as 'false – fatally false'. Purity, it is held by the academic circle, cannot coexist with knowledge: 'a pure woman should be absolutely ignorant of a certain class of evils in the world, albeit those evils bore with murderous cruelty on other women.' Above all, she summarises, 'Silence was thought to be the great duty of all in such subjects'.[18] Once again, the academic and assertive voice is exclusive and essentialist; knowledge, ironically enough, is presented as contaminating, like the 'malarial miasma' which Butler regards as possessing Oxford itself. But a rich and creative silence emerges out of this miasma.

Liminal Prophecy

It is no surprise that Butler should have made discussion of this nameless novel so significant in her autobiographical account, for there was common ground between herself and Gaskell. Both shared a basic liberalism of approach, which issued in a commitment to individual rights, informed also by a broadly Christian understanding of where such rights originated: in the gift and example of Christ. Both also, struggle with the question of how to write about sexuality in a context that denies it a voice. In the section from the *Memoir* already mentioned, Butler goes on to describe her attempts to alert 'one of the wisest men' to the plight of a 'very young girl', to which he 'sternly advocated silence and inaction'.[19] Such a dismissal leads, Butler tells us, first to amazement and discouragement, within which 'echoed in my heart the terrible prophetic words of the painter-poet Blake – rude and indelicate as he may have been judged then – whose prophecy has only been averted by a great and painful awakening – "The harlot's cry from street to street, / Shall weave old England's winding-sheet"'. The quotation goes unreferenced in the *Memoir*, but comes from the concluding section of Blake's poem 'Auguries of Innocence', which begins with the famous lines, 'To see a world in a grain of sand, / And heaven in a wild flower, / Hold infinity in the palm of your hand / And eternity in an hour'.[20] Butler characteristically seems to distance herself from Blake with the genteel caveat, but also reaches out in solidarity with him, finding solace amidst her own 'discouragement', in Blake's social exile. Two kinds of wisdom are in tension here: the wisdom of the worldly 'sage' in Oxford, militates against that of the more destructive yet also more substantial prophet, Blake, whose prophetic truth is confirmed by what Butler first sees and then describes. Silence, furthermore, is the condition, even the prerequisite, of this process of self-identification with an exiled, prophetic community. It is as if the silencing Butler experiences, first from the young adversary of Mrs Gaskell's novel, then from this old sage, opens up in her heart space for the disclosure of prophetic truth: an opportunity, that is, to resound with sympathetic understanding with words at which social delicacy might have reason to balk.

As has been observed, Uglow writes somewhat disparagingly of the seemingly unselfconscious, emotional identification that often inspired and fed into Butler's social involvement. It is as if, in this view, such a response leads to unconsidered equivalences being offered, where difference in social status and opportunity is all-determining. However, what may also be observed here is an imaginative entry into a discursive space and time where the inarticulate cry of pain stands in judgement and may overturn social order; but may also, in the transformation of prophetic vision, attain to a level of understanding which transcends the limiting polarities of worldly discourse. Blake's worldly mysticism locates the eternal in the immediate; subjective, imaginative vision becomes the means by which contraries are brought together, by which one offence against life is avenged by an unlikely opponent. Thus, the harlot's cry is one both of pain and of protest; both of witness to victimisation, and also a rallying to justice. The vision of the seer provides a liminal space, in which wordless pain is transformed into powerful social change. A conversation across time is enacted, as it were between exiles from differently normative structures, so that Oxford's recoiling from Gaskell's shocking novel provokes thought of the 'rude and indelicate' Blake, and provides an alternative context of discussion for the nineteenth-century woman, 'silent' but revolving inwardly. A 'literary autobiography' that took its own processes of thought more seriously might have wanted to set out the 'influences' on Butler's thinking in a more deliberate, systematic manner. Butler's casual, associative way of writing, however, avoids the construction of such a linear 'tradition' of thought, preferring to use a more lateral, visionary form of allusion, one in which the material divisions of time, class and place are momentarily dissolved in the awakening to witness.

Butler's allusion to Blake also leads into a further anecdote, in which Butler relates the struggle of a circus woman to 'leave the life in which she was plunged, the most innocent [part] of which was probably her acrobatic performances.' Here as often, Butler's writing seems to act out an inner, spiritual drama. While the woman's body performs the 'plunges', the falls from grace, demanded of her by society and circumstance, the woman herself:

> had aspirations very far beyond what is expected of a circus
> woman. She wanted to serve God. She saw a light before her,
> she said, and she must follow it. She went secretly to churches
> and chapels, and then she fled – she did not know where – but
> was recaptured. [...] I had been sitting for some time at my open
> window to breathe more freely the sultry air, and it seemed to

me I heard a wailing cry somewhere among the trees in the twilight which was deepening into night. It was a woman's cry, a woman aspiring to heaven and dragged back to hell – and my heart was pierced with pain. I longed to leap from the window, and flee with her to some place of refuge. It passed. I cannot explain the nature of this impression, but beyond that twilight, even in the midst of that pitiful cry, there seemed to dawn a ray of light and to sound a note not wholly of despair. The light was far off, yet coming near, and the slight summer breeze in those tall trees had in them a whisper of the future. But when the day dawned it seemed to show me again more plainly than ever the great wall of prejudice, built up on a foundation of lies, which surrounded a whole world of sorrows, griefs, injustices and crimes which must not be spoken of.[21]

It is the liminal moment of twilight at which prophetic vision occurs: and the vision, which the daylight world condemns, is also a means of delivery and liberation. During day and night, however, the world of academic rationalism defends itself from the true through words and illusion, driving to its peripheries all those who seek to challenge or question it.

Once again, Butler challenges and seeks to open up an image of enclosure, here the 'great wall of prejudice' that both declares and also seeks to deny human suffering. Her prophetic vision, discovered at the 'window' of desire and prayer, is liminal in the sense that it involves a momentary solidarity with the 'circus woman', as stylised in her role as the prostitute and therefore equally remote to Butler as to her culture. But despite such stylisation, Butler discerns hope for social change, on the edges of certainty, at twilight, within the 'wailing cry' and amidst the 'slight stirring breeze' – all of these offering a 'whisper' of a better future.

Helen Stoddart has observed that the female acrobat is often presented in Victorian culture as a focus for sexual ambiguity, both eroticised and also idealised; furthermore, she suggests that the circus has 'a self-image that is at heart a paradoxical one since it promotes an idea of itself in the popular imagination as embodying a lifestyle unfettered by conventionality or social restraint', and yet, 'behind this image lie levels of physical discipline, bodily regulation and hardship which are unrivalled by any other western performance art.'[22] Butler often emphasises the muscular discipline underpinning contemplative and vocational activity, work both sustaining and also ridiculing the idealised and ethereal image of saint or sex-worker. It is not, I suggest, simply that Butler 'identifies' with the remote and unseen acrobat; rather, she perceives a momentary affinity in their otherwise different lives, a difference whose pathos is not overlooked. The contemplative moment in which she reaches out towards this ambiguous figure acknowledges its potential to stir desire in the beholder; but it is a desire that Butler, like the disciplined acrobat, channels into visionary effort.

What these early anecdotes suggest, is that Josephine Butler made creative and unsettling use of the stark oppositions on which she perceived her culture as being based, and came gradually to see herself in the role of mediator between them, by virtue of her occupation in different capacities within both spheres. Her sensitivity to and determination to overcome, pain drew her close towards figures, such as the circus woman, who both courted and also eluded abjection, blurring gender categories;[23] moreover, she openly acknowledges the closeness she feels to the 'refuge' of self-destruction. Uglow's assessment, following that of Judith Walkowitz, that this was just emotional 'identification', misses the subtlety with which Butler attempts to approach an inherently antagonistic situation. Butler retains an awareness of the civilised status from which she speaks, and which she must use if social change is to be effected. Enacting the movement between one position and the other becomes the means by which the harmful polarity in society may be challenged and dissolved, through the creation of a space in which the representative of one stereotype – the fallen woman, in *Ruth* – may be shown at successive moments in other lights, as moral exemplar, and even 'prophet'.

'united wail [...] reaching to the heart of God'

The final anecdote I shall cite from the *Recollections* concerns the sudden death of the Butlers' only daughter Eva, who tumbled from a high staircase at the age of five. The loss of children was not unusual in this time, yet Butler's heart-rending and also troublingly dramatic account moves in a particularly vivid and poignant way: 'Never can I lose that memory – the fall, the sudden cry, and then the silence', Butler writes, and describes Eva in her father's arms, 'her beautiful golden hair, all stained with blood, falling over his arm'.[24] Later, Butler comments on her 'flight from earth', the word which she had earlier used of the circus woman, which leads into the semi-mystical trance and vision she has earlier described. The section here also concludes that the 'sorrow seemed to give in a measure a new direction to our lives and interests', a surprising comment perhaps given the natural experiences of perplexity, dismay and disorientation to which Butler also alludes.[25] Eva and the circus woman both become channels for prophetic activity, though one is stylised as an angelic presence and the other, a 'fallen woman'. Butler, like Gaskell, seeks to bring the two polarities into one, and indicate the area of continuity between them within the economy of salvation. Both offer a vision of – express the desire for – an 'alternative consciousness' as Brueggemann called it. Both are equal channels for the prophetic process.

In due course, the 'direction' that is taken leads the household to Liverpool, where, after further depression, Butler turns to 'plunge into the heart of some human misery, and to say (as I now knew I could) to afflicted people: "I understand: I too have suffered"'.[26] In other words, the tragic loss of Eva is perceived as an answer to her earlier sense of unease at her own good fortune, and at the unjust inequality between rich and poor, male and female, on which she had silently reflected in Oxford. There is an unsettling appropriation here, always a risky potential in such narratives, that the objective reality of death has been in some way transformed in the discovery of her calling: it is as if suffering has allowed Josephine kenotically to cross a bridge into humanity.

The account of Butler's visit down into the oakum sheds, in which many prostitutes were enclosed, is a particularly memorable instance of this pilgrimage into the world, not least for its transformation of a kind of hell, the dark and stagnant sheds, into a place of play. Her own suffering becomes her, the respectable woman's, passport; she demonstrates her good will by sitting 'among them', and by tolerating their laughter at her uselessness; and 'while we laughed we became friends'. She relinquishes the status and privilege of class, therefore, and from that dispossession a meeting and an exchange occurs. But power is discovered in an unexpected, and significantly non-verbal form. In response to the suggestion that they learn a few verses 'to say to me', one girl 'standing up in our midst', spontaneously repeats words from John 14, commanding silence with her authority; prayer follows: 'it was a strange sound, that united wail – continuous, pitiful, strong – like a great sigh or murmur of vague desire and hope, issuing from the heart of despair, piercing the gloom and murky atmosphere of that vaulted room, and reaching to the heart of God'.[27] Here, Butler compares (with explicit self-irony) the slightly awkward, middle-class 'leader', attempting to redeem the masses, with the self-selecting, nameless, effortlessly authoritative 'prophet' who arises out of their prison, 'among the damp refuse and lumps of tarred rope', redolent of death, rejection and captivity, and speaks to the moment. Her voice 'united' with those of the other women and with Butler's in an utterance transcending the confinement both of words and of their dismal prison, 'reaches' to God. It is clear which of them has authority, and yet both are interdependent: prophetic utterance arises out of the exchange.

Turning the oakum shed into a place filled with strange sound and also a place of play throws into question Uglow's view of Butler's relation to the women as either custodial or falsely identifying. Instead, as they laughed they became friends. Consequently, this incident offers an alternative to the forms of social behaviour and individuality available within the educated life of Oxford and Cheltenham. The women's prayer is corporate, non-verbal, both poignant and 'strong'; the 'tall, handsome girl' betokens a natural authority, free from desire for power, and rooted in the equality of friendship. Furthermore, when the narrator tries to convert, to instruct 'them' in performing to her, the self is asserted and the narrator becomes an 'I' with designs on the audience. Countering this danger and the anxiety it provokes, the tall and dark girl becomes like the Baptist: she 'had prepared the way for me', so that Josephine is then able, as it were seamlessly, to declare, without loss of integrity or integration with her audience, 'let us all kneel, and cry to that same Jesus'. There is a moment here when Butler is claiming that identity has briefly disrupted the alienating structure of power and privilege, when her own experience of suffering enables her, through humility and confidence, both to ally with and give leadership to 'suffering humanity'. The episode suggests that such leadership is mobile, and can be assumed by anyone: it is not particular to herself, or to the 'other', though both share in it at different moments.

Prophecy, Humility, Soul-leisure

This moment of corporate understanding is made possible by Butler's distinctive understanding of prophecy and the prophetic role, and it was a role to which Butler gave considerable thought. In her essay, *Prophets and Prophetesses,* she works to overturn customary expectations of what prophecy entails, and in doing so herself offers, perhaps, a kind of prophecy.[28] For Butler, prophecy calls for courage; she emphasises its heroism, the courage which commitment to solitude and the inner battle against egotism calls for. The prophet is, thus, forged not in the sphere of action, the world, but in the desert, in the space beyond the parameters of the civilised and the known. Jesus goes into the wilderness, and emerges a prophet of a particular, and original, kind. Butler descended into the wilderness of the oakum shed, to establish herself as a spiritual authority.

She goes on to identify two particular characteristics associated with the prophet; humility and, surprisingly, what she calls, soul-leisure. The first she proceeds to define in a way that, again, challenges conventional if distorted understanding of the term. It connotes, not a weak dependency on another; rather, the reverse. The 'truly humble person is the most independent of men: he bears himself with dignity among his fellows.' He appears, further, to possess 'self-reliance and confidence', qualities deriving not from success in the world, but solely from God.[29] He is ready to undertake 'the smallest thing, unknown and unnoticed, as to undertake some great, difficult and (to the world) apparently ambitious enterprise'.[30] His indifference to esteem gives him a 'strange dignity and calm', yet also an emphatic 'humanness'. In contrast to the 'feverish competitiveness' of the world, manifesting as much in good works as in self-interested ambition, he declines to 'rush to the front'. [31]

For this reason, Butler refrains from calling the prophet a spiritual 'leader', a word that might have seemed appropriate. Rather, such a word is 'terrifying' to her; by virtue of its connotations with human power, it insists on a relation with the other that cannot but subordinate. The terms 'seer' or 'prophet', however, Butler sees as lacking this coercive design, and as more exactly embodying a contemplative attitude to others and to God. Furthermore, the prophet does not only speak with his or her eye on the future, on a utopian condition that cannot be realised in the present. The prophet speaks into and from the present, intending to realise the 'fulness of promise' in the now. However, such a stance is a gift, bestowed only on one committed to 'standing aside' from the present.

The prophet is, in one sense, neither exceptionally privileged, nor an outcast, and the role is potentially available to anyone, as Blake had said, male or female. Butler's use of the gendered version of the term, 'prophetess', suggests however that while gender difference is not erased, neither is it obstructive to the process of prophetic vision; for being absorbed into the mind and heart of God calls for an equal degree of transformation and transcendence from both genders. Similarly, Butler points to a quality of inward vision which is not affected by worldly distinctions of power or status; for a humility which is not an inversion of pride, a weak dependency and self-abasement, but rather 'stands aside' from such considerations of difference in self-reliant confidence, able therefore to see what she regards as the false conventions of society with clarity. Such independence of spirit differs, I suggest, from the idolatrous pursuit of rational autonomy derived from enlightenment thought, reducing objects of vision to mechanical similarity. Butler therefore emphasises the prophet's capacity for 'humanness', employing the feminised term 'tenderness' to suggest the degree of social involvement that becomes possible, indeed imperative, for such a figure. The prophet does not exclusively occupy the margins of society; for society is constructed itself as a 'wilderness', as Butler so often declares; the prophet, rather, stands to remind society of the possibility for a resolution of hostile contraries, first in her own role, free of the fantasised constructions of gender, and then in her activity.

The prophet has, historically, offered a means of authority and speech to women. The role was particularly frequently employed in mid-seventeenth-century religious culture, by figures like Anna Trapnel. In her case and others, disembodied freedom from femininity is the condition for authoritative speech; and that speech is explicitly perceived as the speech of God, for which the prophet is a vessel. Butler speaks comparably of divine possession, but her stress on humanity and her gendered term 'prophetess' remains in touch with the flesh. However, the emphasis on soul-leisure and its focus on the disciplined battle with evil reminds us that independence from worldly difference, which leads occasionally to what she terms friendship with God, comes at the cost of an inner battle whose demands and rigours should not be underestimated. Leisure, or freedom from the hurtling compulsions of business – an activity she once again renders as a repetition of the fall – is far from its opposite, indolence, though may very often be confused with such emptiness. Both terms, leisure and humility, therefore, are defined against and apart from their apparent opposites and associates; humility is neither pride nor self-abasement but independence of either success or failure; leisure, is neither action nor indolence, but an effortful freedom from both.

Similarly, Butler writes that the prophet speaks to the present moment: just as she offers 'thoughts for the present time', and offers God's promise of fullness of life 'here', as she says, while bearing in mind still the 'catastrophe' that is to come. In this sense Butler's eschatology is, to use a distinction explored by J. F. C. Harrison, 'existential' rather than 'apocalyptic', focused on the needs of the present.[32] It is also carefully denuded of those elements that have consistently made prophetic speech disreputable: its strains of anti-intellectualism, its simplifying dualisms, its association in particular with highly feminised emotion, though traces of all these remain.

Conclusion

Butler's concern to rehabilitate prophetic speech and find a way in which it may come into dialogue with 'worldly dialectics', is most successfully worked through in her two sacred biographies, *Catherine of Siena*, one of her most popular works, and *Saint Agnes*. In both, the protagonist embodies the quality of courageous independence and relational fluidity to a remarkable degree.[33] Butler's writing more widely seeks to bring abject and oppressor, female and male, into fruitful relation with one another, at moments which certainly acknowledge the presence of hierarchy and imbalance in language as in society, but which look to the non-verbal – whether in the inarticulate cry of prayer or the silent example of George Butler – as a means both of protest at the tyranny of speech, and also as a way of bringing both more closely together. For Butler, as Sarah Coakley argued, contemplative or mystical prayer offered not a passive acquiescence to conventional understanding of femininity, but, in its 'heroic', 'severe', 'discipline' of inwardness, rather an 'enlarging' of the self, a dedicated embrace of all that might be offered.

As Butler argues in *Prophets and Prophetesses*, such inner enlarging of the self requires an active courage even greater than that involved in external, worldly conflict: and it also requires an independence from such involvements. Her writing illustrates the enormous capacity for bringing together people or social units generally separated by social prejudice which results from such inner contemplative activity; it is itself not in opposition to worldly involvement, but becomes the means by which such work can effectively be done.

❧

Endnotes

[1] Milbank, 'Christianity, Feminism and Social Action', p. 154, Jenny Uglow, 'Josephine Butler: From Sympathy to Theory', *Feminist Theorists*, ed. Dale Spender (London: Women's Press, 1983), p .160, Judith R. Walkovitz, *Prostitution and Victorian Society* (Cambridge: Cambridge University Press, 1994), Moberley Bell, *Josephine Butler: Flame of Fire* (London: Constable, 1962), Glen Petrie, *A Singular Iniquity* (London: Macmillan, 1971).

[2] Even the recent and richly comprehensive study, Lisa Severine Nolland, *A Victorian Feminist Christian: Josephine Butler, the Prostitutes and God,* Studies in Evangelical History and Thought (Carlisle: Paternoster, 2004), takes a somewhat apologetic tone in accommodating Butler to today's culture.

[3] Walter Brueggemann, *The Prophetic Imagination* (Augsberg, Minneapolis: Fortress Press, 2001), p. 3.

[4] *Swallowing a Fishbone: Feminist Theologians Debate Christianity*, ed. Daphne Hampson (London: SPCK, 1996).

[5] Josephine Butler, *Woman's Work and Woman's Culture* (London: Macmillan, 1869).

[6] Butler, *Woman's Work*, p. ix.

[7] Butler, *Woman's Work*, p. xxxvii.

[8] Butler, *Woman's Work*, p. xxxviii.

[9] Josephine Butler, *Autobiographical Memoir*, ed. George W. and Lucy Johnson (Bristol: Arrowsmith, 1909).

[10] Margaret Cavendish, Duchess of Newcastle's autobiography, *A True Relation of my Birth, Breeding and Life […]* (London, Martin and Allestrye, 1656) is one of the earliest examples of a woman's autobiography containing a hagiographical account of her husband. This has been traditionally understood as a trope of female modesty (see Sidonie Smith, *A Poetics of Women's Autobiography: Marginality and the Fictions of Self-representation* (Bloomington and Indianapolis: Indiana University Press, 1987), pp. 84-101). Butler is distinctive in her openness about her husband's secondariness in many of her crusades.

[11] Starkey, 'Saints, Virgins and Family Members', p. 150.

[12] For example, Liz Stanley has written of the feminine self 'enmeshed with other lives which give hers the meaning it has' (*The Autobiographical I: the Theory and Practice of Feminist Auto/biography* (Manchester: Manchester University Press, 1992), p. 14.).

[13] Johnson, *Autobiographical Memoir*, p. 28.

[14] Johnson, *Autobiographical Memoir*, p. 30.

[15] Johnson, *Autobiographical Memoir*, p. 30.

[16] Ibid.

[17] Johnson, *Autobiographical Memoir*, p. 35.

[18] Johnson, *Autobiographical Memoir*, p. 31.

[19] Johnson, *Autobiographical Memoir*, p. 31.

[20] William Blake, *The Complete Poems*, ed. W. H. Stevenson (New York: Longman, 1985), pp. 585-57. Blake repeats this assertion in 'London': 'But most through midnight streets I hear / How the youthful harlot's curse / Blasts the new-born infant's tear, / And blights with plagues the marriage hearse' (Blake, *Complete Poems*, p. 154.) and quoted in Johnson, *Autobiographical Memoir*, pp. 31-32.

[21] Johnson, *Autobiographical Memoir*, p. 33.

[22] Helen Stoddart, *Rings of Desire: Circus History and Representation* (Manchester and New York: Manchester University Press, 2000), p. 175.

[23] Stoddart quotes the diarist Arthur Munby who relates his attraction to one acrobat and his consternation on discovering that 'she' was, in fact, a boy.

[24] Johnson, *Autobiographical Memoir*, p. 49.

[25] Johnson, *Autobiographical Memoir*, p. 52.

[26] Johnson, *Autobiographical Memoir*, p. 59.

[27] Johnson, *Autobiographical Memoir*, p. 60.

[28] Josephine Butler, *Prophets and Prophetesses: Some Thoughts for the Present Times* (Newcastle-on-Tyne: Mawson, Swan and Morgan, 1898).

[29] Butler, *Prophets and Prophetesses*, pp. 11, 23.

[30] Butler, *Prophets and Prophetesses*, pp. 16-17.

[31] Butler, *Prophets and Prophetesses*, p. 19.

[32] J. F. C. Harrison, *The Second Coming: Popular Millenarianism 1780-1850* (London: Routledge, 1979), p. 228.

[33] Butler's portrayal of these saints makes them into prophetesses, therefore; both Butler's contemporary prophetic women and her medieval heroines share he qualities found by subsequent feminists in the tradition of medieval mysticism, which Laurie Finke, for instance, describes as 'a site of struggle between the authoritative, monologic language of a powerful social institution and the heteroglossia of the men and women who came under its sway and sometimes resisted it.' (Laurie A. Finke, 'Mystical Bodies and the Dialogics of Vision', *Women, Autobiography, Theory: A Reader*, ed. Sidonie Smith and Julia Watson (Madison, WN and London; University of Wisconsin Press, 1998), p. 404.

5

Josephine Butler's Apocalyptic Vision of the Prostitute and Modern Debates on Prostitution

Alison Milbank

Over twenty years ago, Alison encountered Josephine Butler while in charge of the library at Mary Sumner House, the Mothers' Union Headquarters, and went on to write an article on Butler as a Christian, which was an early attempt to understand and value a figure then maligned by feminists as matriarchal and custodial in her approach to work with prostitutes. A scholar of the Victorian period, Alison has published Daughters of the House: Modes of the Gothic in Victorian Fiction *(1992),* Dante and the Victorians *(1998) and* Chesterton and Tolkien as Theologians: The Fantasy of the Real *(2007). Lecturer in Literature and Theology at the University of Nottingham, and curate of the Holy and Undivided Trinity, Lambley, Alison attempts to unite theology and practical engagement. As her title indicates, she discerns in Butler's vision of the prostituted woman a sign of eschatological inbreaking, in which as enslaved but about to be freed, the woman stands as sign of the working of the kingdom.*

I long to have a hundred voices, that with all of them I might pray without ceasing that Christ will come quickly, and deliver for ever the poor groaning world: the slaves from all their woes, the victims and slaves of lust in our own land, the poor women who are driven as sheep to the slaughter into the slave market of London; prisoners, captives and exiles.[1]

In old age Josephine Butler looked back to the 'sweet visions' of her childhood, when she 'used to sit under the shade of the trees of my father's home and read of the holy martyrs and dream of a golden age'.[2] Her identification with the female saints of an epic past echoes that of George Eliot's Dorothea Brooke, who compares herself to a latter-born Teresa of Avila and whose 'loving heart beats and sobs after an unattained goodness'.[3] The heroine of *Middlemarch* is unable to realise her heroic potential within the confines of Victorian convention. Dorothea is 'Foundress of nothing', and the narrative of her life is one of containment within a social labyrinth, a 'walled-in maze of small paths that led no whither'. The novel ends with her life sublimated in that of her husband.

Despite a similar awareness of the walled-in character of female experience, Josephine Butler would indeed found organisations and lead a public life of epic proportions. She had the advantage of being the offspring of a scion of the great Whig dynasty of the Greys, and of an intellectually nourishing home life. Furthermore, John Grey was a strong supporter of the abolition of slavery, providing her, as was the case for American feminists Lucretia Mott and Elizabeth Cady Stanton, with an emancipatory narrative that would justify her own campaigns against the Contagious Diseases Acts, which she termed 'our Abolitionist Crusade'.[4] The quotation used as an epigraph to this essay begins with the sufferings of actual slaves in the American Civil War, and then goes on to extend the language to include those enslaved by prostitution. Thirdly, she inherited through her mother's Huguenot ancestry a radical Protestantism that was evangelical in piety yet relatively liberal in doctrine and Biblical interpretation, and which gave her access to a scriptural hermeneutic that could speak directly to her own age.

For the difference between the young Josephine and Dorothea emerges through their divergent attitudes to the relation between past and present. In *Middlemarch*, despite the imminence of the Reform Bill of 1832, Dorothea's eyes are upon the past for the possibility of action, and she interprets the present as a site of lack and constraint. In contrast, Josephine Butler's use of the term 'golden age' is more mobile, since it refers both to the dawn of Christianity and to an expected, indeed imminent future reality.

The term 'golden age' was central to the apocalyptic discourse of radical protestant groups from the Anabaptists in the seventeenth century to millennial groups in the nineteenth, and it referred to the time of the so-called millennial Sabbath, a thousand year rule of peace and justice foretold by Revelation 20.4. Various competing models of this golden age were current, with the premillenarians expecting the *parousia* of Christ and the last judgement before this period, and others seeing it as the prelude to the coming of Christ: the postmillenarians.[5] There was, however, a shared acceptance that the birth-pangs of the New Age had already begun and that an outpouring of the Holy Spirit, as among the Irvingites, was revealed in gifts of healing, prophecy and other charismatic signs.

Since the young Greys, as well as attending their parish church, were also taken by their governess in a cart to hear the Irvingite preachers, Josephine Butler would have had direct access to this tradition, which believed in the need to return to apostolic doctrine and practice in preparation for the imminent coming of Christ: hence the title, 'Catholic Apostolic Church'.[6] Although Butler claimed to prefer the simpler teaching of the Methodists to Irvingite excess, there too apocalyptic expectation was often accompanied by ideas of sanctification in the Spirit. Sandra and Paul Zindars-Swartz have pointed out that the categories of post and premillenarian are too rigid to describe the fluidity of Victorian apocalypticism, and this essay will not seek to situate Butler precisely between Darby, Irving or Frere.[7] What I wish rather to demonstrate is the importance of apocalyptic as a rhetorical mode of representing prostitution for Butler, and to move to suggest that it has something to contribute to debates about the nature and treatment of street workers in our own day.

Apocalyptic is a genre shared by Jews of the intertestamental period and Christians alike, and takes its title from the Greek verb meaning to uncover or reveal. Such writings, often in the form of a dream vision, aim to uncover spiritual forces at work in human history, as well as to predict a future that has an element of judgement. The book of Revelation in the New Testament goes so far as to collapse time and space, so that the seer John of Patmos is presented with the reality of a divinely enacted catastrophe, in which Babylon and all forces of evil are destroyed in a crisis in which the just will be saved and a new heaven and earth emerge from the cosmic upheaval. Throughout Christian history, oppressed groups have claimed this discourse for themselves, since it not only reveals the hegemony of the powerful as Satanic and the oppressed as victims but foretells the latter's imminent victorious restoration. Women have had particular recourse to the role of the seer who is instructed by the angel to write, as a means of establishing their right to speak and prophesy. Indeed, Butler's biography of Catherine of Siena draws attention to this aspect of Catherine's appeal to the Pope and other authorities. Women seers were a feature of the English Civil War period, such as Lady Eleanor Davies, who was instructed by the prophet Daniel himself to announce the writing on the wall for King Charles I. Nearer to Butler's own time was Joanna Southcott who in 1792 claimed to be the woman clothed with the sun of Revelation 12, and whose box of secrets successive Archbishops of Canterbury have rather unsportingly failed to open as she instructed them.[8]

Southcott's visions were coterminous with the French Revolution, which inaugurated a century of quite general apocalyptic expectation in society at large that has yet to be studied with the detail it warrants. 1789 as the opening of the seventh seal was followed by 1815 as the date of the woes of the sixth vial, prompting even the worldly Lord Byron to write the apocalyptic poem 'Darkness'. Moreover, as I have noted elsewhere, even 'progressive' Whig historians could discuss the proximity of the second coming with confidence in the 1840's.[9] Josephine Butler's participation in the campaign to undo the Contagious Diseases Acts began in the late 1860's, just after the time presaging the cosmic battle according to the dating of John Cumming, James Frere and Edward Irving, and continued through the millenial expectations of 1876-8.[10] The titles of many of her addresses and books have a millenarian edge: 'The Hour Before the Dawn', 'The New Era', 'Prophets and Prophetesses', 'A Sabbath Rest for the Soul on Earth', etc. Helen Mathers criticised earlier remarks I made about Butler's employment of millenial language, claiming that she is only premillenial (meaning that she looks to a gradual and progressive development of the Kingdom), but there is evidence of a stronger belief in nearly every text she wrote, long before the Pentecostal interests of her old age.[11] For example in her 1871 address to the Ladies' National Association, *Sursum Corda*, she wrote:

*I believe that the conflict between God and evil, so far from dying
out, will become keener and fiercer as time goes on, but that
the faithful and uninterrupted efforts of the servants of God to
establish the supremacy of conscience, and the bringing of every
impulse of man's lower nature into subjection to God's laws,
will be finally crowned by an act of the Divine Will, whereby the
principle of evil itself will be expelled from the earth, and the
reign of righteousness will be established.*[12]

This direct reference to the millenial Sabbath is not the smooth
march of the secularised postmillenarianism of Imperialism but is to
be accompanied by 'signs of terror', 'a national exorcism', a Divine
judgement with sword and pestilence and 'the rising of the Sun of
Righteousness'.[13]

Butler's extensive recourse to resurrection discourse as in accord
with this sense of the last days and with a quasi-Irvingite and Holiness
belief that a new era of the Holy Spirit was being inaugurated. *Prophets
and Prophetesses* takes its impetus from the speech of Peter in Acts 2.
16-21:

16 But this is that which was spoken by the prophet Joel;

*17 And it shall come to pass in the last days, saith God, I will
pour out of my Spirit upon all flesh: and your sons and your
daughters shall prophesy, and your young men shall see visions,
and your old men shall dream dreams:*

*18 And on my servants and on my handmaidens I will pour out
in those days of my Spirit; and they shall prophesy:*

*19 And I will shew wonders in heaven above, and signs in the
earth beneath; blood, and fire, and vapour of smoke:*

*20 The sun shall be turned into darkness, and the moon into
blood, before the great and notable day of the Lord come:*

*21 And it shall come to pass, that whosoever shall call on the
name of the Lord shall be saved.*

The prophets here are indeed, as Butler wrote, 'to show forth the mind of God on any matter' but their words are part of the 'latter days' presaging the coming of the Lord, of which event they are a sign like the portents in heaven. They proclaim the resurrection indeed but as the first fruit of the harvest. It is not the end of the story but in one sense the beginning. Hence at Pentecost and again in the New Pentecost the golden age is both active but also yet to be achieved; the prophet bears this double perspective. Similarly, *The Hour Before the Dawn* of 1876, published in the middle of the 1876-78 millenial expectation, has a liminal quality, reminding the Christian reader of the time when the women brought spices to anoint the body of Christ while it was still dark, and the time between the night-time crossing of the Red Sea by the Israelites and the arrival of the Egyptian hosts in the morning. *The Hour Before the Dawn* is subtitled by the Vulgate version of Romans 13.12, translated by the King James version as 'The night is far gone, the day is at hand'.[14] Not only is this verse was often interpreted apocalyptically but the address includes an open call for the return of Christ: 'VENI DOMINE JESU'.[15]

For resurrection is first and foremost an apocalyptic event (insofar as one may speak of it as an event), and the beginning of cosmic renewal. Butler follows St Paul's (and Revelation's) association of the creation with the female and maternal body, so that in the abrogation of the Contagious Diseases Acts and the end of prostitution 'the groaning and travailling earth shall be released from her bondage, and the rod of the oppressor be broken'.[16] Like the artist Stanley Spencer, who painted so many general resurrection scenes of his Cookham neighbours clambering awkwardly out of their tombs, Butler found in the tropes of Revelation a means by which both body and soul could be addressed together, and a liberation that could be offered to the whole person. In her discussion of Christ's dealings with women in the gospels Butler stresses their bodily needs and specifically female ailments and puts the body at the centre of her critique of the Contagious Diseases Acts: 'God has given to woman, for good and wise ends, an <u>absolute sovereignty over her own person</u>, and of this no man, no legislation on earth has any right to deprive her.'[17] Apocalyptic is a mode which allows the restoration of the body in the form of a cosmic marriage.

The figure of the New Jerusalem descending like a bride is one in which all may participate. So not only does Butler look to the recovery of full personhood in the resurrection of the prostitute but she occasionally compares the dying prostitute to Christ's affianced bride, and famously, like Catherine of Siena, Butler herself experienced a spiritual betrothal.[18] This mystical marriage, however, is linked to Butler's baroque conception of the heart of God. As she is betrothed to God, so she shares his heart – that is, his love for all creation. In this way, use of the marriage metaphor does not set up an exclusive relationship of the individual soul with God, but renders every such union a proleptic anticipation of the New Jerusalem.

Apocalyptic discourse is important for Butler for a second reason: that it enables the integration of those other strands in her rhetoric that I alluded to in the beginning of this essay. The quotation above about the sovereignty of the body comes from a Whig discourse of rights akin to that of Butler's friend and supporter, John Stuart Mill; in *The Constitution Violated* Butler makes frequent use of the Gothic perception of the woman as entrapped heroine at risk from rape and oppression by a degenerate and oppressive aristocracy. Apocalyptic allows both the emancipation of the Gothic heroine from imprisonment and the restoration of the free subject of liberal politics. Furthermore, it prevents the liberatory act from being one out of subjection to autonomy in the modern sense of the atomised individual because the apocalyptic bride is holy as a sign of the sacredness of creation. Her integrity is revealed *in* rather than beyond the movement of deliverance itself, as the revelation of an always already accomplished emancipation, made evident to all in the liberatory moment. The slave loosed from his or her chains is an analogous example, in which the loosing of the chains allows the God-given humanity to be revealed.

A third way in which apocalyptic energises and directs Butler's rhetoric is in its dissolving of physical barriers. The apocalyptic eye of the seer breaks down all divisions between earth and heaven, spiritual and physical realities. Since prostitutes (and other women) were actually forcibly detained in lock hospitals or brothels (especially under the Continental system of legalised prostitution), a Gothic narrative of escape from imprisonment was a natural mode and Butler described a 'half-waking vision' in terms of 'huge walls blocking the way and darkening the daylight on every side.' At the appearance of the face of God however, the walls get lower and lower, until Butler is able to spring on top of them and shout for joy and victory.[19] In *The Hour Before the Dawn* she announces: I have found the door of hope: he has the key to all the mysteries', quoting from Revelation 3. 7-8, which refers to the open door which no-one can shut, and the rescue of the blessed from coming destruction.[20]

This apocalyptic removal of oppositions has a twofold function in Butler's work. First, by pointing out a machinery of oppression at work in society, apocalyptic is a device for addressing social forms of sinfulness *as* structural at a time when sin was increasingly individualised, and most people would have viewed the prostitution problem primarily in terms of the wrongdoing of the individual woman. Butler might be aware of the damage prostitution exacted on the woman involved, but she was always clear about its social and economic basis. Secondly, in its unmasking of power and breaking down of barriers between time and eternity, apocalyptic allows other dualities to be questioned from its quasi-divine perspective. Hence Butler can both draw attention to the barriers placed between 'pure' and 'fallen' women and attack their ideological separation. In *The New Godiva* dialogue Victor addresses directly William Lecky's suggestion that the prostitute has a priestly function in bearing the sins of society, by suggesting that if prostitution is so necessary a condition for social health then the middle and upper classes should offer their own daughters for this service to the community. Elsewhere Victor deepens this sacrificial understanding by describing the enslavement of women in prostitution as a 'holocaust' by which a sickly and over spiritualised conception of innocent womanhood is maintained.[21] For Butler the subjugation of one group of women affects the others: 'can the soul of my sister be defiled and my soul not be the worse for it? It cannot' for woman is *'solidaire.'*[22] Her liberatory approach sees all women as in need of deliverance by Christ in different ways and Mary Magdalene is their model, as the woman who was first healed by Christ and then also the witness of his resurrection. Butler does also commend the Blessed Virgin, but even she is presented by Butler as besmirched by scandal and Joseph's lack of belief in her innocence. She can thus stand for the woman in a garrison town, like Mrs Percy, whose reputation is besmirched and her good name taken away. Butler adapted the Magnificat itself to stand for the 'low estate' of all God's 'handmaidens'.[23]

The consequence of this female solidarity is that the prostitute, far from being a figure of outcast status, from whom respectable women keep apart, can instead become representative of all womanhood - or indeed all oppressed humanity - for Butler. Indeed, it is because of her enslavement that the prostitute can function as apocalyptic sign and witness. First, she is a judgement on society: in her own person she functions as a form of 'writing on the wall' like the Divine message to Belshazzar in Daniel 5:

> *The handywork of ruined women is visible in the blasted walls of the Tuilleries. Their history is written in black smoke on the crumbling walls of our palaces in flames. There is no need of a Daniel here to decipher the writing on the wall. All the world can read, plainly, written there, the words, La femme déchue – the ruined woman.*[24]

Elsewhere Butler quotes William Blake's poem, 'London' and 'the youthful harlot's curse' which 'blasts the new born infant's tear/And blights with plagues the marriage-hearse'.[25] The prostitute reveals all that is awry in human sexual relations.

Secondly, the prostitute as victim reveals the presence of hell on earth. This is a trope much used to describe the indescribable nature of poverty in Victorian Britain and often as a means of avoiding engagement with it. In contrast, Butler does invoke Revelation 9 in her description of a visit to a foreign brothel – 'Hell hath opened her mouth. I stand in the near presence of the powers of evil. What I see and hear are the smoke of the pit, the violence of the torture inflicted by man on his fellows, the cries of the lost spirits, the wail of the murdered innocents, and the laughter of demons' – but she does so in order to precipitate action: to uncover and to liberate.[26] Indeed her model of apocalyptic is more mobile and dynamic than that of the book of Revelation itself because she combines it with an equal attention to a gospel inauguration of the kingdom. Although any direct and detailed account of the life endured by the women and children in this brothel would have been unacceptable, apocalyptic - even lurid apocalyptic language - was possible and a way of speaking the unspeakable.

A third way in which the prostitute becomes a witness is as a recipient of liberation in which the eschatological promise has been already achieved. In *Sursum Corda* Butler makes this position explicit: '"Even so, Lord Jesus *come quickly*!" is the last record we have in the inspired writings, of the appeal of the waiting Church to her Lord; and we may not deny that he does, many a time, come quickly, and may do so again.'[27] Josephine Butler and her husband took a number of sick and dying prostitutes into their own home, including one significantly named Mary or Marion, whose own death was accompanied by the same words of Revelation: 'Oh, come quickly, Lord Jesus' and by a desire to burst limits, asking for the window to be opened, perhaps in alliance with the belief that this represented the escape of the soul from the body.[28] Butler had Marion's coffin filled with white camellias, which, in the Victorian symbolism of flowers, represented achieved perfection. Her narrative, later published as a booklet, 'Marion, histoire véritable', was itself a witness both of society for condemning her and of the kingdom already active in her salvation. Marion even became a prophet to Butler herself, warning her of struggle and difficulties ahead.[29]

It should be emphasised here that although Butler saw death as one form of liberation from prostitution, and she and her sister Harriet imagined their own dead children welcoming prostitutes to heaven, she was not like most Victorian novelists whose narrative, however sympathetic, saw the only resolution for repentant Magdalens beyond the grave.[30] Butler founded a home for former prostitutes and hoped that they could engage in honest and healthy work and marry and have children. Her support for women's employment in all trades and professions is well-attested, although even here she conceives the employment of women as an act of specifically religious liberation. In *Woman's Work and Woman's Culture* Butler foregrounds the importance of women as the first witnesses of the resurrection, and conceives this liberating act as analogous to female emancipation both from the private home and the public brothel.[31]

The importance of these death-bed narratives of Marion and

others is also due to the fact that they allow the objectified woman to achieve subjectivity and a voice, 'the voice of the slave herself'.[32] Butler records the dying words of one seventeen-year old orphan who had been hustled from prison to the streets and back: '*I will fight for my soul through hosts, and hosts, and hosts,*' and comments on 'that sense of the dignity and true worth of the self in her – the immortal, inalienable self – found expression in that indomitable resolution'.[33] Indeed, the combination of abolitionist and apocalyptic rhetoric allows the sin to be decried but the prostitute herself fully accepted in all her personhood. Butler's attitude to individual 'fallen women' was always one of love and acceptance, not only of those forced into the trade but even of those whom she describes in *The Moral Reclaimability of Prostitutes'* as involved through affection (for a pimp/boyfriend) or 'excess passion'.[34] In each case the method of approach is the same revelatory uncovering: 'delicately and frankly to elicit the God-given character, and to give it permanence'.[35] This, Butler goes on to stress, is more difficult with the male clients, whose divine image is obscured further by hypocrisy and denial.

It is with Butler's stress on giving a voice to the voiceless that she comes closest to contemporary ethnographic approaches to prostitution. Cecilie Hørigård's *Backstreets: Prostitution, Money and Love* seeks to give a voice even to pimps and clients to understand their perspective, and Maggie O'Neill in *Prostitution and Feminism: Towards a Politics of Feeling* spends much of the book seeking for a model in which to study prostitute lives without rendering them mere objects of knowledge.[36] She evolves a model that she entitles ethno-mimesis, which involves a degree of emotional immersion in the subject of study, which is in dialectical relation to the 'constructive rationality' that understands the subject in relation to the practices and processes by which we structure our knowledge of the world.[37] In practice this seems to mean that the ethnographer is fully prepared to listen and accept the life-story as offered by the other, even to the extent of being moved by it and changing his or her ideas. This model of ethnography has emancipatory potential as observer and observed have their conception of reality challenged. So the women described are not a separate race of victims viewed as objects and the researcher is brought to 'the recognition of that which binds me to other women as well as that which separates me' in a manner reminiscent of Butler's view of female solidarity.[38]

O'Neill obtains her participatory-action model from Spanish sources that are themselves influenced by Marxist consciousness-raising and involve a level of commitment both to those studied and to emancipation.[39] This is also the epistemological model of Latin-American Liberation Theology in which the base community reflects upon its experience of oppression and finds resources in scripture to lead to emancipatory praxis.[40] Liberation Theology makes extensive use of Christ's message of liberation in his first sermon and the coming of the kingdom, and it follows Butler in using apocalyptic to demystify oppressive social structures. In O'Neill's nonreligious model there is a similar apocalyptic uncovering: 'As a society we cannot move forward in any enlightened way until we start calling things by their name, until we start seeing things as they are'.[41] She then stresses the need to connect ideological revelation with praxis, commending multiagency work with prostitutes that employs Habermas's 'counter-public sphere' in which 'agencies, individuals and groups can engage in discourse and development and move towards the possibilities of transformative consequences.'[42] This utopian belief in an alternative civil society is again close to that embraced by Liberation Theology in the period after Marxist revolutionary hopes were somewhat given up.

The problem with both models is that they are not apocalyptic enough. Liberation Theology sees theology as 'critical reflection on praxis'. A given social experience is assumed and set apart from the theology, which uses it as its basis upon which to reflect, and which it must then mediate back to faith. Ethno-mimesis similarly takes prostitute experience as a given, even if it understands it as a self-conscious performance – taking seriously and giving a positive valence to the dissociation reported by a number of studies on prostitute subjectivity.[43] Butler, despite her acceptance of the economic basis of prostitution, never accepted it as a given fact in this way, but rather as a sinful opposition to the created order.

For contemporary study of prostitution is highly problematic. On the one hand there is still an enslavement model, represented by the 1949

United Nations Convention on Trafficking in Persons as 'incompatible with the dignity and worth of the human person' and prevalent in studies of the globalisation of prostitution and people-trafficking.[44] This position is represented in this volume by Carrie Pemberton. Certain feminist approaches share this perspective, even going so far as to decry all male/female sexual relations as abusive, while others seek to justify prostitution as a form of free choice or even as a mode of resistance to male power. [45] The centrality of child prostitution and abuse has rendered the subject even more confusing, with organisations such as the Anti-Slavery International seeking to distinguish child from adult and coerced from free prostitution, the last of which is regarded as a legitimate form of work.[46] Joanne Phoenix, in an empirical study, *Making Sense of Prostitution* is convincing when she argues that prostitute identity is a paradox in which she is *both* worker *and* commodified body, victor and survivor, who both chooses and does not choose prostitution.[47] After a nod at the deconstructive ability of prostitution to 'penetrate the veils of ideology' Phoenix concludes despairingly by lamenting that our millenial Britain contains women 'who lead lives so utterly circumscribed by penury, violence and enforced dependency that going to sell sexual services in a social context whereby they are at increased risk of further destitution and exploitation and violence comes to be seen as offering the choice of future stability'. [48] The circular convolutions of this sentence reflect the bind in which those who attempt to theorise prostitution have found themselves.

In her own day Butler was quite radical in refusing to condemn individual prostitutes, for example in Winchester, when the Cathedral ladies sought her support for a purity campaign. In the prostitute she sought not conversion and repentance but 'delicately and frankly to elicit the God-given character, and to give it permanence'[49] and she offered love and acceptance. Apocalyptic in relation to the individual offers a revelation of the self as beloved. Structurally, however, what Butler has to offer that O'Neill's feminist theory and Liberation theology seek unsuccessfully is a truly apocalyptic perspective, which does not accept any 'secular' separate from the ethical and religious as Gutiérrez and Boff tend to do in accepting 'the autonomy of the secular'[50] as a given that theology and religious praxis must work with. Nor does she accept the narrative of prostitution within its own paradigm as O'Neill wishes to do, despite the latter's attempt to connect with something beyond the empathic. Butler's rhetoric offers another narrative of self-understanding that both allows dignity and agency to the woman (and to the male prostitute whom a modern Butler would have included equally) but offers a way out, not into some utopian future but to a kingdom active but not yet fully achieved.

Butler saw very clearly that the problem of prostitution from the worker side was one of economics and lack of self-worth, and from the client's side one of objectification and also a lack of self-worth. *The Hour Before the Dawn*, from which I have quoted so frequently, is an appeal to men, to whom also it has a message of hope: the open door is also for them. They need liberation and deliverance just as much as the prostituted women. Butler describes the male clients as self-appointed cathedrals reflecting the light back – a form of whited sepulchres – when their real status is a Gothic ruin. It is, however, through the desolation and decrepitude of the ruined abbey that the sun can truly reach and light up 'with a new beauty every torn and broken fragment'.[51] Butler, a universalist, looks to a time when men will become brothers to women in more equal relationships and to the salvation of all.

Through her apocalyptic rhetoric of emancipation Butler can offer a *telos*, a goal that includes men and women, clients and prostitutes, which is lacking in the moral relativism of the twenty-first century, when the most that can be looked for is a self-conscious performance of prostitution that privileges alienation as knowledge, or a puritan withdrawal from sexual relations. Only a religious perspective such as that of Christianity can offer this hope, in the days beyond the demise of the master-narratives, precisely because of its apocalyptic function, which reveals the violence endemic not just in economic sexual exchanges but in all attempts to instrumentalise people, and treat them as things. The answer is not the western embrace of choice and individual autonomy, whereby the person enters a world of competition and substitutionary violence, of which prostitution is but one example, but the Christian vision in which people are not means to an end, or even ends in themselves, but signs of the liberating Kingdom of God.

Endnotes

[1] Josephine Butler, 'Private Thoughts', 18 April, 1865, quoted in Helen Mathers, 'The Evangelical Spirituality of a Victorian Feminist', p. 300. Jane Jordan, who cites the same passage in her biography of Butler (p. 65), believes it to be the very first reference in Butler's writings to the sufferings of prostitutes.

[2] Josephine Butler, *The Lady of Shunem* (London: Horace Marshall and Son, 1896), p. 142.

[3] George Eliot, *Middlemarch*, ed. David Carroll (Oxford: Oxford University Press, 1988), p. 3.

[4] Josephine Butler, *Personal Reminiscences of a Great Crusade* (London: Horace, Marshall and Son, 1896), p. 8.

[5] See Bryan Wilson, 'Millenarianism and Sect Formation in the Nineteenth and Twentieth Centuries' in *Apocalyptic in History and Tradition*, edited by John Barton and Chris Rowland (Sheffield: Sheffield Academic Press, 2002), p. 316.

[6] On this movement see Columba Graham Flegg, *Gathered Under Apostles: A Study of the Catholic Apostolic Church* (Oxford: Clarendon, 1992). Butler's remarks are quoted in A. S. G. Butler, *Portrait of Josephine Butler* (London: Faber, 1954), p. 200.

[7] Sandra and Paul Zindars-Swartz, 'Apocalypticism in Modern Western Europe', in *The Continuum History of Apocalypticism*, edited by Bernard J. McGinn , John J. Collins and Stephen J. Stein (New York and London: Continuum, 2003), pp. 607-627, p. 610.

[8] On Lady Eleanor Davies see Stevie Davies, *Unbridled Spirits: Women of the English Revolution, 1640-1660* (London: Virago, 1999), pp. 51-3; on Southcott, see Val Lewis, *Satan's Mistress : the Extraordinary Story of the 18th Century Fanatic Joanna Southcott and her Lifelong Battle with the Devil* (Shepperton : Nauticalia, 1997).

[9] Studies of apocalypticism in English Romanticism include E. S. Shaffer, *Kubla Khan and the Fall of Jerusalem: The Mythological School in Biblical Criticism and Secular Literature* (Cambridge: Cambridge University Press, 1975), Steven Goldsmith, *Unbuilding Jerusalem : Apocalypse and Romantic Representation*, (Ithaca : Cornell University Press, 1993), *Romanticism and Millenarianism*, edited by Tim Fulford. (New York and Basingstoke : Palgrave, 2002), Morton D. Paley, *Apocalypse and Millennium in English Romantic Poetry* (Oxford : Clarendon Press, 1999). On Arnold and Blackstone's expectation of the second coming see Alison Milbank, *Dante and the Victorians* (Manchester: Manchester University Press, 1998), p. 49.

[10] On dates of millenial expectation see *The Continuum History of Apocalypticism*, pp. 610-11.

[11] Mathers, 'Evangelical Spirituality', pp. 300-01.

[12] Josephine Butler, *Sursum Corda* (Liverpool: T. Brackell, 1871), p. 6.

[13] *Sursum Corda*, pp. 11, 13.

[14] Josephine Butler, *The Hour Before the Dawn: An Appeal to Men* (London: Trubner and Co., 1876), p. 1.

[15] Butler, *Hour Before the Dawn*, p. 111.

[16] Ibid.

[17] Josephine Butler, 'An Appeal to the People of England on the Recognition and Superintendence of Prostitution by Governments' (Nottingham: Banks, 1870), p. 17.

[18] 'One day He brought to my heart and my soul's listening ear...these words, "I will betroth thee to Me for ever, in judgement and righteousness, in loving tenderness and mercies. I will betroth thee to Me in faithfulness'. Quoted in Butler, *Portrait of Josephine Butler*, p. 178.

[19] Quoted in *An Autobiographical Memoir*, p. 235.

[20] Quoted in *An Autobiographical Memoir*, p. 155.

[21] *The New Godiva: A Dialogue* (London: Fisher Unwin, 1885), p. 25. A copy at Vassar used by the Indiana Victorian Women Writers Project attributes this to Butler and has it bound with another Butler pamphlet. The British Library copy is anonymous. Jane Jordan attributes this pamphlet to Butler in her bibliography (p. 349).

[22] Josephine Butler, 'Address at Croydon, July 3, 1871' (London: Office of the National Association, 1871), p. 3.

[23] See *Personal Reminiscences*, p. 182: 'We can echo the words of that which is written: "My soul doth magnify the Lord, and my spirit hath rejoiced in God my Saviour, for He hath regarded the low estate of His handmaidens." And remember, women, if we are faithful unto death, all men shall call us blessed.'

[24] *Personal Reminiscences*, pp. 246-47.

[25] Quoted in Glen Petrie, *A Singular Iniquity: The Campaigns of Josephine Butler* (London: Macmillan, 1971), p. 40, from Butler's letter to Benjamin Jowett.

[26] Butler, *Recollections*, p. 479.

[27] *Sursum Corda*, p. 37.

[28] *Recollections of George Butler* , p. 190. On the meaning of white camellias see *Colliers' Cyclopedia of Common and Social Information* (London: P. F. Collier, 1882), p. 453.

[29] Butler, *Recollections of George Butler,* p. 191.

[30] As, for example, Elizabeth Gaskell's *Ruth* (1853), Dickens's Nancy in *Oliver Twist* (1837-9) Wilkie Collins's *The New Magdalen* (1873).

[31] Butler, *Woman's Work*, p. xxix.

[32] Butler, *Personal Reminiscences*, p. 280.

[33] Butler, *Recollections of George Butler,* p. 69.

[34] Butler, *Moral Reclaimability of Prostitutes*, p. 5.

[35] Butler, *Moral Reclaimability of Prostitutes*, p. 4.

[36] Cecilie Hørigård and Liv Fristad, *Backstreets: Prostitution, Money and Love* translated by Katherine Hanson, Nancy Sipe, and Barbara Wilson (University Park, PA.: Pennsylvania State University Press, 1992); Maggie O'Neill, *Prostitution and Feminism: Towards a Politics of Feeling* (Cambridge: Polity, 2001).

[37] O'Neill, *Prostitution and Feminism*, pp. 55-59.

[38] O'Neill, *Prostitution and Feminism,* p. 48.

[39] O'Neill, *Prostitution and Feminism,* p. 47.

[40] Stavo Gutiérrez, *A Theology of Liberation: History, Politics and Salvation*, new edition, introduced by Chris Rowlands (London: SCM, 2001), pp. 50-57. See also Juan Luis Segundo, *The Liberation of Theology*, translated by John Drury (London: Gill and Macmillan, 1977), pp. 125-53.

[41] O'Neill, *Prostitution and Feminism*, p. 184.

[42] O'Neill, *Prostitution and Feminism*, p. 185.

[43] For a critique of the idea of civil society in Liberation Theology and also of its claiming an arena of 'pure nature' see Daniel M. Bell, Jr., *Liberation Theology After the End of History: The Refusal to Cease Suffering* (London and New York: Routledge, 2001), especially pp. 51-59.

[44] See Sheila Jeffreys, 'Challenging the Adult/Child distinction in theory and practice on prostitution. Sheila Jeffreys. *International Feminist Journal of Politics*. November 2000. Accessed online at http://mc2.vic.net.au/home/catwaust/web/myfiles/adultchild.htm on 9/6/06.

[45] For the slavery approach to prostitution see Kathleen Barry, *The Prostitution of Sexuality* (New York: New York University Press, 1995), and Sheila Jeffreys, *The Idea of Prostitution* (Melbourne: Spinifex, 1997); on the positive valency of sexwork see Jill Nagle (ed), *Whores and Other Feminists* (London: Routledge, 1997).

[46] Jeffreys, 'Challenging the Adult/Child Distinction'.

[47] Joanna Phoenix, *Making Sense of Prostitution* (London: Macmillan, 1999), p. 186.

[48] Phoenix, *Making Sense of Prostitution,* p. 187.

[49] Butler, *Moral Reclaimability of Prostitutes*, p. 4.

[50] Gutiérrez, *Theology of Liberation,* p. 56.

[51] *The Hour Before the Dawn*, p. 12.

6

Religious Motivation and the Abuse of Women: Some Reflections on the Concerns of Josephine Butler

Ann Loades

Professor Emeritus at the University of Durham, Ann Loades is a theologian with wide research and teaching interests, which include the relation between philosophy and theology, Christian ethics, and sacramental spirituality. She has a particular interest in feminist theology and ethics. Among her most recent books are a study of the spiritual writer, Evelyn Underhill *(1997) and* Feminist Theology: Voices from the Past *(2001), which includes a chapter on Josephine Butler. In the essay below she celebrates Butler's attention to sex trafficking and the domestic abuse of women, while also arguing that traditional religious understanding of female self-sacrifice can undermine the care of the self necessary to oppose such practices.*

Josephine Butler lived through momentous changes to the lives of women in the course of her own long life (1828-1906), most notably access to independent economic resources and to better education, which at least in principle made a difference to their power to earn their own livings. In turn, these changes had an impact not only on their relationships with men but on the importance given to children and their lives, so closely intertwined as they were and are with the well-being of their mothers in particular. She was not of course alone in her concern for the fate of mothers who gave birth to illegitimate children, the struggles of poverty-stricken women in prostitution and women's ability to get their voices heard on these and other issues. She was, however, particularly well placed to provoke women more fortunately placed to take these problems seriously, thus raising some very difficult issues for themselves as well as the most unfortunate, about the place of women in their family groups and kin networks, and their capacity for self-governance and for 'care', about which so much is sometimes made in writing on feminist ethics. Women's ability or inability to protect themselves and their children from violence and abuse within a household, their own capacity for inflicting such abuse, and their responsibility for situations where children run from home, for instance, remain painful problems difficult to address. Our concern at this juncture, however, is to reflect on Josephine Butler's distinctive contribution to changes in the lives of women during the course of her long life.

We need not be squeamish at recognising that Josephine Butler's particular embodiment of imagination, compassion and intellect were fired by religious conviction, though like other women she had to negotiate with care her relationship to religious institutions, given the 'in principle' recognition in some Christian theology of women's spiritual equality with men. Coupled as such recognition was with women's religious, social, economic and educational subordination to males it was unsurprising that it was possible to sustain the illusion of their inherent inferiority. Despite the deplorable expression of women's inferiority in common law, Josephine was blessed by coming from a home imbued with the spirit of reform characteristic of the branches of the Greys of Northumberland. In these families women were well educated and fostered in self-confidence, moral and physical courage, the ability to discern fundamental moral principles, and then to work at putting such principles into practice. She also enjoyed a long and fulfilling marriage to a man who came from a family whose men found their own vocations in education as well as the church and public service of various kinds. George Butler, her husband, found his particular vocation both as an ordained minister of the Church of England and as one of the educational innovators of his day, and committed himself to Josephine's causes wholeheartedly. She was also fortunate in being able to secure the support of some senior and experienced politicians, as well as having a talent for inspiring loyalty and developing friendship across social and denominational limits. This was vital for her campaigns, since Nonconformist women had considerable experience of organising philanthropic movements, and of managing petitions on a large scale, making good use of the development of railway, steamship and postal service connections, both within and well beyond national boundaries.

In discerning Josephine's own convictions we may properly rely very largely on her own published comment, sometimes writing as a contemporary of the events which provoked her to publish, sometimes engaged in a retrospective review of the course of things from the perspective of her old age, when much had been achieved, although much remained to distress her. It is also worth bearing in mind the legacy of Mary Wollstonecraft's 1792 *A Vindication of the Rights of Women*[1] on the one hand, and on the other, the way in which women were able to appeal in their own case to the USA Constitution at the famous meeting at Seneca Falls in 1848, which focussed their campaigns for the right to the vote and the transformation of women's legal status in relation to men.[2] The *Vindication* continued to be read despite the troublesome legacy of her husband, William Godwin's, 1798 *Memoirs* of Mary. Careful readers of the *Vindication* might well notice her pleas for clean hearts, well-furnished brains and personal modesty, and her point that arguments for equality supported the role of mothers and the importance of families for the rearing of children. And in what was for her to become the crucial transitional year of 1869, Josephine Butler received a letter from the great American Quaker campaigner, Lucretia Mott, recalling the importance of the Seneca Falls meeting for establishing women's conventions, her own reading of the *Vindication*, and the fact that women would no longer rest 'satisfied in the circumscribed limits with which corrupt custom and a perverted application of the Scriptures had encircled her...'[3]

And when Josephine came to write her own *The Constitution Violated* (1871)[4] she may well have had both precedents in mind, with the difference, of course, that in the absence of a constitution she had to work out the principles which she believed should underlie British legislation. Only then was she able to articulate what had been happening and continued to happen to women, precisely in terms of such principles not being applied. Not only had their 'rights' not been vindicated, they had systematically been disregarded. To show how such a position cohered with principles she had worked out earlier in her life, however, we turn to some clues from her earlier years, as well as providing some examples of how these affected her position on a range of issues.

Some Moral and Spiritual Principles in Action

Josephine gratefully acknowledged the importance of both her parents, but especially of her father, as well as her husband in shaping who and what she was. Hannah, her mother, came from a family which had fled France when legal protection was removed from Protestants in late seventeenth-century France, and had been educated by Moravians whose missionaries had see all too much of the conditions of slaves. Making sense of biblical material (where possible) whilst discussing major issues of the day in a domestic context was notably characteristic of both Methodists and Moravians and was a significant feature of Josephine's education as it was for her siblings. The interpretation of texts about both slavery and women raised major problems.

In her memoir of her father she recalled that he was wholly free of what Josephine denounced as 'a peculiarity of modern, as of ancient barbarism, *i.e.* the undervaluing of the female sex'[5]. She also cherished the memory of 'the purity of his character' as she grieved to hear women tell their daughters 'that all men are corrupt, that we must expect nothing else, that we must judge them leniently, and resign ourselves to fellowship through life with persons about whose past and present life the less we know the better'.[6] Given such doubts about men, and the existence of circles where it was fashionable for men 'to dwell continually upon, and to make literary merchandise of, the folly, the weakness, or the wickedness of the female sex', she thought it important to speak boldly of the existence in women and men alike 'of purity of heart, of innocency of life, of constancy in love'. We may perhaps suppose, however, that the memory of her father, however, in effect left her with a difficulty about finding her own 'voice', as indeed she did in the course of her marriage to George. For her father was so 'pained and puzzled' by even the slightest allusion to 'the vileness of the times, or of fashionable vice or villainy', that his wife and daughters and those who knew and loved him learned never to speak of certain matters in his presence.[7] The modesty of person and mind advocated by Mary Wollstonecraft and expressed in the lives of Josephine's parents had somehow to be represented in her own person whilst she found ways to raise questions about some of the perversities of human sexual behaviour which it might have been impossible to discuss with her father. On the other hand, we might suppose that had he lived to see it, his trust in and admiration for the women of his family might have enabled him to support Josephine once he understood, as her husband did, the crisis of confidence to which she was eventually brought when faced with the invitation to become President of the Ladies' National Association for Repeal of the Contagious Diseases Acts (or as she preferred to say, for their abolition), since the degradation of women and analogies with slavery and its violence had became clear enough to her by then. A major task for everyone in her time was to dislodge from white as well as from black consciousness the conviction that it was God, and not human beings, who had instituted slavery and that it was therefore meant to be a permanent feature of human society. If the Deity was indeed to be worshipped as 'Father of humanity' then both the slavery of colour and the slavery of sex had to be extinguished.[8] And if one apparently immovable institution could be shifted, so could others.

Living in an age when women were not greatly encouraged to take action independently of men Josephine did of course know of exceptions. Thus she wrote of 'our brave Northumbrian girl, Grace Darling, who could never understand the sensation caused by her heroic deed, saying (and truly) that there were girls all along the coast who would and did accompany their fathers and brothers to sea in great storms, when there was a chance of saving life'.[9] Nonetheless, backing up her father in his campaigns against slave-holding was one thing, but to take the lead in a women's organisation as an independent being, and especially in a leading position, was something altogether. On the other hand, not only in respect of the abolition of slavery but on other issues too, women, like men, could be faced with some inescapable matters of conscience. For instance, one of Josephine's aunts had married as her second husband a certain Dr Duncan, whose most important social reform had been the establishment of a Savings Bank from his position as minister at Ruthwell, and both he and Henry Grey (married to another aunt) seceded from their original ministries into those of the Free Church of Scotland in the so-called Great Disruption over issues of patronage in 1843. To Josephine's father, those who seceded provided a noble example of 'moral courage and consistency, one which gives to it the stamp of no ordinary event, and to the men the value and character of martyrs'. They had acted 'in obedience to the dictates of a strong moral obligation to do the right, and despise and reject the expedient'.[10] As she was later to write, 'principles know not the name of mercy'[11] when something of crucial importance seemed to be at stake, and there were a number of instances in her life when she and George took an unfashionable stance on some situations. Thus in regard to the Civil War in the USA (1861-5) where a vital issue of justice was at stake (freedom from slavery) she was to write that this was one of several occasions when they found themselves in a minority, learning to stand firm as the tide went by, maintaining a charitable attitude to those who conscientiously differed from them, and towards those who simply went along with fashionable opinion. 'In this case, the feeling of isolation on a subject of such tragic interest was often painful: but the discipline was useful: for it was out lot again more emphatically in the future to have to accept and endure this position, for conscience' sake'.[12] By the time George died in 1890, Josephine was a seasoned enough political campaigner to be able to write quite unambiguously her own opinion of another war, that between Boer and non-Boer in South Africa. In her 1900 *Native Races and the War* she appealed, as one might expect, to the 1834 bill for the abolition of slavery launched by Charles, second Earl Grey, to make the point that however brutal the English could be to 'weaker human beings', they were at least committed in principle to treating the non-white inhabitants of South Africa with some measure of human decency. For this reason, a deeply unpopular war had to be endured on a continent where 'black ivory' (a hideous euphemism for slaves) was still for sale.

As indicated above, Josephine did indeed find her own voice in the course of her marriage to George, and no less a person than Elizabeth Cady Stanton was to note that Josephine's style was not unlike 'that one hears in Methodist camp meetings from the best cultivated of that sect; her power lies in her deeply religious enthusiasm'.[13] George's stint as a Public Examiner for the University of Oxford (1852-1857) taught her both lessons in humiliation and forged her determination both to speak and to act. Josephine was used to the society of both women and men, and had not appreciated the distortions in perspective which came about in a predominantly single-sex and male society such as Oxford was in her day. Sometimes she was the only woman present in her own drawing-room, where she learned to sit silently and sore at heart as her guests 'would speak of things which I have already revolved deeply in my own mind'. Discussions of Mrs. Gaskell's *Ruth*, for example, led to expressions of opinion that a moral lapse in a woman was 'an immensely worse thing than in a man'. It was also affirmed that a pure woman 'should be absolutely ignorant of a certain class of evils in the world, albeit those evils bore with murderous cruelty on other women'.[14] From such experiences she became clear that 'not only must as many men and women as possible severally understand the truth concerning their relations to each other, but also [...] they must learn the lesson in each other's presence, and with each other's help'. A deep-seated mutual sympathy must replace 'the life-long separation and antipathetic sentiments' of the past.[15] In the meantime, there were cases of injustice and distress known to Josephine personally, and some of these she and George could mitigate, as, for example by providing employment in the Butler household. So Josephine learned to attend less to the representatives of the 'highly educated, masculine world' and to address herself much more to God.[16] In her Oxford society, her appeal to a God in whom she believed 'all truth centred, and who is willing to reveal it to those who ask, knock and seek' apparently counted for little or nothing where women were concerned. Occasionally even here, however, she found her voice, as when hurt to hear 'a distinguished college tutor' claim that 'a woman's face when engaged in prayer could never wear any other expression than that of insipidity'. Josephine retorted by employing an analogy from the expression her own face might wear 'when one converses with a man of high intelligence and noble soul' (clearly not her conversationalist) which, when finding an answering chord to one's own, beams 'with increased intelligence and exalted thought'. How much more must that be the case, she argued, 'if one converses face to face with the highest Intelligence of all! Then every faculty of the mind and emotion of the soul is called to its highest exercise'.[17] One of her greatest tributes to George was that he prevented her from doing her later work with 'a solitary, wounded, and revolted heart', which would certainly have limited her usefulness.[18] And central to their lives together was the conviction that 'in regard to certain vital questions, the sayings and actions of Jesus were....revolutionary'. A crucial example here was the way he responded to a particular woman and her accusers in John 8. In this case, she wrote, he emancipated a woman from 'legal thraldom' whilst imposing upon the men present 'and upon all men by implication', the higher obligation which they had attempted to force on one half of society, 'and breach of which their cruel laws visited with terrible severity on women alone'. They were convicted by conscience; the woman remained free not only from 'the harsh, humanly-imposed judgement' but from 'inward moral slavery'.[19] Just as both black and white had to be freed from the supposition that it was God, rather than humanity, who had instituted slavery, both women and men alike had to dislodge from their consciousness the supposition that some women deserved nothing better than the contempt in which some if not all of them were held.

As a major contribution to being free of belief that they deserved nothing better, women clearly needed education and employment, and in her capacity as President of the North of England Council for the Higher Education of women (1867-1873) Josephine produced her first public manifesto, *The Education and Employment of Women* (1868), education being what slave owners most dreaded, since it was the road to emancipation. She herself needed to believe that she and other women of her social position were capable of earning their own living; and she had found that by 1861 some 2.5 million women were already working for their own subsistence, with more than 43,000 of them working as labourers, 'a fact worthy of remembrance when it is said that women are too weak to serve in haberdasher's shops'.[20] She knew perfectly well that women's being without a vote contributed to public indifference towards the injustice served them at work, as well as their own cowardice when asked to help tackle the problem. She gave a moving analysis of the profession of teacher and governess, craving as they rightly did both enough to eat and the ability to access knowledge. With certificates of university education, she hoped that many would avail themselves of education, and this, she hoped, would break down the division between 'ladies' and governesses and teachers. She even hoped that talented women of any social class would teach, so that the evidence of such 'disinterested zeal' and the 'energy of voluntary choice' would help transform the standing of the teaching profession.[21]

That apart, women of her own class were in for a further shock, for the same text produced Josephine's first published comment on prostitution. Enlightened and educated women were not only to demand respect for themselves, but were to claim it also for poor women 'whom it is too often deemed a light matter to injure in the worst way'. Further, women who were 'ladies' were also to demand such respect for the 'fallen', who through the voice of their happier sisters shall yet demand, not only compassion, but the respect due to every human being, however clouded with misery and sin'.[22]

The Problem of Abuse

The example of Christ in defending a woman from stoning and in releasing a woman from 'bonds of infirmity' (Luke 13.10-17) was to be crucial in another respect than release from 'inward, moral slavery' however, because as Josephine knew perfectly well, violence of one person against another, and not only of slave owners against slaves but of men against women, was common enough, and indeed continues. When she came to shelter some of them in her own home, she saw on their very bodies the scars of the violence some of the most courageous had experienced, when virtually imprisoned in brothels, as part of the process of making them 'submissive'. For instance, one girl was found to be in pain 'from unhealed stripes on her back and shoulders', a fact certified by the Butlers' own physician. Josephine was rightly appalled. 'We seemed to stand before a victim of some cruel overseer of slaves in the cotton plantations of one of the Southern

States of America in the past times'. She persuaded the girl to tell her story: because she had refused to co-operate with her brothel-keeper the girl had been immured in a basement, starved and scourged with a leather thong. Yet she had comforted herself with the knowledge that 'Jesus had himself been cruelly scourged, and that he could feel for her', having seen an engraving of this incident in a shop window'.[23] Josephine endorsed her view.

She may in fact have lived through one of the periods when woman-battering was 'flowing' rather than 'ebbing', since there is some evidence that it was particularly common in the 1830's and 1840's, and again in the late nineteenth century, when movements for women's emancipation gathered strength. Such an increase may also have been true of 'domestic violence' in 1970's and subsequently, which has perhaps enabled us to see more clearly some of the factors involved in the phenomenon as adults negotiate or renegotiate their unpredictable and ambivalent relationships. Certainly there are difficulties in finding out how extensive woman-battering was or is. It needs also to be acknowledged that there are some cases of 'battered husbands' and that women may find the means to retaliate with 'man-slaughter'. That said, there seems to be sufficient evidence that women have by far the greater chance of being on the receiving end of domestic violence than do men, and it is clear that in the nineteenth century they had very great difficulty in getting some sort of justice in respect of their suffering. Yet some had learned that there was nothing inevitable about the social acceptability of such behaviour, or of the forms of marriage that seemed to leave women so powerless. Moves simply had to be made to secure conditions of life for women that made things more tolerable, and depending on their degree of economic independence, the ability to separate from, or better, divorce intemperate and violent husbands. A major problem was that securing such freedom might require a degree of intervention in a woman's life that would be refused on other occasions, if it were to be men in control of the intervention. At least some women were shrewd enough to doubt that men could necessarily be relied upon to discern women's best interests, when those same women had so little opportunity to think and act for themselves, or voice their needs as they identified them.

With the group who wrote *Legislative Restrictions on the Industry of Women* (1872), Josephine observed that those who proposed to control women's work hours seemed, as ever, to be assuming 'that women are irresponsible beings, incapable of judging for themselves, and consequently requiring to be judged for and to have their actions regulated by the sole responsible human agent – man'.[24] On the contrary, some of them were sufficiently responsible to know that, for their children's sake, women were sometimes better off unmarried.

For all the most laudable intentions, one of the problems about pleas for women's freedom were integrally associated with centrally important values which rendered them acutely vulnerable, and thus the argument for their freedom depended on continued advocacy of the very qualities and characteristics that could entrap them. The problem is exemplified in Josephine's 1868 manifesto on the education and employment of women where she is scrupulously careful to argue that emancipation will not destroy women's 'nature'. For she wrote that 'it will always be in her nature to foster, to cherish, to take the part of the weak, to train, to guide, to have a care for individuals, to discern the small seeds of a great future, to warm and cherish those seeds into fulness of life. "I serve" will always be one of her favourite mottos, even should the utmost freedom be accorded her in the choice of vocation'. Christ himself exhibited 'in perfect beauty the distinctive virtues of the feminine character'.[25] She seems never to have made the connection between those distinctive virtues and the possibility of being 'scourged' despite the evidence under her very eyes.

Even when it is possible for women to be economically as well as socially largely independent of men, it is possible to experience 'partial extinction' as a result of the paradigm of women's 'nature' Josephine admired. The 'good mother' may suffer in consequence of the limitlessly self-sacrificial image offered to her by some Christian rhetoric. A distressing example of the complexity of the issues is given by sociologist Bernice Martin[26] in her account of the behaviour of her daughter's partner. A thoroughly abusive situation developed from her daughter's total commitment to him, and her desire to show care and concern for him. This then became his justification for her never being free from his surveillance, except at work, so long, at least, as she was still fit to go to her work. Thereby, he effectively sabotaged any efforts on her part to do anything for herself independently. She came to a stage of putting up with being brow-beaten to avoid physical violence either to herself or their small daughter, believing herself to be worthless and incapable of getting anything right. She even forgot how to spell. When he threatened to beat up 'her gentle and much loved youngest brother', she somehow summoned up her last shreds of energy to flee, having found a first stage 'safe-house' to which to run. With such an example in mind, no wonder that there remains much concern about 'the female self and how it might be better defended'. Re-capitulating Josephine's paradigm (still alive and well in Christian rhetoric) is not sufficient.

At one level, Josephine recognised that there was a problem, and that it was intrinsically connected to what was in her day understood by a marriage, in which men might generously refuse to exercise their legally authorised powers over wives who were deemed to have no independent existence. There were impressive examples of women and men on both sides of the Atlantic who used the occasion of their marriages to make public protest about the resulting position of women. John Stuart Mill on his marriage to Harriet in 1851 and Henry Blackwell when he married Lucy Stone in 1855 are two well documented examples.[27] George Butler himself held the view that his relationship with Josephine should be 'a perfectly equal union, with absolute freedom on both sides for personal initiative in thought and action and for individual development'.[28] In many cases, however, it seemed that it was precisely when a woman had committed herself to a legal and permanent relationship with a husband that abuse would then take place. In a woman's state of legal nonentity, it must have been excruciating to realise both that the violence would not stop and that a disintegrating relationship could not be renegotiated unless it did. As Josephine commented: 'If we compare the slight penalties inflicted for cruelties practised on women and children with those imposed for injury of property or the wounding of a stag, the property of a Duke, we cannot wonder at the low estimate, in England, of the worth of women'.[29]

We now know much more about the relationship between

domestic violence and possessiveness and jealousy, expectations about a woman's obligations to provide domestic and sexual 'services', a sense of 'right' to punish women for perceived wrongdoing and panic about the maintenance of male authority in a household. It is unfortunately arguable that this unholy cluster received sanction in Christian tradition, as to some extent Josephine came to realise. The 'rule of thumb' indeed put some limits on the extent to which men battered women (beating 'with a stick no thicker than his thumb' was a common adage), but the promise of obedience to a husband in marriage according to the rites of the Church of England, and the appeal to the so-called household codes of the New Testament, reinforced female 'submission'. A text such as 1 Peter 3.1-9 remains one of the most troublesome, urging submission, silence and chastity on wives to aid in the conversion of their unbelieving husbands. Add to this the teaching of forbearance, meekness, forgiveness and self-sacrifice from the pulpit, and the recipe for damage is a powerful one, partly because such characteristics in the lives of both men and women are so essential to the flourishing of any intimate relationship. Without the benefit of clear-minded relegation of certain texts to the Graeco-Roman slave-owning households in which they may have had some point, women remained and indeed remain vulnerable, except in respect of men whose relationships with women would never encompass violence in the first place. I am not of course suggesting that it is only in biblically soaked or post-slavery cultures that women are physically and emotionally abused. There is ample cross-cultural evidence to the contrary.

It remains difficult to evaluate the texts and traditions which create the climate in which abuse may continue. A recent collection of essays,[30] for instance, provides examples of those who somehow want to be constructive in affirming the 'headship' of males and the 'submission' of females, whilst arguing for 'biblical equality' between the two and 'healthy and egalitarian' relationships within families and churches in the post-enlightenment era. The authors have a hard task, for whilst it may have made some sense in Graeco-Roman society to understand by 'headship' that women are drawn from men's very being and are vitally connected with them, it is a belief difficult to sustain in the present. 'Submission' is a recipe for disaster if males believe that God intends them to dominate women, that women are morally inferior to them, that suffering is a virtue peculiarly suited to women, and that women must quickly 'forgive' and be reconciled with those who insist upon differing standards for themselves, or abuse them, perhaps with the underlying view that 'God punished women more' (Genesis 3.16). Even when women find their voices they may be told by pastors and counsellors that the violence would not have occurred had they loved more or less, or been less or more submissive, or stronger or less dependent, or had they not unconsciously desired to be punished.[31] Josephine's practice of providing refuges for the damaged negated such views, and aligns her with those who think that it is God's will for women to be safe, and that a woman is not committing the sin of pride by being concerned for her own physical safety. And now that feminist biblical exegesis has developed, it should be particularly disturbing to read analyses of the extent to which the deity is portrayed as a betrayed 'husband' dealing with a disorderly and disobedient 'female'.[32] It is possible that the habit of portraying God as 'male' and actual 'male' social and political sin as 'female' was employed as metaphor to shock men out of their behaviour by portraying them thus. The sinful 'female' then has to seek forgiveness from her 'husband', whose abuse of her is for her own good. We would be right, however, to think that such metaphors serve only to continue to sustain the devaluation and denigration of women, as does the current rhetoric in some Church of England circles that women are 'equal but subordinate'. Having done so much to establish the point that women were indeed persons, and must be treated as such, there was, unfortunately, much that remained to be done to secure such recognition for them and for their children, beginning with the formation of the Society for the Prevention of Cruelty to Children in 1884 and continuing into our own time. That, however, requires another set of reflections. [33]

For the moment, in recollecting Josephine Butler and just one of her concerns for justice to be done for women, we might hope that we in our time display comparable sensitivities to those who are marginalised, address our own complicity in social wrongs, and if we are associated with or members of ecclesiastical institutions, resist the temptation to suppose that the Christian tradition has all the 'answers' when in so many ways it remains part of some of our most central problems. Josephine Butler might well have been horrified by the indubitable fact that so many of the issues she identified have not yet been resolved. The year of the bicentenary of the abolition of the slave trade in the British Empire at least might be a good time for a fresh start, not least on domestic violence and the 'sex trafficking' to which violence is so integrally related.

Endnotes

[1] Mary Wollstonecraft, *Political Writings* edited by Janet Todd (Oxford: Oxford University Press, 1994).
[2] See Ann Loades, *Feminist Theology: Voices from the Past* (Cambridge: Polity, 2001), pp. 88-98.
[3] Butler, *Woman's Work and Woman's Culture*, p. xlvii.
[4] Josephine Butler, *The Constitution Violated* (Edinburgh: Edmonston and Douglas, 1871).
[5] Josephine Butler, *Memoir of John Grey of Dilston* (Edinburgh: Edmonston and Douglas, 1869), p. 300.
[6] Butler, *Memoir of John Grey,* pp. 337, 341.
[7] Butler, *Memoir of John Grey,* pp. 339-40.
[8] Butler, *Personal Reminiscences*, pp. 257-58.
[9] Butler, *Personal Reminiscences*, p. 5.
[10] Butler, *Personal Reminiscences,* p. 196.
[11] Butler, *Truth Before Everything*, p. 2.
[12] Butler, *Recollections of George Butler,* pp. 141-42.
[13] Elizabeth Cady Stanton, *Eighty Years and More. Reminiscences 1815-1897* (Boston: Northwestern University Press [1898] 1993), p. 368.
[14] Josephine Butler, *Recollections of George Butler,* p. 96.
[15] Josephine Butler, *Social Purity: an Address* (London: Morgan and Scott, 1879), pp. 11-12.
[16] Butler, *Recollections of George Butler,* pp .98-99.
[17] Butler, *Recollections of George Butler,* p. 99.
[18] Butler, *Recollections of George Butler,* p. 101.
[19] Butler, *Woman's Work,* p. lviii.
[20] Josephine Butler, *The Education and Employment of Women* (London: Macmillan, 1868), p. 4.
[21] Butler, *Education and Employment of Women*, p. 10.
[22] Butler, *Education and Employment of Women*, p. 11. In lamentable contrast, see the evidence produced by Frances Finnegan, *Do Penance or Perish: Magdalen Asylums in Ireland* (Oxford: Oxford University Press, 2004), and the lives of penance forced on thousands of girls and women housed under the aegis of some women's religious orders, with the knowledge and connivance of a whole society.
[23] Butler, *Personal Reminiscences*, pp. 386-87.
[24] Josephine Butler and others, *Legislative Restrictions on the Industry of Women* (London: Matthews, 1872), p. 13.
[25] Butler, *Education and Employment of Women,* p. 18.
[26] Bernice Martin, 'Whose soul is it anyway? Domestic Tyranny and the Suffocated Soul', in *On Losing the Soul. Essays in the Social Psychology of Religion*, ed. Richard K. Fenn and Donald Capps (New York: State University of New York Press, 1994), pp. 69-96.
[27] Ann P. Robson and John M.Robson, *Sexual Equality. Writings by John Stuart Mill, Harriet Taylor Mill and Helen Taylor* (Toronto: University of Toronto Press, 1994), pp.47-48; Elinor Rice Hays, *Morning Star: A Biography of Lucy Stone* (New York: Octagon, 1978), pp.128-29.
[28] Butler, *Recollections of George Butler*, p. 56.
[29] Butler, *Constitution*, p. 139.
[30] Catherine Clark Kroeger and James R. Beck eds, *Women, Abuse and the Bible. How Scripture can be used to Hurt and to Heal* (Grand Rapids: Baker, 1999).
[31] Carol J. Adams and Marie M.Fortune eds, *Violence against Women and Children. A Christian Theological Source Book* (New York: Continuum, 1995).
[32] For example, Renita J. Weems, *Marriage, Sex and Violence in the Hebrew Prophets* (Minneapolis: Fortress, 1995).
[33] See Ann Loades, *Voices from the Past*, pp. 73-139 on Josephine Butler, and pp.140-65 on the sexual abuse of children.

Christian Responses to Prostitution in Whitechapel, East London: 1906 to 2006

Kenneth Leech

Ken Leech arrived in the part of London he describes in 1958 as a student at King's College, London, and resident in Cable Street, where he worked with the Franciscans and with the redoubtable Fr Joe Williamson. After his ordination, Ken was based in Hoxton, Soho and Bethnal Green, where he was involved for many years in work with the homeless – founding the charity, Centrepoint – sex workers and drug addicts. He is well known as the historian of the Anglo-Catholic socialist movement in all its varieties, and he was instrumental in founding the network of socialist Christians, The Jubilee Group, in 1974. More recently he was Director of the Runnymede Trust and Community Theologian at St Botolph's Aldgate. His publications involve the same union of prayer and practice as Josephine Butler herself. The classic, Soul Friend, *was first published in 1974, while recent books include* The Eye of the Storm: Spiritual Resources for the Pursuit of Justice *(which won the Harper Collins Religious Book Award in 1995);* We Preach Christ Crucified; Politics and Faith Today; The Sky is Red: Discerning the Signs of the Times *(1997),* Drugs and Pastoral Care; Through Our Long Exile: Contextual Theology and the Urban Experience *(2001). In this chapter Ken reflects on the work of Father Joe, who was himself greatly influenced by Josephine Butler and wrote two books about her life, and those, rather less publicly known, who served in the Cable Street area. Interestingly, Ken ends by showing how exchanges of activists between Whitechapel and the United States have led to a recent project in Oregon.*

✑

O
n 25th January 1962 Fr Joe Williamson, parish priest of St Paul's, Whitechapel, in the East End of London, gave evidence to the Josephine Butler Society on prostitution in

his parish.[1] He claimed that most prostitutes there were teenagers and that the pimps were mostly Maltese. Earlier he had claimed that there were over one hundred street prostitutes operating in the western end of Cable Street, at that time the social centre and 'café quarter' of the London Docks. I worked out that, even if they were packed together, shoulder to shoulder, and even if some were standing on others' shoulders, one hundred would not have fitted in this quite small stretch of street! I worked closely with Williamson, and, while I was devoted to him, he did not always get his facts right. He was a campaigner, not a social analyst. I suspect that this may be true of many activists in this and other fields, and it is worth bearing this in mind in understanding the rhetoric and writing. However, he was certainly correct in stressing that the East End prostitutes were younger than the national average, and that many, though not all, of the pimps in the 1950's and 1960's were Maltese, a criminal network which, while highly significant, was not typical of the Maltese population in London as a whole.[2]

In spite of much 'gentrification', 'yuppification', and commercial developments, the East End remains one of the most deprived areas of Britain. Government data about the twenty most deprived districts in 2000 placed the East End (Tower Hamlets) top, followed by the adjoining areas of Hackney and Newham.[3] I want to reflect on the East End of London from the death of Josephine Butler to the present, with brief comments on some of the offshoots of work with prostitutes in what is in fact a quite small geographical area. I lived in Whitechapel as a student from 1958 to 1964. The house had been a brothel until 1944 when the Society of St Francis took it over, calling it – I thought a little unwisely! – a 'house of hospitality' (Only later did I learn that the term came from Dorothy Day and the Catholic Worker movement.) After years of ministry in Shoreditch, Soho and Bethnal Green (1964 – 1990), I returned in 1990 to live in a flat in Whitechapel Road directly opposite the site of the first of the Jack the Ripper murders of 1888.

I became involved with work with female prostitutes as a student through the ministry of Fr Williamson and his two women colleagues, Nora Neal and Daphne Jones. Later I worked with female and male prostitutes (rent boys) from St Anne's Church, Soho from 1966 to 1971, and, after returning to the East End, chaired the Maze Marigold Project for its first ten years (1988 to 1998), working again in the Whitechapel area. I worked there with some remarkable colleagues who were detached youth workers – Rio Vella, Trisha Mata, Sandra Shanks and others- and later with Fr Brian Ralph who is still in Bethnal Green. Work with prostitutes has been a major part of my ministry in the East End, as it was in Soho, and has given rise to much theological and spiritual reflection, much questioning and many unresolved questions.

Prostitution, like most activities today, is a global reality. It is therefore impossible to isolate Commercial Street and Old Montague Street from the rest of the world. If we look at the situation of women in Central and South America, we see that prostitution is one aspect of a more dispersed exploitation of women. Melissa Wright's study of the murders of over two hundred women in Ciudad Juarez in Mexico towards the end of the 1990's shows the way in which, in this part of the world, women are seen as flexible and, in the end, disposable labour. Many of the murdered women worked in export-processing *maquila* factories, of which Mexico has over 3000. Wright argues that women workers are seen as 'waste in the making'. Often the murdered women are accused of being prostitutes, whether they are or not, since this is a convenient way of saying that they are disposable, and that their deaths do not matter. The known fact is that they have to cross stretches of desert to get to main roads and buses. They are, according to Wright, 'the by-product of a process during which the human beings turn into individual waste'.[4]

The globalisation of 'sexual slavery' has, in recent years, led to claims of very large numbers, ranging from 10 to 30 million.[5] It has been clear in London in recent years that much of the prostitution is organised by criminal syndicates elsewhere, a situation very different from that in the nineteenth century or even in the 1950's and most of the 1960's.

In East London, prostitution occurs 'outside the gate', in an area close to the eastern edge of the City, the financial district. The Church of St Botolph, Aldgate, stands at the point where the financial district, comes to an end, and the East End (or, as estate agents now call it, 'city fringe') begins. The correct title of the church is 'St Botolph *Without* Aldgate', that is, outside the 'old gate', and, for many years, this church was also involved in pastoral work with local prostitutes. Literally outside 'the gate', slightly east of the City boundary in Whitechapel, is one of the major centres of juvenile prostitution, in Commercial Street, Old Montague Street and adjoining streets.[6]

Prostitution was common, indeed notoriously so, in nineteenth century Whitechapel, and in adjacent districts, and the legend of 'Jack the Ripper' continues to this day, with 'Ripper tours' taking place weekly, and sometimes daily, and unending debate about his (or, in recent reports, her) identity. So, in the East End, prostitution is a well established phenomenon. In the early census data for Whitechapel and St George's in the East, from 1851 onwards, many women identified themselves as prostitutes. St George's in the East seems to have preceded Whitechapel as a prostitute area.[7] They were part of a wider process by which this part of the East End became 'the home of the strangers, the shiftless and the derelict'.[8] The building of Rowton House in Fieldgate Street in 1892 symbolised and perhaps intensified the image of Whitechapel as the epicentre of homeless people north of the Thames. By the time Jack London wrote *The People of the Abyss* in 1903, the language of 'abyss' and of 'outcast London' was well established, though it is important to stress that many parts of the East End were very different and resented this kind of language.

When I lived in Cable Street at the end of the 1950's, very few of the working women were of local origin, and this had been true for at least a decade.. While much of the media coverage was both racist and inaccurate, some of the points made were correct. Thus the *Daily Mail* in 1947:

> *The girls who haunt the cafes and pubs are not London girls, they come from South Shields, Newcastle, Cardiff, Liverpool: many of them are on the run, and some have escaped from remand homes. They are safe in Cable Street. Most of them are teenagers...*[9]

There were many such articles in this period. A few months later Vivien Batchelor wrote: 'Seamen all over the world know of Cable Street, and, if their tastes lie that way, make for it as soon as their ships dock. Some of them are coloured boys just off their first ship. A few months ago they were still half naked in the bush.[10]

There was a massive increase in prostitution in the area after 1946, when there were two convictions. In 1957 there were 795. The London Docks attracted young people from all over Britain, and the British Social Biology Council's study in 1955 referred to 'the Stepney problem' as a type of prostitution which differed from the London norm.[11] The prostitutes in the Cable Street and Commercial Road districts were much younger, and more likely to be mentally ill, than was the case in London as a whole. I note, however, that the Josephine Butler Society claimed in 1964 that there were more young girls working as prostitutes in Britain as a whole, and more who had no contact with social or pastoral workers, since the Street Offences Act 1959, so it looks as if the East London pattern was spreading in these years.[12]

The 1955 study described Stepney as 'a reception area for young, unsettled girls who may eventually swell the ranks of professional prostitutes in districts further west'. It was 'predominantly a young prostitutes' district'.[13] My impression, having worked in Soho as well as Stepney, is that this shift westwards did not occur much. The 'promotion' to the West End was far more common with drug dealers and users than with prostitutes. The study also suggested that gang involvement was slight in these years, a view which had also been stated by Chief Superintendent Hewitt, writing in 1951, and was reinforced by Downes's work, published in 1966.[14]

The 1955 study made two important points which remain relevant today. First, it reported: 'Field work has shown that areas such as Stepney are often the ultimate resort of those girls who fail in Approved Schools and Borstals [...] Almost all the twelve girls known in Stepney through fieldwork are from Approved Schools and four are Borstal girls.[15] Secondly, the study defined what they called the 'Stepney Problem':

Stepney Problem is a special connotation used to describe those girls who were mainly the failures of Approved Schools and Borstals, and went to live in the coloured quarter of Stepney. Mentally, physically and morally, they were in a lower grade than the ordinary prostitute.[16]

Rolph's study used the phrase 'the coloured quarter', a term which had been popularised in the same year by Michael Banton's book of that title. It was a misleading term since the 'coloured' population of the Cable Street area was probably no more than 500. The old Cable

Street café area was finally demolished after 1967. By the 1990's, the prostitute district had shifted slightly northward, a process which had developed with the demolition, and the women were increasingly from the East London area, though not immediately local. A report in 2002 claimed that 93 per cent of the 170 girls and young women working in Commercial Street did not come from the East End.[17] The role of drugs had also changed. In the 1950's the women used Drinamyl (dexamphetamine sulphate with amylobarbitone) as a 'wakeamine'. They were among the first group of users of this drug, manufactured by Smith, Kline and French (now known as Glaxo Smith Kline) in 1956, although its early use by prostitutes is not well documented.[18] By the 1990s, the use of crack cocaine and heroin was a key factor, though often it was the 'boyfriend' (pimp) whose drug use provided the economic motive for the women's work.

I shall restrict my reflections to three phases: the 1920's to 1950, the 1950's and 1960's, and the years since then. As far as Christian, and specifically Anglican, involvement was concerned, these three phases were dominated by some key individuals: Edith Ramsey in the first and second, Joe Williamson, Daphne Jones and Nora Neal in the second, and Rio Vella, Trisha Mata, Sandra Shanks, Brian Ralph, and others in the third.

1: 1920's to 1950's

Edith Ramsey was a remarkable woman who, although she arrived in Stepney soon after World War 1, in many ways belonged to the nineteenth century tradition of social 'maternalism'. She pioneered 'English as a second language' long before most people had heard of the idea. She and Williamson were, I believe, the only people to have been awarded the MBE for work with prostitutes. Edith was documenting prostitution in the East End from 1920, and was once described as 'the Florence Nightingale of the brothels'. She argued that there was a direct link between prostitution and derelict housing and, certainly in the East End, the issues of slums, housing racketeering, cafes, the docks, and prostitution were intertwined. [19]

As a local councillor, Ramsey visited all the cafes and clubs in her ward, was a prolific writer and campaigner, and, as a teacher with a social work background, was in personal touch with thousands of people involved with prostitution and criminal activities. She was particularly involved with 'the Commercial Road girls', some of whom became quite famous.

2: Joe Williamson 1950's and 1960's

From the mid-1950's the issue of prostitution in the west end of Cable Street was associated in the media with the name of Joe Williamson. This was partly due to his own expertise in dealing with the media, and the fact that his churchwarden, Frank Rust, was a press photographer.[20] Williamson became known as 'the prostitutes' priest', though he only ministered in Whitechapel for a short time, from the mid 1950's until the early 1960's. Nora Neal arrived in 1957 from work in Hackney and with Daphne Jones, a nurse and church worker from Poplar, opened Church House the next year, and worked devotedly in this refuge for girls on the street. Father Joe wrote that 'we wanted it to be a real home, without the hostel atmosphere of bare walls and imposed discipline of the convents which are still, to their great credit, almost the only way of escape for girls on the street'.[21] He himself dated his devotion to the needs of prostituted women to a present of a small box of chocolates from a destitute woman, 'Mary': 'accepting Mary's present, I accepted my commission from God to all I could for prostitutes for the rest of my days'.[22] Audrey, Williamson's wife, should also not be forgotten. She was selfless in her care of women whom she put up in her own home, and hid from pursuit by their pimps.

During the 'Williamson era', prostitution was largely restricted to Cable Street, Old Montague Street and Commercial Road, and streets running off them, particularly Hessel Street and Sander Street. Many people in the East End were anxious to dissociate themselves from the image of Stepney in the media as a prostitute area, though some managed to raise money on the basis of that image. Fr Peter Clynick, parish priest of St Mary's, Cable Street, put a regular advert in the *Daily Telegraph* which ended 'Please help our work in Cable Street'. His part of Cable Street was utterly different from that which was linked with prostitution. From the nearby Borough of Bethnal Green, Councillor

Fleet proclaimed, 'There are no prostitutes or pimps in the borough […] Ours is a good borough'.[23] He was writing during the peak period of the control of the Kray twins!

It was during the period of Williamson's work that David Downes did his doctoral research at the London School of Economics on delinquent subcultures in Stepney and Poplar, though it was not published until 1966. Downes was the first criminologist to be allowed access to Scotland Yard files for juvenile crime, and his work was a detailed study of juvenile crime in the year 1960, with a careful analysis of the concept of gang subcultures. He was highly critical of the application of United States gang theory to the British scene. Downes noted that in 1960 'prostitution accounted for more female offenders than all other offences in Stepney'.[24] 48 of the 97 convictions in that year occurred in two streets, Hessel Street and Sander Street, and indeed prostitution offences only occurred west of Sidney Street, with Hessel, Sander and Cable Streets accounting for the majority. As a result of Williamson's publicity, Sander Street attained national notoriety a few years later.

3: 1960-2004

I now turn to the years 1960-2004 during which I worked in the East End. The period needs to be documented in detail, and I have attempted to do this in various books and papers, but much more needs to be done.

The zone of activity of young prostitutes in East London today spreads out north to Stamford Hill and may be diverted, usually by police action, west towards Kings Cross, but the key area is the Commercial Street and Old Montague Street part of Whitechapel. In 1967 Elizabeth Burney described Brick Lane as the 'worst and most neglected district' in health terms.[25] By 1991 a journalist was describing it as 'a neo-Georgian toy-town for a new generation of resident urban gentry'.[26]

The Maze Marigold Project, which I chaired for the first ten years of its life, was based, first, in Commercial Street, and then in Old Ford Road, Bethnal Green In its report on research undertaken in 1999, this project recorded the results of interviews with 100 women engaged in prostitution in the East End. 34 were aged 15-18, and 19 were aged 19-25. The oldest woman interviewed – whom I had known for some years - was 62. The largest single group (27) was white, though there were twelve identified as black British, and, of the white group, twelve were Irish. 15 of the women had begun work at the age of 13, and 19 at 14.[27] In 2002 evidence from vice squad 'swoops' suggested that there were 170 girls working in the Commercial Street area, of whom 73 per cent were drug abusers, almost all of cocaine.

In April 2003 a helpful report on prostitution in the East End, edited by Paula Skidmore, was launched, the result of a joint project by Barnardo's, Providence Row Charity, and Toynbee Hall, the university settlement in Commercial Street.[28] It was encouraging to see so many people gather at Toynbee Hall for yet another meeting on this subject. It brought back to my mind a similar gathering in the same room to launch Edith Ramsey's report, *Vice Increase in Stepney,* in 1957. Since then, there have been many such meetings, but most of them have not included a single prostitute. Human beings have been talked about in their absence.

Paula Skidmore's report was good, but it contained some claims which need examining. Fr Williamson, she says, was 'assisted in his campaigns by W. Edwards', the MP for Stepney at the time. She also claims that, after the Street Offences Act, 'the vice trade moved more decisively to Soho'.[29] I doubt if either of these claims is correct. Walter Edwards was not at all supportive of Williamson who once described him as 'no more use than a sick headache', and invited MPs from other areas to visit Stepney because of Edwards's incompetence. As for the claim about the shift to Soho, I refer back to my comments on the Rolph study of 1955. Prostitution continued in the East End from 1959 to the present day. I see no evidence that there was a shift to Soho, where the trade was already well established.

The Situation Today

The data suggest that the 'Stepney problem', as defined in 1955, is now more widespread. Research in Wolverhampton and Nottingham, for instance, in 1998 indicates that child prostitution is more common than was once thought.[30] Work in the East End of London itself suggests that this is correct.

Reflections

Ministry with sex workers raises two issues in social ethics which appear in a wide range of other questions. The first is the issue of how Christians minister with people who are involved in activity of which they personally disapprove. Prostitution, drug taking, banking, involvement with armaments and the pursuit of war, collusion with capitalist finance –all these raise the same kind of dilemmas, though their similarity is not always recognised. The second issue is whether the Christian task is simply to bear witness to a different lifestyle and a different set of values, or whether we are also to work, with all its mess, ambiguity and imperfection, with trying to make the best of what we have. I suspect that even those who opt for the former find themselves in practice working with the latter.

What is crucially important is that Christians recognise that prostitute women are valuable, important women, made in the image of God. They must not be despised, must not be seen as victims of 'our' compassion, must be treated with respect, and seen as equals. When this happens, all kinds of things can change. The ministry of Fr Brian Ralph, based in Bethnal Green, is a dramatic and important example of pastoral care of women in prostitution which is not patronising, and which has certainly helped many women to recognise their own dignity, worth and potential.

One important aspect of the East End work has been the spin-offs into other districts, and, indeed, other countries. There were such spin-offs from the Williamson era into Balsall Heath in Birmingham, and into Kings Cross in London. Kings Cross was to take over from the East End to some extent as a centre for young prostitutes in the 1970's and 1980's, and in 1982 the English Collective of Prostitutes occupied the Church of the Holy Cross in Cromer Street as a protest against police harassment.[31]

In 1979 I set up a link between the East End and the South Side of Chicago which continued until 2004. Within a few years it had grown to involve other parts of the USA. Many people from London went to the USA, and many Americans came to the East End. As a result of her experience of working with Brian Ralph and Maze Marigold,

Sara Fischer, now a priest in Oregon, founded a group called Rahab's Sisters which works with prostitute women in the Portland area, while Judith Whelchel, who had also spent time in East London, founded the Church of the Advocate in Asheville, North Carolina, which is working with homeless people including prostitutes. During the same years that I have discussed, people like Edwina Gately – originally from Lancaster - and Fr Depaul Genska, OFM, began important work in Chicago.[32]

Rahab's Sisters: A Recent Overseas Development Related to the East End Work

One of the features of the East End work has been a link between East London and the USA. Many theological, medical, social work and youth and community work students came to work with us between 1978 and 2004. A number of them became involved with the work with young prostitutes. One of them, Sara Fischer, now an Anglican priest in Portland, Oregon, founded Rahab's Sisters, based on work in East London. Below she describes the nature of the work with which 'Rahab's Sisters' has become involved.

'Rahab's Sisters, which has been going since Advent, 2003, was inspired by the Maze Marigold project in East London, by the way the staff of that programme cared for each and every working woman with whom they came in contact, 'without judgment and without reproach'. We learned early on that flavoured condoms are just as important in East Portland as in East London. (Our first night, we offered someone condoms and she said 'flavoured'? Anyone can get those awful health department condoms! You gotta have flavoured!!) Ditto with candy and plenty of sugar for coffee.

'We provide an open house in a church on a busy street and serve about twenty women on most Friday nights. The church is in an ideal location for this ministry, and the parish hall is right on the street. We put candles in the window and our logo proclaims a light in the window. We provide a hot, nutritious, home cooked meal, hot drinks, condoms and lots of other health products (hand soap is very popular), along with underwear, hairbrushes, toothbrushes, etc. Most of these come from in-kind donations made by volunteers and others. We occasionally have specific donation drives at churches. In Advent we had a 'Sock Sunday' and on the Sunday closest to St. Valentine's Day we have 'Undie Sunday'. In each case we have collected hundreds of pairs of new socks and underwear.

'Over and over we say that ours is a ministry of hospitality and presence. We are not trying to evangelize or convert or rehabilitate, except insofar as we hope that if the women we serve understand that we see them as human beings of equal worth and meaning as any other woman that they might come to see themselves that way. I believe that the way Jesus healed was to see people as God made them. The quality of interaction that our Friday guests have with our volunteers is unique in their lives: where else can they sit down and be waited on? Where else does someone ask them how they like their coffee? And my favourite image is of a group of women sitting around a table eating and drinking, some Rahab's Sisters volunteers and some guests from the street, talking about various disasters they'd had making gravy!

'We do not currently have any paid staff, but are staffed by wonderful volunteers from 4-5 different churches. Interestingly, most of the women drawn to this ministry are in their late 40's or older; those of us with gray hair seem to be most comfortable with the lives of the women we serve. Ours is a ministry for women by women; if men want to participate we encourage them to make a donation or tell other people about Rahab's Sisters. We do pay an armed security guard (this is America, after all!) because we assume that most pimps are armed and we were told early on that prostituted women will intuitively know how far we are willing to go to protect them. We have gotten a grant from the Episcopal Church's United Thank Offering which is being used to expand from 2-4 Fridays a month and to broaden our volunteer and donor base.

'The women we see along 82nd Avenue are at the very bottom of the 'food chain'. They are all extremely poor and drug-addicted. Many are referred to us from the needle exchange van which parks outside the church. They range in age from 15 to 50, and many have lost children and home many times over. All lead a violent life, with little memory or hope of anything different. Someone has described our ministry as hospice care. The church is in a neighbourhood which is trying to 'better itself' and the neighbours do not want the women around and do not want us to minister to them. We see only a small portion of the women that walk up and down 82nd Avenue, however, and it is a long time before we will be 'out of business'.[33]

Endnotes

[1] I have tried to use the term 'East End' quite precisely to refer to the area immediately adjacent to the City of London, which used to consist of the three boroughs of Stepney, Poplar and Bethnal Green, and now forms the London Borough of Tower Hamlets. The term is often used loosely to include such places as Hackney and Canning Town which are more accurately termed 'East London'. There is similar confusion in many books including Geoff Dench et al., *The New East End*, (London: Profile 2006). Robert Jenkins, MP for Dulwich in 1963 even saw Bermondsey –in South London- as part of the East End! (Hansard, 22nd July 1963, col. 1154).

[2] See Geoff Dench, *The Maltese in London: A Study in the Erosion of Ethnic Consciousness* (London: 1975).

[3] *Indices of Deprivation 2000*, DETR September, 2000.

[4] Melissa Wright, 'The Dialectics of Still Life: Murder, Women, and Maquiladoras', in Jean Comaroff and John L. Comaroff (eds), *Millennial Capitalism and the Culture of Neoliberalism* (Durham NC: Duke University Press, 2001), pp. 127, 139.

[5] See Kevin Bales, *Understanding Global Slavery* (Berkeley CA: University of California Press, 2006) and Martin A. Lee, 'The Globalisation of Sexual Slavery', in *San Francisco Bay Guardian*, 5 March, 2001.

[6] The word 'prostitute' is disliked by many people who favour the term 'commercial sex worker'. The debate about terminology is not trivial, and it has split the world of the working women themselves. I do not propose to go into that debate here, but it seems important to register its existence. It exposes and opens up an area of contempt towards women, viewed as objects of male desire, as commodities

[7] W. J. Fishman, *East End 1888* (London: Duckworth, 1988); John Hollingshead, *Ragged London in 1861* (London: Smith and Elder, 1861), pp. 291-93.

[8] Michael Banton, *The Coloured Quarter* (London: Jonathan Cape, 1955), p. 28.

[9] *The Daily Mail*, 31 October 1947.

[10] *John Bull*, 14 December 1947.

[11] C. H. Rolph (ed.), *Women of the Streets: A Sociological Study of the Common Prostitute* (London: British Social Biology Council/Secker and Warburg, 1955), p. 245.

[12] Reported in *The Guardian*, 11 November 1964.

[13] Rolph, *Women of the Streets,* pp. 12, 51.

[14] C. R. Hewit, *The Police and the Prostitute,* Alison Neilans Memorial Lecture (London, 1951), p. 6; David M. Downes, *The Delinquent Solution* (London: Routledge and Kegan Paul, 1966); Kenneth Leech, 'Human Casualties in a Crisis District', *East London Papers*, 11, pp. 3-19.

[15] Rolph, *Women of the Streets*, p. 223.

[16] Rolph, *Women of the Streets*, p. 245.

[17] *East London Advertiser*, 18 January 2002.

[18] See Kenneth Leech, *Pastoral Care and the Drugs Scene* (London: SPCK, 1970).

[19] *East London Advertiser*, 8 July 1960.

[20] Father Joe [Joseph Williamson], *The Autobiography of Joseph Williamson of Poplar and Stepney* (London: Hodder and Stoughton, 1963), p. 12.

[21] Father Joe, *Autobiography*, p. 153.

[22] Father Joe, *Autobiography*, p. 130.

[23] *East London Advertiser*, 7 November 1958.

[24] Downes, *Delinquent Solution*, pp. 140-47.

[25] Cited in Charlie Forman, *Spitalfields: A Battle for Land* (London: Hilary Shipman, 1989), p. 75.

[26] Article by Mike Berlin in *Tribune*, 31 May 1991.

[27] See *Maze Marigold Project Research February 1998-August 1999* (London: YWCA, 1999).

[28] See Paula Skidmore (ed.), *Report of the Working Party on Prostitution and Commercial Sex Work in E1* (London: Providence Row Charity and Toynbee Hall, 2003).

[29] Skidmore, *Report*, p. 20.

[30] Article by Jason Bennetto, *The Independent*, 29 June 1998.

[31] See Selma James, 'Hookers in the House of the Lord', in *Feminist Action*, ed. Joy Holland (London: Battleaxe Books, 1983), pp. 180-203.

[32] See Edwina Gateley, 'A Good Catholic Girl', *The Tablet*, 3 July 1993, pp. 851-52 and John Paul Szura, OSA and DePaul Genska, OFM, 'Ministry with Persons in Female Heterosexual Prostitution with Emphasis on Ministry Education', *New Theology Review*, 4, 2, pp. 105-07.

[33] Personal communication to the author by Revd Sara Fischer, Rector of St John the Evangelist Episcopal Church, Oregon, MS, USA in 2006.

Sex Work and
the Politics of Rescue

Janet Batsleer

Janet Batsleer is Head of Youth and Community Work programmes in the Institute of Education at Manchester Metropolitan University. She was a co-founder of the sadly missed Women's Studies Programme at that University and authored Working with Girls and Young Women in Community Settings *(Ashgate, 1996), a feminist discussion of youth work practice documenting activism from the 'second wave' of that movement, as well as a number of other publications. She is actively involved with community-based work with young women, including work with vulnerable and exploited young women in Manchester and the North West. She worships as an Anglican in Manchester. Janet approaches her topic with a dual focus both on practical engagement but also on a philosophical understanding that is influenced by French feminist thinkers who seek new understandings of subjectivity.*

᠆ᡋᢂᠥ

F ree at last. After seventeen years of brutal campaigning she was able to turn her attention to the even more hellish matter of the international slave trade in underage girls.

How, the commissioners had asked her, could it be right for a lady to have such familiarity with the techniques of professional prostitution and brothel keeping? How could a lady of her social standing and breeding bear to contemplate such degradation and wickedness in members of her own sex?

'There is no evil in the world,' she said, 'so great that God cannot raise up to meet it a corresponding beauty and glory that will blaze it out of countenance.'

The awful abundance of compassion had made her fierce.[1]

Some contemporary debates among feminists about the ethics of sex work are immensely fierce also. This chapter outlines, in brief, some contemporary issues in relation to the sex trade, and then presents some ethical resources for responding to sex work and sex workers. I am writing from a professional perspective, as someone who educates community workers and supports projects and staff engaging with street prostitution. I write also as a feminist and an Anglican concerned with the nature of a loving response to those engaged in the sex industry.

The sex industry in the context of globalisation is one of the starkest examples of the extension and deepening of the power of market forces, even in the sphere of personal relationships. Prostitution- taken to mean the consensual exchange of money for sex –is implicated in the existence of global sexual tourism, the feminisation of poverty, the development and management of the 'sex trade' in the so-called third world, the spread of AIDS, and the problems consequent on the political and economic transformation in Eastern Europe.[2]

Nevertheless, it is also important to recognise the significance of the local in relation to this global perspective. Most young women who sell sex do so first of all in their own national and indeed their own neighbourhood context. There are thought to be about 1500 people trafficked into the UK for the purposes of prostitution currently, although it is also estimated that up to 80% of off street prostitution in London and in Glasgow involves women from Eastern Europe and the Baltic States. Street prostitution is the most visible and most 'problematic' form of prostitution. It is therefore the most quantified and the most analysed. It is impossible to know how many women work privately, being self-employed as escorts for example. It is equally impossible to know how many men use the services of prostitutes and whether these are routine or occasional visits. The term prostitution encompasses women and also a small number of men who work for £150 an hour as 'escorts', engaging clients through the internet, at one extreme, and young women and men who are offering sexual services for £10 a job on the streets at the other. In other words, sex work encompasses a real variation in experience and in degrees of victimisation, control of working conditions, agency and choice.

Most women who become involved in selling sex on the streets do so at a young age – between 16 and 21 years. A significant proportion is addicted to heroin and crack cocaine. Many are precariously housed, often living with the pimps who control their earnings. A significant number of young women involved in prostitution have grown up in the care system and their lives have been troubled from the start. There is a strong likelihood that they have begun to sell sex after being introduced to 'the game' by a friend. It is more likely to be members of their own peer networks than kidnappers who introduce young women (and young men) to sex work. As well as occurring on the streets, sex work happens in massage parlours, saunas, as part of the lap-dancing club network, and in the porn industry. Pay rates for street sex are not high but the act does not take long to perform and a woman can charge more highly if, for example, the client asks to spend thirty minutes with her. It is not unusual for a street sex worker to service ten clients a night, if business is good.

The legal framework for responding to prostitution, which is the basis of so much political controversy, is complex globally. In the UK, prostitution is not a criminal offence, but there are currently 35 arrestable offences related to prostitution including offences of 'soliciting' 'loitering', 'brothel keeping' and 'kerb crawling' (which was added recently.) It is illegal to buy sex from any-one under the age of eighteen. Young people under eighteen selling sex are responded to through the child protection system rather than prosecuted for the above offences. There is evidence of the increasing use of Anti-Social Behaviour Orders in the UK against street sex workers. An Anti-Social Behaviour Order is a civil order which may carry a prison sentence if breached. The practice of 'carding' telephone kiosks and other public places to advertise sexual services has been a particular focus for the use of ASBOs. There have however been some dangerous precedents which go beyond the prohibitions on carding, such as women being given ASBOs preventing them from carrying condoms in particular areas. This use of ASBOs is raising many concerns for the safety of women working in the sex industry who may be facing more difficulty by moving to an unfamiliar beat. In Germany, prostitution is legalised and regulated. In contrast in Sweden prostitution has been made entirely illegal, since 1999.

There is fierce political controversy which surrounds the issue of prostitution. It is a practice and politics, which draws out ferocity, just as with Josephine Butler, for whom (as the quotation from Maitland and Mulford at the beginning suggests) 'the over abundance of compassion had made her fierce'. What may have constituted such fierceness in Butler? What might be the source of so much ferocity in the current debates? What else is in these fierce exchanges, alongside compassion? And where might such ferocity be found today? Certainly it is there in the feminist debate, the contestation between those who see prostitution as 'the oldest oppression' rather than 'the oldest profession' and those who emphasise the capacity of sex workers for agency and self-determination; the contestation between abolitionist and sex workers' rights perspectives.[3]

There is debate at every point, even about the nature and extent of the sex trade. Home Office statistics are inevitably based on the criminalised part of the industry. The evidence of organisations campaigning against trafficking tends to suggest that most women involved in the sex trade are illegally coerced, kidnapped and abused and that therefore criminalisation (or abolition) of the whole industry would be the best measure to stem the global trade in and abuse of women and men. This elision of trafficking and prostitution is open to debate. Some writers suggest that such an elision stems from a moral ideology which views prostitution as 'vice' pure and simple, rather than a recognition of the variation of practice involved in prostitution.[4] Others, who support the regulation and/or decriminalisation of prostitution, suggest that coerced prostitution represents only a small corner of the sex industry, and that many women who work in the industry are there voluntarily or choose to make money this way as it is a considerably more lucrative form of employment than other jobs available to them, such as employment in cleaning or caring. There is a view that many if not most who work as prostitutes are caught up in drug addiction particularly in relation to heroin and crack cocaine and that the dealers are also part of criminal gangs particularly based in Eastern Europe and Albania. Alternatively, however, it is suggested that off-street prostitution, based in massage parlours, saunas, escort agencies and at private addresses is comparatively safe as a form of work and reasonably paid compared to other low paid employment to which women might have access.

The ferocity of debate is a particularly feminine fierceness. It is inevitably bound into a historic patriarchal account of 'honour' and 'shame' which bears heavily still on women.

> *Women's honour (*and, I would add, in the current context, women's shame JB*) [is] something altogether else: virginity, chastity, fidelity to a husband. Honesty in women has not been considered important. We have been depicted as generically whimsical, deceitful, subtle, vacillating. And we have been rewarded for lying.*[5]

There is to this day a notion of 'protecting virtue' (in women) and 'exposing vice' (in men and women), which is a sexual construction and which is rooted in a particular Christian view of sexual morality and sexual sin. At times it can seem that the preservation of such morality is the Christian Church's primary contemporary social concern. To speak of morality seems to be only to speak of acceptable and unacceptable sexual relationships. Despite this, I believe strongly that broader ethical perspectives on the work are a necessity for all who engage in intervention. Implicit or explicit ethical narratives are an essential ground of practice.

Such ethical resources will include an insistence upon a *situated* engagement with sex work. An ethical stance is necessary because without it pastoral responses take the form either of 'first aid' or 'social control'. By first aid, I refer to a practice common throughout welfare and care in which wounds are patched up and further damage prevented, but nothing is done about the factors causing the damage in the first place. Indeed, the work of care is so time and compassion consuming that such causes are frequently altogether forgotten. In the case of care for sex workers, such 'first aid' includes the distribution of clean needles to injecting drug users and the distribution of condoms, as basic harm prevention measures. We might think of this as a 'health and safety' vision.

By social control, I mean the view of the sex trade as a social nuisance, even as 'dirt' needing to be cleaned up. Sex workers themselves, along with punters, dirty needles and used condoms, need to be removed from residential areas and if possible off the streets altogether and into brothels and massage parlours. Out of sight, out of mind. Such strategies are implemented via the use Anti-Social Behaviour Orders and by periodic sharp enforcement of the law on kerb crawling. They are often accompanied by calls for the criminalisation of the entire sex industry. The vision of society that seems to accompany such perspectives is that it should be clean.

Beyond these pragmatic responses lies a political debate. The fiercely contested perspectives can be represented as the 'abolitionist' versus the 'harm reduction' or sex workers' rights perspectives. In campaigning terms, there is little love lost between the two positions. In the rest of this paper, I seek to outline contemporary ethical responses to prostitution; to say something about the resilience of may young women involved and how this might be strengthened ; and suggest something of the nature of an ethics of solidarity with women involved in the sex trade.

The Liberal Response

First, then, to outline a contemporary liberal consensus in relation to prostitution, which can to a certain extent be associated with harm reduction and sex workers' rights perspectives. From this perspective (which is one which I share to some extent but which I also propose to critique) the exchange of sex for money is seen as a hidden aspect of so-called 'normal' heterosexual and to some extent homosexual relationships. The existence of prostitution as a trade is predicated on the existence of a certain view of marriage. The traditional Christian encouragement of 'abstinence' outside marriage (and the limitation on the acceptable forms of sex within it) creates a moral boundary. This moral boundary also forms the border of the market place in which prostitution can flourish, providing those 'immoral' services for which it is impossible to ask your wife and girlfriend. At the same time that the distinction is drawn between 'good' and 'bad', 'respectable' and 'rough' sex, so honour is given to the virtuous and shame to the vice ridden. In the public imagination (as exampled in the tabloid press, for instance) sex work is a crime against standards of decency and morality. (Sir Paul McCartney's ex wife Heather Mills McCartney has fallen from saint to sinner in the tabloid headlines: the representation of the heroine campaigner against landmines exposed as a 'shameful' former porn star provides a vivid example of this public morality at work.) The fact that prostitution is associated with dirt and disease, that it is shameful and is taboo is the most serious source of difference between prostitution and other forms of work. It is the 'whore stigma' which is the root of the problem.

The stigma associated with prostitution is therefore, liberals argue, what needs to be removed. One of the most significant steps in this direction was the development of the term 'sex work' as a deliberate intervention to challenge stigma. The Oxford English Dictionary records the first use of the term, in the *New York Times*, in 1971.

> **sex worker**, *a person who works in the sex industry, esp. a prostitute (usually used with the intention of reducing negative connotations and of aligning the sex industry with conventional service industries).*[6]

This is clearly distinct from meanings associated with the noun 'prostitute':

> *A person entirely or abjectly devoted to another; a 'slave'. Obs*

> *A woman who is devoted, or (usually) who offers her body to indiscriminate sexual intercourse, esp. for hire; a common harlot.*

or with the adjective: prostitute

> *Offered or exposed to lust (as a woman), prostituted; also more generally, abandoned to sensual indulgence, licentious. (Sometimes const. as pa. pple.) Now rare or Obs. (exc. as attrib. use of B. 1).*

The term 'sex worker' was therefore developed in order to mitigate the identification of prostitutes with abjection. The issue of the abjection, and the devotedness of the prostitute, will return in this chapter. However, by adopting a perspective which sees women as sex workers it is possible to ascribe a dignity to them as workers and to support a view that, as workers, like other workers, they have rights.

They are no longer abject. As prostitutes they are abject. As workers, they have rights to health care, housing and education as well as rights to protection from violent clients and rights to engage in prosecutions for rape and sexual assault, and to be believed.

It is possible too from this perspective to recognise the ways in which sex workers develop informal systems of mutual support: codes of honour which challenge the dishonour projected on to them by the wider society. In one influential article, Gail Phetersen suggested the following as sources of sexual dishonour imputed to prostitutes:

1. Having sex with strangers
2. Having sex with multiple partners
3. Taking sexual control and initiative and possessing experience
4. Asking for money for sex
5. Being committed to satisfying impersonal male lust and fantasies
6. Being out alone dressed to attract male desire
7. Being in the company of bad, aggressive, abusive men whom they can handle (common) or cannot handle (shameful)[7]

However, the construction of 'good' and 'Christian' femininity is at the very least in part responsible for such a code of honour/dishonour. Another way of thinking of this splitting is through the discourse of madonna/whore, in which 'badness' is projected on to the whore as it cannot be contained within the imagined 'good' body of the woman. A significant body of social research suggests that sex workers develop their own code of honour in response to such projections. 'Good whores' maintain a code of fair work; ask for money in advance; leave clients feeling satisfied; wash clients; use condoms; remain detached; do not provide non-negotiated services; keep off alcohol while working; warn others of dangerous clients. While some of this code is to do with sex, sexual competence and experience, it is just as obviously a discourse of mutuality and well-being, offering some basic sense of fair treatment and a concern with safety and with health.

The powerful liberal view of the need to counter or at least minimise and equalise sexual stigma and to resist further criminalisation and prosecution of prostitutes is worth re-stating in a climate in which Anti-Social Behaviour Orders are regularly used to clean up areas and women. The huge difference in the numbers of Anti-Social Behaviour Orders issued in the London Boroughs of Camden and Islington can easily be explained by the existence of a longstanding 'red light' district close to Kings Cross Station, which is in the London Borough of Camden. The use of the discourse of 'anti-social behaviour' usually contains a projective identification of a 'badness' belonging to the whole social body on to specific groups, in this case sex workers. Any ethics which starts from a commitment to interconnectedness, as will many forms of Christian ethics, must mean recognising and countering such projections. It does however, from a feminist perspective, leave a number of important questions begging.

Feminist Questions

The most obvious question frequently posed by feminists is the question of what it is about 'normal' heterosexual relations and about some gay relationships which creates the demand for prostitution. Prior to the Football World Cup of 2005, the Salvation Army attempted to organise a mass leaflet of football grounds publicising the illegality of both trafficking and of the use of the services of 'trafficked' women in regulated German brothels. I had the experience of being invited – through various Christian networks - to take part in a mass leafleting of the Old Trafford Ground of Manchester United Football Club (the 'Theatre of Dreams') – asking men not to pay for sex with trafficked women in the brothels available during the World Cup. The authorities called off the leafleting activity, on the grounds that it was causing 'too much litter'. But it was clearly too much in all sorts of ways. The proposed activity made abjection visible too close to the theatre of dreams. 'Being on the game' was being made visible too close to 'the beautiful game'. The fact that the use of sexual services has apparently moved into the mainstream of leisure and purchasing activity for stag nights, hen nights and holidays made uncomfortably visible a worm at the heart of family leisure time. There is a difficulty still for many heterosexual relationships. What still seems unimaginable to most women - sex without attachment - seems all too attractive, at least once in a lifetime, to a small but significant section of men.

The feminist argument against prostitution is not and in my view should never be an argument against prostitutes or rooted in contempt for them. The feminist argument against prostitution is rooted in sadness and anger about what the demand for prostitution reveals about the general character (both private and public) of relations between the sexes. It also requires imagining what will make for better heterosexual relationships and a close attention to issues of coercion and consent. I will argue that coercion and consent, free choice and control by others exist on a continuum rather than in the polarised forms ('trafficked women versus voluntary prostitution'; 'prostitution versus casual sex' ; 'prostitution versus unwanted married sex') indicated so often in the current debate. While there is a significant feminist support for abolitionist perspectives, it is also possible to argue against prostitution from a feminist position without supporting current abolitionist campaigns.

The case of the Cuddles Massage Parlour indicates some of the tensions and contradictions involved. On October 1, 2005 West Midlands Police as part of a clampdown on trafficking raided Cuddles Massage Parlour and 'rescued' women believed to have been kidnapped, raped, drugged and sold into prostitution. 19 women from 10 countries were put under police protection following the raid. Six of the women were taken as illegal immigrants to Yarls Wood Immigration Removal Centre to face deportation within days. (At that time the United Kingdom had not yet signed the European Convention on Trafficking, which would allow a 30 day respite period for women seeking to leave the sex trade prior to deportation proceedings being invoked.) The following day a number of the women being held demanded and secured their release from detention on the grounds that they were working at the brothel of their own free will. On their account, it was the British state rather than their husbands/brothers/cousins/the pimps who ran the brothel, who were their kidnappers. For migrant women, faced with claiming to have been trafficked and therefore being subject to deportation and claiming to be working voluntarily, the risks must be hard to weigh.

Attention to the extreme cases associated with trafficking can lead to the neglect of the situation of street sex workers within the UK who have not been trafficked. Just as it has been argued that the 'Maiden Tribute of Modern Babylon', the repeal of the Contagious Diseases Acts, and the raising of the age of consent were part of a 'remoralisation' directly connected to the criminalisation of homosexuality in the 1880's, so we need to pay attention to the question of where the rhetorical figure of the 'trafficked woman' leads the gaze of policy makers now. We also need to ask what, in turn, this rhetorical figure renders invisible. The focus on extreme victimisation may make the more mundane issues facing many involved in sex work considerably less visible.

A Children's Society Report on street prostitution suggests that 90% of sex workers who work on the streets start under the age of twenty-one; 83% are addicted to heroin and crack cocaine and perhaps 50% are people who have come through to the teenage years as 'looked after children'. They have been 'in care' and may well have been introduced to selling sex or turning tricks by older friends who have also been in the care system. They are highly vulnerable young people, by no means the 'freely choosing' autonomous individuals proposed by liberal ethics, but, equally, they are not selling sex because they have been kidnapped and sold into sex slavery. Either/or distinctions between voluntary and coerced prostitution are of little use here. The idea of a continuum of agency is most helpful. Young people may be practising a vitiated agency, but retain some agency nonetheless.

One account of the experience of trafficked women suggests that 'trauma' may lead women to deny the experience of kidnap and abuse and to suggest that they are 'freely choosing' something into which they have in fact been coerced.

During the travel and transit stage women may experience an 'initial trauma' that is usually acute and triggers survival responses that engender symptoms of extreme anxiety that inhibit later memory and recall. The impact that trauma can have on memory may have significant effects later when women are questioned by law enforcement officials, asked to provide criminal evidence or participate in criminal proceedings.[8]

This argument concerning trauma means that notions of women's 'freedom of choice' are largely undermined. The key issue for those concerned with whether there is consent on the part of women involved in the sex industry is sidestepped. Taken together with a recognition that 'trafficking does not necessarily involve force but can include a range of control strategies and coercive contexts which vitiate consent', this leads to a turn of attention away from debates which polarise voluntary and coerced activity. The attention of analysis and it is hoped action turns to the need to understand the extent and range of control and of coercive contexts and to what needs to be done to undermine them.

At this point in the discussion however, the issue of self-determination returns. The question of the self-determination of women involved in the industry is vital not because they should be seen as the freely choosing autonomous individuals of liberal political theory but because without an engagement with sex workers` own voices and perspectives, the transformation of heterosexual relationships which is needed, and which needs first to be imagined, cannot occur. In the same way, and as a consequence, individual personal 'escape' can only become real if it can first be imagined and desired from within a person's own context.

Whilst recognising and acknowledging that much that is painful is blessedly erased from our consciousness, the cases of 'extreme victimisation' should not be argued and cannot be argued mainly on the basis of trauma/repression. This is in part because such arguments open up the danger that feminist solidarity will be based on a projection of our voice on to the silence of the prostitute. Just as the projective identifications of 'badness' onto the whore in the madonna/whore dichotomy need to be dismantled, so do the victim/rescuer dichotomies on which feminist action has sometimes been built. It is to this problem that the final section of the paper now turns.

Dialogic Ethics

It is vital that there is a dialogue between feminists and sex workers about the nature of campaigning in relation to the laws governing prostitution as well as in relation to other social policy initiatives. Otherwise, compassion, like other forms of caring, may reinforce the very patterns of economic and political subordination responsible for such suffering. Compassion as a form of 'suffering with' may not in and of itself provide the energy to move out of subordinated relationships. In fact, it may freeze existing positions and subjectifications. In order to create new positions, to imagine heterosexuality differently and to transform existing relationships, the 'compassionate self' may need to be abandoned. Perhaps in the 'excess of compassion' which made Josephine Butler fierce were other energies, emotions that move rather than transfix: griefs, losses and angers.

The view that such a dialogue is possible is testified to in the work of feminist researchers who have engaged in participatory research with sex workers. It is also to be found in the more intimate accounts of prostitution in which there is regular evidence of the distance which women create between themselves – their 'integrity' as it were - and their activities with punters. There is a 'proper distance' which protects integrity. The distancing and separation which prostitutes create between personal relationships and sex with punters shares I think in the sense of 'proper distance' which belongs to all relationships with 'the other.' This may be thought if as a form of self-protection, and of the protection of the desire for loving relationship, rather than a commercial one.

This 'proper distance' extends to the distance between the one who works to offer solidarity and the one who receives solidarity. The emotional and physical barriers and boundaries which sex workers use to protect themselves against personal involvement with clients already speak of a desire *not* to be reduced to a sex object. Just as humans should not be reduced to sex objects, neither should sex workers be reduced to being objects of pity. An object can be appropriated and used. Between two subjects there is always a gap, a distance.

That there is no *automatic* identification with suffering- for example by women with women just because we *are* women – is also that which opens up the possibility of finding a connection. There is something to be discovered, some thing to be learned, something to be wondered at and be amazed by. The lack of automatic connection means exploring both the nature of common ground and the nature of unlikeness, in what I will name, following a number of feminist writers, as a politics of love. A politics of love is involved with wondering and asking questions, opening up new possibilities rather than reproducing those repetitious practices of the 'norm' which are so in need of transformation.

A politics of rescue repeats and affirms existing social relationships and in particular reinforces a position of victim in the dynamic of persecutor, 'victim' and rescuer. A politics of love seeks to be a politics of transformation of such social relationships, and it is on this basis that feminists speak of solidarity. 'Am I not a woman and a sister?' was written on the medal stamped in the anti-slavery movement, which yet portrayed the English woman as maternal and the slave as child-like, and so has been analysed as a form of cultural racism, even while speaking of and practising emancipatory politics. I argue that it is possible to move against these positionings of 'victim' and 'rescuer' by acknowledging and working with hidden aspects of each position, in particular the resilience of the 'victim' and the pain/woundedness of the 'rescuer'.

In the context of the discussion of solidarity between non-prostitutes and prostitutes it is particularly important to recognise, name and acknowledge sexual woundedness imposed or experienced in the context of acceptable, normal and legitimate heterosexuality. This means a refusal to speak from 'normal' to 'deviant', from 'whole' to 'sick'. It is also vital to recognise and value all forms of resilience, mutual care and agency that can be found among sex workers/ prostitute women.

Love, pain and woundedness are closely connected, and as Sara Ahmed has argued, 'love is often conveyed by wanting to feel the loved one's pain, to feel pain on her behalf'.[9] I want to argue that in responding to prostitution from a position outside prostitution it is necessary to recognise our pain, sadness and anger that exists within 'normal' heterosexuality and what the nature of our investment in the pain of prostitution, and in the desire to remove it, might therefore be. It is also vital to be open to wonder and delight. It is amazement which opens up the world to transformation, to being imagined differently. If the capacity to feel amazement and delight in response to others is repressed, they are again objectified and 'frozen' in existing relationships.

In moving away from the victim/rescuer dynamic, it is necessary to move away from the cultural and professional investment which is often made in the wound as an identity. The confessional and testimonial culture which accompanies much work with survivors needs to be extended. The narrative of the 'repentant whore'/reformed prostitute is a common narrative in professional projects. For example, many projects use personal testimonies to build support for their work. It is important to ask what the work of such representations is and to what extent they enable transformation of existing social relationships to occur. This is difficult territory, concerned with how work with sex workers is represented in the public domain and to what extent representations of pain and suffering are used to mobilise a politics of pity and horror rather than a politics of love, anger and transformation. Whilst it is very necessary to mobilise support for such projects, and this rhetorical strategy is far preferable to the 'naming and shaming' of the 'common prostitute', I believe it is necessary to develop a range of representations and mediations which can shift the terms of our understanding. What, we need to ask, is involved in being 'moved to pity' or 'moved to anger'? What moves and where to in such representational strategies? Perhaps being 'moved to pity' can lead more readily to a desire to rescue? I am looking for public representations of work with sex workers which may 'move to love' in the sense I am using the term here.

The feminist politics of love I am describing is not necessarily, or perhaps not yet, an abolitionist politics but is a politics which is attempting a dialogue about alternative possibilities for relationships between men and women, and which works in alliance with welfare support. Projects have therefore been established which offer safe housing; popular education; access to good health care; midwifery services; support with children; alternative employment opportunities. Such projects respond to the dignity of the persons of sex workers and recognise men and women as sexed and sexual bodies in the image of God, created for mutuality and delight.

Distance and the refusal of over-identification is necessary part of such practices, but it is not, primarily, a distance of avoidance or self-protection. It may be that in this distance is also the 'gap' of ethics when ethics is understood as an encounter with alterity. The discussion of pain, suffering and love of course resonates with the central preoccupations of Christian faith. It is with the turn to ethics among some feminists that the concluding section of this paper engages. (The paper is indebted at this point to the discussion of Julia Kristeva and Luce Irigaray by Elisabeth Grosz).

The impact of feminist thought influenced by psycho-analysis, philosophy and theology is often treated with suspicion by those involved in practical politics and pastoral work, but it is, in my view, a significant resource for the practice of dialogue between sex workers and those who propose ourselves as allies.

In brief, these are engagements with ethics which seek to move beyond the practice of the law, and social control, to explore the nature of engagement with the 'Other'. For Julia Kristeva, for example, her engagement with the marginalised feminine voice has led to a commitment to voicing the feminine not as politics but as 'her/ethics'; an encounter with alterity: 'a herethics – perhaps no more than that which in life makes bonds, thoughts and therefore the thought of death, bearable: herethics is undeath (a-mort) love.'[10] This love in Kristeva's account is close to madness, holiness and poetry. I suggest it is the space for such love which is being protected /created by the distancing activity in which sex workers are said to engage when undertaking their work. (Kristeva goes on to say that when this love is voiced in the symbolic order it refers to God in religious discourse; to beauty in art; to meaning and narrative in literature; and to copulative sexual union.) Such love may then form a bond , a common ground between the woman sex worker and her allies, as it is not given by one to another but is a connection which is accessible to all, and which is not 'chosen' but rather accessed.

The quite different account of the nature of the ethical relationship with 'the other' proposed by Levinas (and developed by Irigaray in `I love (to) You.') is also potentially a resource for this practice. Firstly, there is the emphasis on wonder, and on an activity originating with the Other in relation to which the subject is passively positioned. The other astonishes and fills the subject with wonder and surprise. How will it be to be amazed and astonished by an encounter with prostitute women, rather than simply moved to pity and to a desire to rescue and save? Strangely, our response to the other woman, the other voice of the whore in the Christian tradition, that of the woman with the jar of ointment, who becomes Mary of Magdala, who becomes 'the one who has loved much', 'the tart with the heart of gold', tells us something of what such wonder and surprise might be. The prostitute is abject, but also devoted, set apart, and participates thereby in an aspect of the sacred. This too may arouse an excess of love in us that can make us fierce.

> *The first word of the face is the thou shalt not kill. It is an order. There is a commandment in the appearance of the face, as if a master spoke to me. However, at the same time, the face of the Other is destitute. It is poor for whom I can do all and to whom I owe all. And me, whoever I may be, but as a 'first person', I am he who finds the resource to respond to the other's call.*[11]

A feminist response rooted in such traditions of ethics and in the practice of love in the public world have much to offer those responding to sex work in the here and now.

To believe in the possibility of seeing the sex worker as the (other) woman who astonishes and amazes and provokes to wonder may enable, alongside stories of pity and rescue, narratives of collective suffering and collective hope to emerge; hope for a more generous and hospitable world, and hope, in that world, for more generous and hospitable relationships between men and women. This is a work of imagination and of story telling as well as of collective practice in new forms of project work and campaigning. Whilst this is happening, a politics of love creates a space for the both the liberal and the abolitionist discourses to exist alongside one another in mutual critique. Perhaps offering an example of a penultimate ethics alongside an ultimate ethics. An ultimate ethics might desire and long for a world in which prostitution no longer exists. A penultimate ethics seeks to build up the dignity and worth of those who work as prostitutes in the here and now. And this can only be done through dialogue with them, in the sense I have argued.

Not yet the heavenly city. But enough it is to be hoped to make us fierce once more.

Endnotes

[1] Sara Maitland and Wendy Mulford, *Virtuous Magic: Women Saints and their Meanings* (London: Mowbray, 1998), p. 230.

[2] O'Neill, *Prostitution and Feminism*, p. and Maggie O'Neill, 'Prostitute Women Now', in *Rethinking Prostitution: Purchasing Sex in the 1990's,* ed. Graham Scrambler and Annette Scrambler (London: Routledge, 1997), pp. 83-90.

[3] On the abolitionist side J. Bindel and L. Kelly, *A Critical Examination of Response to Prostitution in Four Countries: Victoria, Australia; Ireland; the Netherlands; and Sweden* (London: Child and Woman Abuse Studies Unit, London Metropolitan University, 2003); on the liberal side, see O'Neill, *Prostitution and Feminism*.

[4] Teela Sanders, *Sex Work: A Risky Business* (Collumpton, Devon: Willan Publishing, 2005).

[5] Adrienne Rich, 'Women and Lying: Some Notes on Honour', in *On Lies, Secrets and Silences* (London: Virago, 1980), pp. 185-94, p. 186.

[6] *Oxford English Dictionary*, second edition and revisions (Oxford: Oxford University Press, 1989), http://dictionary.oed.com , accessed on 27 March, 2007. All further references are to this edition.

[7] Gail Phetersen, *The Whore Stigma: Female Dishonour and Male Unworthiness: Report Sponsored by the Dutch Ministry of Social Affairs and Employment* (The Hague: Emancipation Policy Co-ordination, 1986).

[8] *The Health Risks and Consequences of Trafficking in Women and Adolescents: Findings from a European Study* (London: London School of Hygiene and Tropical Medicine, 2003).

[9] Sara Ahmed, *The Cultural Politics of Emotion* (Edinburgh: Edinburgh University Press, 2004), p. 30.

[10] Elizabeth Grosz, *Sexual Subversions: Three French Feminists* (London and Sydney: Allen and Unwin, 1989), p. 132.

[11] Levinas, quoted in Grosz, *Sexual Subversions,* p. 143.

Josephine Butler and the Trafficking of Women Today

Carrie Pemberton

Carrie Pemberton is the Chief Executive of the counter trafficking and support-service providing charity CHASTE – Churches Alert to Sex Trafficking across Europe. An Anglican Priest for the last ten years, Carrie worked for three years in D. R. Congo establishing a women's development centre and establishing with her husband the Institut Theologique Anglican (ISTHA) in Ituri. A Women's National Commissioner developing the programme on Violence against Women and briefing the government on Trafficking issues, Carrie is a board member of the UKHTC and has developed the Virtual University of research on Trafficking based in Sheffield. Her monograph on the incipient conversation between women contextual theologians of Africa, Circle Thinking: African Women in Dialogue with the West, *is published by Brille. Her chapter responds with enthusiasm, from an abolitionist perspective, to Butler's ideas.*

&

The body of this essay was inspired by reading the letters, speeches and writings of Josephine Butler, collected and edited by Jane Jordan and Ingrid Sharp, from the perspective of an academic caught in the heat of the forge rather than in the quiet cooling and finished hardening process in the library. In the fourth volume of Jordan and Sharp's multi-volume edition, Butler's 'Letter to the Mothers of England (commended also to the Attention of Fathers, Ministers of Religion, and Legislators)' raises the realities of a contemporary 'white slave trade'. Her clarity in this appeal, which asserts that 'fair England – [continues] – to present the most tempting field to these kidnappers and slave dealers', invites the attending mothers and the fathers, ministers and legislators listening into the conversation, to engage in resistance to this hidden and insidious form of enslavement driven by the uninhibited sexual demand of men. She engages the women's emotional intelligence and proper accountability stating, 'If you cannot extend your sympathies to the children of other lands, you at least can feel for those of your own […] Do not imagine you are powerless – if once we consent to know, – do you believe it is possible that the just and merciful God will leave us helpless, or refuse to help us?'[1]

Today there is a contemporary cultural uncertainty of how to respond to the growing realisation that the United Kingdom receives an estimated minimum of 4,000 women who have been trafficked for sexual exploitation from across the world and currently an unspecified number of children, though feared to be running into thousands.[2] The popular understanding of trafficking has been significantly enhanced by media commitment to telling the story of those who have been trafficked. Recent significant offerings include docudramas such as 'Sex Traffic', popular series such as *The Bill*, and the recent Canadian Broadcasting drama *The Real Sex Traffic*, which tracked the extraordinary story of one woman's abduction at the hands of her husband's colleague in Istanbul. All these have paid attention to the rise of trafficking in Eastern Europe, from Russia, the Balkans, Albania and the recent European Union accession countries, all feeding into the old European Union countries and ultimately the United Kingdom. This trafficking explicitly for the purposes of enforced sex, profits traffickers, pimps, trolleys, madames and sometimes even members of their own families, but always leaves the deceived women and children indebted, traumatised and brutalised by their experiences.

The Palermo Protocol, adumbrated by the UN in 2000 and adopted in September 2003, defines trafficking for sexual exploitation explicitly but somewhat inelegantly as

> *the recruitment, transportation, transfer, harbouring or receipt*
> *of persons, by means of the threat or use of force or other*
> *forms of coercion, of abduction, of fraud, of deception, of the*
> *abuse of power or of a position of vulnerability or of the giving*
> *or receiving of payments or benefits to achieve the consent of*
> *a person having control over another person, for the purpose*

*of exploitation. Exploitation shall include, at a minimum, the
exploitation of the prostitution of others or other forms of sexual
exploitation, forced labour or services, slavery or practices
similar to slavery, servitude or the removal of organs.*[3]

In February 2006 the British Government ratified this Protocol and
consequently entered into a phase of active co-operation with its goals.
These include legislative transformations for effective enforcement
against traffickers and the adoption of new standards of victim and
witness care. The British Government has now published a UK Action
Plan on Tackling Human Trafficking.[4] The Churches Alert to Sexual
Trafficking across Europe, CHASTE, is part of a wider movement of
lobbying and consultation which has brought about these significant
changes – and by doing so stands in the line of outrage and political
engagement exemplified in the life of Josephine Butler and the work
of the Ladies National Association (LNA), and the wider dispersed
movements which encompassed Working Men's Associations, Ladies
Guilds, and church meetings across Britain; all of which agitated for
the abolition of the Contagious Diseases Acts.

I am interested in uncovering some of the continuities and
discontinuities in the current challenges experienced by those
campaigning against trafficking for sexual exploitation and those faced
by Josephine Butler in her decades of activism from 1866 to her death
in the closing days of 1906. As the current Executive Officer of CHASTE
I am both aghast and heartened that Butler the campaigner directed
her supporters to attend to issues that lie at the heart of contemporary
exploitation in enforced prostitution and trafficking for sexual exploitation.
Heartened, because many of her suggestions, particularly the presence of
a double morality which allowed punters and clients to escape public
censure and left women being exploited and at the bottom end of the
criminal justice system, have found an echo in CHASTE's hit list for
change. Aghast, because more than a century later British culture and
social economy still renders the male client virtually free from censure
or culpability for a trade which is claiming thousands of young women's
lives and futures in the United Kingdom and hundreds of thousands world
wide. In a circular sent out to the Ladies' National Association in August

1885 Josephine Butler announced that any engagement with

> *enthusiastic agitation like the present* [the Hyde Park
> demonstration of 1885 where women were invited to dress in
> black in remembrance of those caught up in White slavery]
> *there will perhaps only be one who will possess that good gift of
> perseverance and fidelity to the death in the pursuit of a worthy
> end. Therefore let us labour to promote that spirit of patient
> perseverance and ask God to give us the continued and unbroken
> inspiration which is imparted in the fullest and highest by His Holy
> Spirit alone – yours in the cause of Justice.*[6]

Butler was in no doubt that the challenge which faced British society in addressing the scourge of 'State regulation of vice' was one which would take the best energies of women and men for a substantial period of their lives. Like Thomas Clarkson the pamphleteer, researcher and lobbyist for the Abolition of the Slave Trade, who started his crusade for justice in 1785 and came to understand in the course of engagement that it would be his life's work, these paradigm shifts in culture can take generations of the committed to establish. Butler saw a cascading catalogue of disaster in British Society being set in train by the 'State regulation of vice', whereby a class of women were set aside for the pleasure of men, both in the armed services and in civilian society. Butler also attributed the patterns of 'white slavery' as a direct impact of state regulation, with young women and children being 'sourced' from the countryside in Britain, Austria, Belgium and Switzerland to serve in houses dedicated to sexual exploitation across Europe. The practices of brothel keepers in London, Liverpool and Newcastle, the grooming and abuse of domestic servants and maids driven into enforced prostitution, recruitment of young English girls for the brothels of Brussels, Antwerp and Paris, a supine State and an inert and at worst corrupt police force; all these were the matters she brought to the public at large, and over which she tirelessly lobbied Parliament. She was aware that the harm done by normalising the abuses of prostitution and violence against women in the domestic context would take decades to heal and transform. In 2007 we are still looking at many of the challenges which she faced, but with a canvas which has been transformed by modern developments in technology, communication and transportation. A transformation which leaves contemporary Britain with an estimated 79,800 women and children caught in prostitution and a global sex industry which now vies with military expenditure as the largest generator of financial movement, a staggering $7000 - $12,000 billion dollars a year. [7]

I am going to look in this paper at three aspects of the environment of Butler's engagement with the business of prostitution in both its national and international dimensions, and her analysis, methods and strategies to combat this 'social and moral evil'. First, there is her experience of direct lobbying of parliament and the ecclesiastical hierarchy as someone belonging to a gender which was not represented directly within the democratic processes of governance, and which she saw required commitment to the suffrage and an improved status for women. Secondly, I shall examine the role of the state, which Butler believed to be critical in informing or developing a moral, healthy, just and equal environment for men and women and all classes and thus the importance of legislation. The third aspect is Butler's challenge to the churches to become involved as those with an immediate apprehension of moral commitment to equality and non-degradation of the individual, and with divine resources of hope to counteract the sense of ubiquitous evil.

Lobbying and the Need for Equality

As an activist, I have been encouraged by the practice of Butler herself. Her reflection on her strategy and the requirements for the overhaul of the polity of vice in the nation and in Europe was developed in 1896 away from the heat of the immediate political battle in Britain, but still in the midst of engaging the Abolition movement in Geneva. She comments to friends and family about its outward beauty but with oppression just below the surface. 'Geneva' she comments 'is such a beautiful City, with a volcano underneath --- a moral volcano, full of fire and mud'.[8]   In her *Personal Reminiscences of a Great Crusade*, Butler was concerned that the principles of the crusade should not be forgotten by succeeding generations – i.e. those of absolute equality in all human laws. In *The Principles of the Abolitionists* she rehearsed again some of those principles: based upon the highest law [the Law of God] , and the 'pure' standard of womanhood; the institution of the family founded on the marriage tie; the resistance of lax principles and the absolute right of people to live in accordance with natural instincts and not the sternness of moral law; the requirements of a moral revolution to reduce prostitution in the cities – particularly the southern towns; the need for 'armies of people (women as well as men) to take to heart and take in hand the reformation of their own towns (local activism); that nothing can be undertaken in this arena without the 'moral support and active co-operation of citizens' (local and global activism) [9] There should be no 'licensing of the trade of prostitution' . This was the conviction that sent Butler across the length and breadth of Britain, particularly engaging the student bodies of Cambridge and Oxford and working men's forums and women's networks.

The emotional leverage of provoking a sense of horror and shame was part of her armoury of response. She was aware of, but did not spend substantial time developing, the idea of 'those men who are left free to tempt and insult women and girls'; she was much more committed to undoing the effect of the Police des Moeurs developed in Napoleonic France and the compulsory examination of women and children for the state management of the health of its soldiery. This part of her concern, – the unravelling of unjust laws established to facilitate leisure sex for men within the armed forces and colonial civil service – was made most explicit in her work on the management of cantonment brothels in colonial India. For despite the repeal of the Contagious Diseases Acts on British soil in 1886, they effectively remained in force in India through the Cantonments Act and the Contagious Diseases (India) Act and there were threats to re-introduce them in areas such as Guernsey after an increase in venereal disease in the 1890's.[10]

The league was a school of principle: of persuasion and argument – with patience, friendliness and firmness; principled determination to see the end of prostitution; to enable appropriate resistance to vice for women and to address the legal immunity for men as those who pimped, groomed and used those prostituted as clients; refusal to punish the prostitute and clear on the need for equality to see any penalties meted out to those whom the law viewed as persistent offenders applied to men as well as women. For Butler, the campaigner of clear principle, to sin legislatively and imperially against the womanhood of the nation was for the Empire to sin against God.[11]

She enshrined in her work and her thinking a clear sense of the rights of womanhood – regardless of creed, colour or class, which all those of sound mind and sound spirituality should and would embrace. Allied to this pillar is her conviction that the rights of children should always be embraced and incorporated in the legislation of the state and the way in which it promoted and protected the rights of family and household. Again, her spirituality drives her understanding of women's sacred, i.e. God-given, rights, so that when these are violated by the body politic, it is that body, the political body which needs to be overhauled. Of course in Britain at that time women were not entitled to vote even with the passage of the Parliamentary Reform Bill in 1884. Even in the supposedly enlightened halls of the world anti-slavery congress of 1840, women did not have the right to be voting members and American women had no right to be seated in the voting chamber, being removed to the gallery. Such unegalitarian behaviour drove the likes of Elizabeth Cady Stanton and Lucretia Mott to move on and organise the Seneca Falls Women's Rights Convention in 1848. They used the Declaration of Independence for their model, calling for equality of the sexes before the law, an end to male oppression of women, better educational facilities, greater employment opportunities, and women's suffrage. Butler, who was no less politically radical than Stanton and Mott, understood the right of 'every woman to the sovereignty of her own person' to be 'a most sacred right'. She was clear that this had been violated by the state in the Contagious Diseases Acts, and she was entirely alert to the requirement for eternal vigilance over this.[12] It was the role of government to afford security of person and property to all men and women and never to undermine that – for that way lay blood feuds and lynch laws. [13] In her discussions of the breakdown of the State and its inability to protect all its citizens against attack, Butler could have been making a contemporary plea for the non return of those violated through Trafficking for sexual exploitation to present day Albania, or regions of Nigeria or the Sudan. Behind all this, of course, is concealed the powerful basis for an argument for universal suffrage; and the extension of the idea of equality of representation within parliament, not only to men but to 'sovereign women'. Indeed, it was her view that a parliament of rich men was unfit to legislate for the poor and unrepresented on issues that pressed so intimately upon their personal integrity. However unlike Stanton and Mott, Butler did not explicitly mobilise her supporters and networks around these issues. It was the outrage over the multiple abuses within enforced prostitution which was her public face, alongside the work on developing educational opportunities for women, which was the less explicitly political expression of her religiously formulated commitment to equality.

For Butler, it was the fact that humanity is made in the image of God from which the full 'horror' of prostitution emerges, stating that 'it is for human beings alone, made in the God's image that that horror is possible'.[14] The logic of her determined opposition to prostitution and the inevitable degradation of women within that trade to being used as beasts and not as women equal in stature and respect to men, that impelled her to see that alternatives must exist. The implementation and expansion of the trade by the 'stronger portion of humanity' – (the male/wealthy) to 'embrace and wreck the weaker' was precisely the degradation and mechanism of enslavement which occurs within prostitution and indeed in the newly outlawed trade of African enslavement. But resisting this meant a developing understanding of the importance of de-restricting the labour market for women at the height of the industrial revolution in Britain. Allowing women to earn, to work in factories, to be able to support themselves and their children would all help avert the 'moral dangers' implicit in pauperism according to Butler. Butler's was a very practical and socio-economically grounded analysis of the forces at work which made prostitution a quotidian and unremarked option in every city for young women who found themselves in the poverty trap or sold on by unscrupulous employers into brothel work.

'White Slavery' and State Regulation: The Need for Legislation

The architecture of 'white slavery' was played out in the recruitment of young women, many of them just children, of the rural poor of English villages. One of the clearest articulations of the circumstances and mechanisms of the process are in the Deposition on oath made by Butler in 1880 to the Stipendiary Magistrate of the City of Liverpool.[15] Responding to a summons by a warrant from the Home Office, Butler recounts the sequestration of English girls into brothels in Brussels and opens up a world of procuresses, pimps, brothels, rapes, violation of minors, deception, kidnap (the enforced holding of young women against their will with no freedom of egress) and the involvement of young children – twelve to fifteen years old - from Germany, France, the United Kingdom, Scotland, and Ireland. She recounts the illicit alteration of birth certificates at Somerset House, of buying and selling of young women between brothel owners from addresses in Tottenham Court Road to Rue St Laurent in Brussels, to Rouen, Limoges and Queret in France, of aliases, and falsified passports. Describing the conditions of the young prostitutes she tells of chronic illness suffered by those prostituted, of the debt bondage of nationals in Belgian, of indecent torture, unnatural orgies, of windowless brothels, of mattresses placed against windows to block the sound of screams during rape and cries for assistance, of mounting indebtedness and lack of freedom of movement.[16]

Victims were only permitted escorted movement outside of the brothel under the watchful eye of the madame; there was a shameful crossover between labour exploitation and sexual exploitation of female employees (a practice widespread today in trafficking for domestic servitude). She testifies to the sense of shame and desperation felt by the young women embroiled, the collusion of police forces in both the British jurisdiction and other countries, the lack of safety and rescue interventions by the state and the haphazard intervention of pastors, doctors and consuls in chance encounters with these young women in the course of their work. [17]

In her letter to *The Shield* in 1880, Butler describes French, German, Swiss and Belgian minors being exploited in 'maisons tolerées' which Butler sees as the reason for the extension of the trade.[18] The young girls in question also included British children – 'innocent creatures, stolen kidnapped, betrayed, got from English country villages by every artifice and sold to these human shambles' – never seeing the sun – concealed from all but their buyers – with the presence of these children unknown to the ordinary visitors the house, known to none but the 'wealthy debauchees who can pay the 'vast sums of money for the sacrifice of these innocents to their fastidious and shameful lusts'.[19]

The inclusion of medical men arranging abortions, certifying virginity, mending the range of genito-urinary diseases that these young women would have fallen foul of is hinted at; and Butler calls down a malediction on those cities where nothing is done about the problem. Butler also alludes to the time and high commitment given by those managing refuges or for the running of any recovery programme for young women who have been caught in the activities of 'maisons tolerées', and of the long walk back to wholeness at both a psychological and physical level. This has much of the tenor of the recent *Stolen Smiles* report commissioned by the Home Office and funded by EU finance, where the range and extent of a woman's recovery time from the impact of contemporary trafficking is examined at length.[20] It is also very much the experience of those involved in raising the finance to fund extra safe housing space for women today as part of the CHASTE round table network of housing providers, which includes the heirs of Florence Booth's work in the Salvation Army and amongst the Conference of Religious.[21]

The range of issues touched on by Butler is similar to those encountered by the victims of the trafficking of women today. The differences, however, are that the blight which struck impoverished families in the 'rural idylls' of England have moved to the devastated villages of Romania and of Moldova; the outskirts of Lagos and Benin City in Nigeria, the paddy fields of Vietnam and the holiday vistas of Thailand. Butler's concerns in late-Victorian Britain, a Britain in the throes of the second wave of industrialisation, were related to the feminisation of poverty due to inappropriately gendered state interventions placing restrictions on the uptake of women into the industrial labour market. This concern was allied to that of the question of suffrage, more particularly in Butler's later writings. There is an uncanny and perturbing parallel to be drawn between the female poverty and lack of full blooded incorporation into the employment market, the lack of educational opportunity, the foreclosure of political representation, a regulated and state approved market in prostitution, (as the state had undertaken during the years of the CDA), the desperation of impoverished parents, and the recurrence of all these themes in the lives of those who will broker their children into the sex markets of southern cities in the United Kingdom and abroad. Today in the global context of trafficking, the 'white slave' trade of yesteryear has moved beyond the permeable borders of France, Belgium and Switzerland to countries as far ranging as Thailand, Vietnam, China, Brazil and Africa. The resemblances between those who were trafficked then and those who now are being moved around nations now are more striking than the differences, except that cocaine and crack replace the champagne and laudanum discussed in letters and articles produced by the Vigilance campaign of the nineteenth century in their concern for the movement of young women into brothels in their time. For those now trafficked across international boundaries the violence of guns, beatings, rapes and threats against family members serve to bring the compliance which shame, social ostracism, political insouciance and police inertia did then. But yet more direct parallels continue in many countries where policing and religious cultures of the primal blame of Eve have not moved on.

The kidnap, grooming, deceit, offers of false employment opportunities in domestic work or low paid factory work, offers of marriage, presentations of work in education as governesses or teachers, all these continue as part of the modus operandi of the deceivers of the trafficked. Added to this, and beyond the categories used by Butler, are those thrown into the forcible subjection of 'money grasping traders' through the impact of civil war, or natural disasters such as earthquakes, tsunamis, ecological degradation, famine, and floods.[22] With modern air and sea travel, and communications and money transfers now operating at an unprecedented global level, the reach of the market of trafficking has exponentially expanded. Britain is now perceived as a country of demand, with the occasional working British girl finding herself at the violent end of the prostitution industry in the Middle East and in Japan.

The misery of the victims of the trafficking are similar, with false imprisonment by state authorities whether because of perceived immigration violations in countries of demand or source, and the associated horrors of multiple rapes, food deprivation, intimidation, loss of autonomy and fear of one's ability to survive, horrors which now as then 'it is impossible to exaggerate'.[23] After Operation Pentameter, during which eighty-four victims of trafficking for sexual exploitation emerged, twelve of whom were minors, there has been a seed change in understanding the range of criminality and depth of violence associated with trafficking for sexual exploitation, which previously had been absent in the broad spectrum of policing in this country.[24] Victims came from countries as diverse as Thailand, Malaysia, Brazil, Congo, Nigeria, the new EU accession states and the countries of the former Soviet Union, China and Pakistan: they were found in towns as apparently idyllic as Beverley (within sight of the Minster), and as ordinary as Surbiton.

Butler called the fact of the white slave trade 'hell on earth' and commented that 'even if one rose from the dead' people would not believe what was happening. Now, as then in Butler's time, victims are indeed 'rising from the dead', in Butler's words 'to tell what they have endured, and I trust that these pale spectres will trouble the peace of every honest man until he has put forth his hand to do what he can do in the work of holy vengeance'. The Police forces of the UK have been so moved by what they have found during Operation Pentameter that the Association of Chief Police Officers and those involved in Operation Reflex, the United Kingdom-wide funded initiatives on immigration associated crimes, have lobbied successfully for a new government funded centre to be established in Britain to research, respond to and launch targeted operations against the new wave of trafficking unearthed in the country. Supported by victim-centered approaches captured in the Palermo Protocol along with the Council of Europe Convention on Trafficking, the police are moving forward co-ordinated responses to the fact of trafficking in cities and towns of the United Kingdom, and using the legislative powers available in the Sexual Offences Act and anti-trafficking legislation to prosecute those seen to be complicit in the trafficking of minors and women into the UK.[25]

There are a couple of reflections I want to make at this juncture. The horror of sexual exploitation, the brutality of the trade, the inhumanity which those who are embroiled in it manifest towards their victims, the complexity of the way in which the trade is managed and the complicity of the end user, the male who seeks sexual relief or the enactment of fantasies by payment, are all strikingly similar to those of Butler's time. However, Butler's stereotyping of the typical user being debauched older and wealthy men are not (and may not indeed have been then) the typical punter of today. Punters who are at risk of purchasing sex from a trafficked young woman today are from all walks of life, from every creed, ethnicity and language group, from all classes in our classless society, but the overwhelming feature which joins them all together is the fact that they are male. The price of a woman varies between £2-12,000 for first time buy in. Their value diminishes fairly rapidly as they move from virginal to second, third and fourth hand sales. One woman I met in the course of work with CHASTE had been sold on three times, with her final price the transfer of a beaten-up Corsa. The health of women is put at profound risk by client usage of up to 16 –20 enforced sexual encounters – or in other words, rapes - a day with prices ranging from £25 a half hour in some of the provinces to £50-60 in the capital. The articulation of the trade is as complex as in the nineteenth century, indeed it is more so, with an increased number of diverse agents involved from a variety of countries: procurers, trainers, transport logicians, drivers, groomers, enforcers, managers, finance collectors, financiers and money launderers, fraudsters, state officials, fixers, promotion managers, brothel keepers and forewomen.

What Butler did not encounter in fully fledged articulation was the context of immigration law which is now in place, through which antipathetic state legislation – antipathetic, that is, to the victims of the trade - makes things considerably worse than they need be. There maybe some continuity here with Butler's sense that the intervention of the state in the regulation of sex was in fact, as she frequently points out, the state's intervention to protect vice. It was clear that Butler had made the connection which still evades so many people today, between regulation, and its profoundly negative effects, through the development of a normalisation of the availability of women for sale, of commercial terms for the accessibility of sex for men from regulated, medicalised, approved and organised sex workers – whatever their pay, health and conditions. Butler, who traced the intrusion of what she called a 'plague' from the shores of Europe commencing in France through the Napoleonic organisation and state regulation of prostitution, was in no doubt that whatever the short term arguments for the health of women working in prostitution (from the development of whole cantonments designated for prostitution services for the standing army of the Empire, to the range of Contagious diseases interventions by medical personnel made compulsory in the initial Contagious Diseases Acts in the 1860's in the metropolis), this legislation and its attendant regularisation of prostitution was all about servicing the sexual leisure 'needs' of the military and those whose lives had been eroded by the vice of sex for payment.

For those of us working to counter trafficking today it is important to see how the State can be worked with to transform the environment which enables this trade to flourish, whilst retaining Butler's appreciation of the fundamental role of religion and moral revolution. Butler was anxious to see the gains of revival movement across Britain actually deliver hard returns in terms of a change in cities and towns in what churches and their leadership were prepared to endure in the incursions of sex for sale in their parishes and communities. As with CHASTE's experience, the first wave of letters which Butler sent to members of Parliament and Church leaders about the issues of CDA met with very little interest. It was at this stage that Butler went to a wider constituency and appealed not only to parents alongside Ministers of Religion but also to Working Men's Associations as well as developing the Ladies National Association which became a key driver for Butler and the whole movement for Abolition of the Contagious Diseases Act to mobilise public support through a newsletter and a substantial programme of public speaking.

Just as Butler found fellow travellers in the UK police force, who went to Brussels to expose practices of trafficking in minors for sexual exploitation, CHASTE has found itself working in an environment where a few pioneering police officers have developed a response to the outrage of trafficking and are pushing forward police activity to turn what was formerly only a strategy of 'escape' to 'rescue'. This has meant that CHASTE is working in very close relationship with the police in the new United Kingdom Human Trafficking Centre (UKHTC); supporting the government in its creation, and lobbying the government for the next generation of legislation designed to protect and enable victims of trafficking to move towards some level of recovery and rehabilitation after their traumatic and frequently life-threatening experiences.

But the State has been a source of difficulties in other arenas, in the regulation of migration, a context which Butler did not share. Today's white slavery is rainbow coloured and multi national. The women who are its victims are Eastern Europeans brought in from both Accession countries and members of the former USSR, Nigerians, Ugandans, Ghanaians, from India, Pakistan, Thailand, Malaysia, from South America, Brazil and Venezuela, following the transport routes developed through the trafficking of drug, illegal armaments trading, and enabled by a panoply of organised crime fund transfers of billions of dollars – now estimated at over $40 billion dollars globally – with between 1-2 million women and children caught up in the trade.

And today the global movement of urbanisation and the draw of the metropolis, has a vector which sources far beyond the wicked cross channel ferry trip of Butler's time. Nowadays the enslavement triangle resembles a polygon – with journeys from the heart of Africa or from China taking months, tracing inconvenient and elaborate routes to arrive at the destination state, with the onward trading of women and children's lives taking place en route alongside freeloading rapes and indiscriminate intimidation. I have not yet met a woman who has been shackled on her journey, but the rapes, intimidation, beatings, uncertainty for the future, loss of autonomy and privacy which characterised the journeys of those enslaved in the brutal West African slave trade of over two centuries ago are securely in place in this new global scourge. They are the new shackles. Even those who are just flown in on standard flights into Heathrow, Gatwick, Stansted or Glasgow airports, or brought across on the ferry from Northern Ireland via Stranraer or Holyhead whose travel has been less dramatic and gruelling, will end up within hours of their arrival in Britain, in circumstances of brutalisation which it is truly disturbing to consider as part of modern day Britain's provision of leisure, pay-as-you-go sex for men with money to dispense for access to flesh.

A mathematical proposition has now been developed to unpack the movement of people over certain distances and times, which defines migration behaviour by the concept of intervening opportunities. That is the movement of migrants over distance and time is proportional to the number of opportunities in the centre, and inversely proportional to the development of intervening opportunities produced by the economic expansion in the hinterland of larger conurbations. So rural to urban and frontier movements have been increasingly superseded by urban to urban movements and in some forms which we now see migration superseded by circulation within and between large metropolitan centres. These traditional, early transitional, late transitional, advanced and super-advanced stages of migration are with us today, and are present in the movement of women, men and children for trafficked exploitation, in particular sexual exploitation. Migration experts have now accepted that there will be always an element of mystery as to why some people move, the volume of people moving and their trajectory, and this sense of mystery must prevail in the understanding of why some women and children become caught in the abuse of trafficking for sexual exploitation.

Of course, many are subject to the bright lights and better life syndrome, though most of those with whom we have had to do have been lured by deceit: the promise of a job with opportunities for self development; of the intervention of a protector (frequently female) in the realm of the initial deception; the hope of gaining employment in domestic work or in au pair-like assistance with children; the promises of a apparently loving boyfriend delivering the young woman concerned from a patriarchal environment where her autonomy and individuality was not recognised; or the removal of all choice which can occur in the environment of refugee camps or on street living.

The circumstances are multiple, but what seems to be a common factor is the intervention of some third party who promotes the movement, fixes the documentation, makes the travel arrangements and secures reception at the end of the journey for the life of promise to commence. The only difficulty is that at the end of that journey, however swift or convoluted it has been, however communal or independent the circumstances, sea crate or seat-belted independent flight, the woman or child concerned is moved into conditions of servitude and multiple bodily violation and violence which are hardly imaginable, so horrific is their reality. And the stage on which these activities take place are places which pride themselves on new heights of human achievement, in technology, in the arts, in education, in political democracy, the extraordinarily sophisticated western democracies, which yet are the locations where women and children can be bought for £25-40 per half hour session against their will, multiple times a day.

The Challenge to the Churches

I think Butler's question in a conversation engaging these realities would be one that asked us to consider what drives this environment of the commercial acceptability of internationally pimped sex? What is it in place in our culture, in our economic activity, in our legislative practices which make this horror possible? We do not know how many women and children in Britain today are undergoing this appalling abuse of their participation in the divine image of the freedom and beauty of God, of their place as fellow human beings free to choose where to walk, whom to love, what to eat and wear, how to pray. Operation Pentameter released eighty-four women in four months, and over the course of three years CHASTE has worked with over eighty seven women and children who have been trafficked into Britain or into our neighbour, Holland. What is taking place, Butler asks us, that such a market in sex has become acceptable? A market which is disseminated through IT, through telephone booths, cabs, hotel concierges, web pages, mobile phone messaging, porn channels, the back of our local papers, ten Thai beauties at your local massage parlour, Scandinavian (read Ukrainian, Albanian, Latvian) blondes available for adult entertainment (read sexual servicing) of our male readership. Open up the pages of private lineage ads in your local paper and the contours of this market begin to become more apparent. In every city in Britain, in every market town, wherever men gather for leisure and entertainment, this market is open and available, becoming for some men as little worthy of remark as going to the pub on a Friday after work for a wind down and the start of the week-end.

Butler clearly placed the responsibility of the increased availability and acceptability of purchasing prostitution at the door of state legislation and capitulation to the 'needs' of standing armies. Some of the responsibility state-wise in the United Kingdom today is the way in which immigration laws have created the opportunity for networks of internationally organised crime to market opportunities to access the West as alternative embassies and travel agencies. In this way they access labour markets otherwise out of reach of those who wish to travel for improved conditions and remuneration in work. Some of the State responsibilities lie in the way in which we work alongside other late capitalist states of the G8 to continue to dominate and serve our best interests in the way in which the global economy is sliced, by turns insisting on the opening up of free markets and the overwhelming of less industrialised economies by our goods, services and knowledge-rich businesses, or through protection of our own markets and patented knowledge.

Some of the State's responsibility has been the laissez faire manner in which the growth of the sex industry in the UK has been allowed to develop without the intervention of police, politicians, or pastoral warnings of the damage done to those who become engaged in its activities physically, emotionally or relationally. We have failed to teach a citizenship vision of radical equality of men and women, of adult and child in the protection and celebration of our bodily integrity, never to be bought or sold, stolen, beaten, or broken in any way. We do not actively educate for this, or expose the extent of its betrayal in our state schools, in our state subsidised media, in our public conversation, whether in secular or religious form. 'There is without doubt' I hear Butler saying 'State accountability and something to be done in our political house about the disorder in the cellar.'

However I also hear Butler insisting that the ability to reverse the area of degraded inhuman practices which we are currently becoming aware needs to be addressed by other cultural drivers, apart from the state. In her own day Butler was clear that there was a responsibility on the part of the churches to bring a spiritual revival which engaged the totality of our humanity, and our interactions with one another and not simply an enthusiasm in the Spirit. Hers was a practically outworked spirituality which insisted on the full humanity of each individual who could own God as Father, and be nominated a child of God, and therefore was not free to be used as anything other than a sacred exchange. Now where commerce has been allowed free reign to commercialise the body – and we have been watching this process since the purchase of bodies in the earliest slave markets of ancient 'civilisations' – commerce itself needs to be taken in hand, and the culture which surrenders itself to the edicts of commerce rather than those of the edicts of God must be taken in hand by those who have been called to be the ministers of religion, the ministers of grace. This is indeed a challenge to churches whose attention has been driven into self protection and maintenance, or into resisting manifestations of sexuality in outbursts of phobic reaction, in particular apparently any manifestations of same-sex erotic which are frequently mutually consensual but do not conform to the heterosexual patriarchal ordering in which the church has been so clearly rooted since its resolution of hierarchies of gendered, racial and age-set identity in the cauldron of the Graeco-Roman world. It is time for the Churches to draw from the well-springs of their spirituality to understand that the heinous crime in the realm of the sexual is that of non-consensuality, of selling peoples' bodies, of rape, of violence and not of the gender of the consenting beloved. That is why the establishment of 'Not for Sale Sunday' promoted by CHASTE across the churches in May each year near the feast day set aside for Butler by the Anglican Church is to be celebrated.[26] This is an engagement with the soul of the country of which Butler would have been a redoubtable champion. 'Everywhere' Butler said 'we see women in chains' – it is time that the Churches in Britain and across the world took up the challenge to resist this enslavement, restore the victims, protect the survivors and develop ways to see the eradication of this pernicious trade in both its international and local instantiations.

Moreover, although Butler co-operated with one or two courageous police investigators, she did not have any co-ordinated state sponsored police activity such as we are now seeing develop through the police response to trafficking in the work of the UKHTC or in the heirs of Operation Pentameter. These operations are vital, and are starting to send one message to traffickers. The message is serious prison sentences meted out in the courts of law for those who traffic. One Albanian recently received a sentence of twenty-two years. Multiple sentences of between seven and fourteen years have been handed down for the offence of trafficking – let alone the potential sentences for any rape, kidnap, intimidation or grievous bodily harm which might be added to this primary crime.

However essential though this responsive police activity is, and to be commended, Butler insisted that there are cultural and personal issues which need to be addressed in order to eradicate the 'squalid activities of vice'.[27] These drivers of 'iniquity' are more profound and spiritual for Butler than any legislature can finally address. Legislature promotes the conditions for the prospering or the diminishing of the societal permissions for the degradations involved in any pursuit of accessing sex from women and the girl child. This degradation can have many guises, through direct wealth transfer (and in this regard we should look more widely at the danger of abuse through asymmetrical marriage alliances between women in Russia, Thailand, and the Near East with British males), through criminalised opportunities in trafficking, through the accessing of paedophilic sex by males on holiday, or the wider accessing of women in prostitution at home or abroad without any consideration of their safety or life circumstances, or the exploitation of power in grooming into prostitution with all its long term consequences on a young woman's future. In order to change legislation one has to address the wider culture which makes acceptable the fact that women's and children's sex is for sale, to bring to the full light of public attention the outrage of anybody having to sell their sexual intimacy, their internal enfleshed identity to another in half hour pieces of their lives.

This is a critical question. As an organisation CHASTE welcomes both the activities of Pentameter and the formation of UKHTC. However we also want to look at State interventions against patterns of demand – to look at the drivers of this contemporary trade in vice. Butler was unable to explore in detail this area of demand. Butler's generation of women were excluded from the portals of democratic governance or parliamentary representation. But Sweden, one of the first democracies to enfranchise women, has led the way in paying attention to the demand factor in the growth of vice, in the growth of multiple abuse in enforced prostitution. In 1998 Sweden after a period of sustained research passed a ground breaking piece of Abolition legislation and placed the clients of pay-as-you-go sex, and those who procure new labourers into the sexual market place, under the penal attention of the state. Women who are found to be prostituting themselves are offered counselling and alternative opportunities for employment and autonomy. Males who are buying are fined, or for persistent offenders imprisoned.

This is a pioneering and crusading piece of legislation protecting the interests of women and the child – with prostitution being clearly identified in Swedish law as violence against women – one of the foundation stones of the Swedish legal system. From this brave legislation a whole range of activity has taken place including the transformation of personal and social education in schools to explore the ways in which violence takes place between individuals in society. In particular students at High School and University explore how women and children are frequently the recipients of this violence. We are looking to bring the Swedish churches over to pursue an active conversation in this matter, and what they have brought to the table of this pioneering piece of legislation which emerged out of a strong and coherent articulation of women's equality and rights from the women's movement.

Butler did not make the move, even from her position of President of the National Ladies Association, to call on women only to find their mind and voice on what was happening within prostitution and the sex markets of her day. She did call on ministers of religion, parliamentarians and mothers and fathers to take responsibility and cognisance of what was occurring, and protested the humanity and inviolable rights located in the space inhabited by any child of a loving heavenly father – as the arena in which those prostituted should be understood and received. She did take the stigma of being a loose woman, or whore from those prostituted. Because she had worked directly, welcomed into her own home, and laboured to develop safe housing, protection and recovery for those prostituted, she brought young frequently illiterate young women from the place of an alienated and ignored group, into people deserving of protection and attention because they became individuals, radically equal with those sitting in the household pews of the aristocracy and the new bourgeoisie of her day.

Today, when the sense of influence and presence of the church in our society is most definitely in decline, frequently more so within the church than in the corridors of power without, Butler and the modern rainbow slave trade in sex, labour, images and organs pose some unnerving questions.

- What is the vision of sexual and interpersonal relationships which the church has as part of its fundamental calling to express the life and divine love of God in its imaged humanity?
- What is the calling of the church in its post-imperial setting in the United Kingdom to the matter of ethnicity and nationhood? Where does the care and accountability of churches stop? At their parish boundaries, in their gathered churches? Or is the orbit of care extended to wherever those imprisoned, beaten and violated are to be found?
- Butler was exercised about the conditions of those in Indian cantonments brought in to service the British Empire's standing army, and about the violence against women run out in other colonies – from the West Indies to the Near East. How is our work internationally with mission partners, and with the government paying attention to the gendered violence which occurs in countries with whom we are connected through either trade or political bilateral or multilateral agreements?
- Butler opened her own home and then moved onto raising finance to run other places of safety, protection and restitution for those caught in prostitution. In the light of lack of capacity in the state financed protection offered through the Poppy Project and Eaves Housing, how are all our churches responding to the challenge to provide safety?
- In a different world of opportunity for women's voices to be heard and expressed in parliament, are equality of worth, value, inviolability being expressed and lobbied for by women's movements in the churches?

- In our global conversations across churches, where is our attention and time spent? Is it to attend to those most violated, intimidated, imprisoned and broken and how our churches can be made better places of healing and reflecting the divine image of mutual equality, respect, dialogue and becoming?
- What is our conversation about the place of sex and the erotic in the ways in which human beings relate to one another, become and enjoy humanity in all its fullness? What is the voice of the church on the provision of safe places for children to be raised – and places of freedom for women to live without fear with men in every sphere of life, at every time of the turning globe; enabled to live without fear of abuse, violence, rape, kidnap, beatings, entrapment, abortion?
- How do we identify the cultural levers of our time, become players in that cultural leverage? What percentage of our lives as individuals and those in community, in our work, church, political affiliations, and leisure activities, do we give to creating a world in which people are valued regardless of ethnicity, age, gender, as being part of our imaging of Divine love and freedom? How does this work with media, press, educational material, liturgical life, synodical life, household activities, in our bedrooms, love-making, child-raising, neighbourhood-nourishing lives? How do we in our church, dioceses, academy and workplace start making these statements and activities which can gather the affiliation and commitment of others?
- Josephine Butler campaigned for the abolition of the Contagious Diseases Act. Nothing less would do. She had done the sums and that was the answer. What is our response to the commercialisation of sex today, and the rainbow sex trade? What has that to say about our contemporary world? And what are we going to DO in response to it?

Endnotes

[1] Josephine Butler, 'A letter to the Mothers of England: Commended also to the Attention of Fathers, Ministers of Religion and Legislators'. April 1881, in *Josephine Butler and the Prostitution Campaigns: Diseases of the Body Politic,* ed. Jane Jordan and Ingrid Sharp, 5 vols (London: Routledge, 2003), IV, pp. 80-94, p. 87.

[2] C. Beddoe, C. *Missing Out: A Study of Child Trafficking in the North-West, North-East and West Midlands* (London: ECPAT UK, 2007).

[3] *Protocol to Prevent, Suppress and Punish Trafficking in Persons, especially Women and Children, Supplementing the United Nations Convention against Transnational Organised Crime* (Geneva: United Nations, 2000), Article 3.

[4] *The UK Action Plan on Tackling Human Trafficking* (London: Home Office, 2003).

[5] 'Letter from Josephine E. Butler to Florence Booth, 26 March 1885', in Jordan and Sharp, *Josephine Butler and the Prostitution Campaigns,* IV, pp. 108-110.

[6] 'Ladies' National Association Circular by Josephine Butler, dated 17th August 1885 (From office of the Federation, Neuchatel, Switzerland)', Jordan and Sharp, *Josephine Butler and the Prostitution Campaigns,* IV, pp. 274-76, p. 276.

[7] H. Kinnell, EUROPAP UK press statement on Violence against Sex Workers (EUROPAP, Department of Epidemiology and Public Health, Imperial College, School of Medicine: London, 2000).

[8] Women's Library Josephine Butler Collection, Josephine E. Butler to Mia [Butler], 1 January 1896 03/24 (II).

[9] 'The Principles of the Abolitionists', Jordan and Sharp, *Josephine Butler and the Prostitution Campaigns*, III, pp. 112-120, p. 116..

[10] 'The Queen's Daughters in India', in Jordan and Sharp, *Josephine Butler and the Prostitution Campaigns*, V, pp. 244-326.

[11] 'Speech Delivered by Mrs Josephine E. Butler to a Vigilance Committee,' in Jordan and Sharp, *Josephine Butler and the Prostitution Campaigns*, III, pp. 123-28.

[12] 'Speech Delivered by Mrs Josephine E. Butler at the Annual Meeting of the Vigilance Association, 15 October, 1874' in Jordan and Sharp, *Josephine Butler and the Prostitution Campaigns*, III, pp. 129-39, p. 133.

[13] Ibid, p. 135.

[14] Ibid, p. 137.

[15] 'The Deposition on Oath of Josephine E Butler, 8th November 1880, made before Mr T Stamford Raffles, Stipendiary Magistrate of the City of Liverpool', in Jordan and Sharp, *Josephine Butler and the Prostitution Campaigns*, IV, pp. 58-79, p. 65.

[16] Ibid, p.66.

[17] Ibid, pp. 70-77.

[18] 'The Modern Slave Trade', in *The* Shield, 1 May, 1880' in Jordan and Sharp, *Josephine Butler and the Prostitution Campaigns,* IV, pp. 20-25.

[19] Ibid, p. 21.

[20] Cathy Zimmerman, M. H., Kate Yun, Brenda Roche, Linda Morrison, Charlotte Watts, *Stolen Smiles: a Summary Report on the Physical and Psychological Health Consequences of Women and Adolescents Trafficked in Europe* (London: London School of Hygiene and Tropical Medicine, 2006).

[21] See further information at our website, www.chaste.org.uk.

[22] 'The Modern Slave Trade' in Jordan and Sharp, *Josephine Butler and the Prostitution Campaigns*, IV, p. 23.

[23] Ibid.

[24] 'Operation Pentameter: an Association of Chief Police Officers' Initiative across 52 Constabularies in Britain 2006'. Accessed at www.ukhtc.org on 24 April, 2007.

[25] The Council of Europe Convention on Action against Trafficking of Human Beings was signed by the UK Government in March 2007.

[26] Established in May 20th 2007, see www.notforsalesunday.org for more information.

[27] 'Ladies National Association Circular 17th August 1885 - from the office of the Federation, Neuchatel Switzerland', Jordan and Sharp, *Josephine Butler and the Prostitution Campaigns*, IV, pp. 274-76, p. 275.

A Chronology of Josephine Butler and Selected Writings

1828   13 April: Josephine Grey born at Milfield, Northumberland, seventh child of John and Hannah (Annett) Grey.

1833   Family move to Dilston, where John Grey becomes overseer of Greenwich Hospital estates.

1846-7   Josephine Grey undergoes religious crisis.

1852   8 January: Marries Revd George Butler, public examiner of Oxford University. George Grey born in November.

1853   Reads Elizabeth Gaskell's novel, *Ruth*, about the redemption of a 'fallen' woman.

1854   Second child born, Arthur Stanley.

1856   Third child born, Charles Augustine Vaughan. About this time the Butlers take a convicted infanticide into their household.

1857   Josephine Butler's ill health forces a move from Oxford. George Butler appointed Vice-Principal of Cheltenham College.

1859   Fourth child born, Evangeline Mary.

1864   20 August: Eva falls to her death from the bannisters.

       Contagious Diseases (not concerned with animals) Act passed, involving forcible registration and regular internal examination of women deemed to be common prostitutes and living within a radius of eleven army camps and naval ports. Those found to be infected with VD to be detained in government certified hospitals.

1865   George Butler appointed Headmaster of Liverpool College. Josephine falls ill and winters in Italy. First reference to prostitutes in 'Private Thoughts Diary'.

1866   Felicia Skene publishes, *Hidden Depths: the Story of a Cruel Wrong*, which is critical of penitentiary approach to rescue work.

       Butlers move to Liverpool. Josephine Butler visits oakum picking sheds at Brownlow Hill Workhouse, where prostitutes and unmarried mothers work.

November: Butlers take dying Mary (Marion) into their home.

6 June: Josephine Butler's name one of 1,500 to petition Parliament for women's suffrage.

Second Contagious Diseases Act passes, which increases the frequency of examination, and confirms the powers of magistrates to order examination regardless of woman's claims to reputation, with a penalty of imprisonment and hard labour for those who resist. Plain clothes police employed to seek out women for examination. Chatham and Windsor added to towns affected.

1867 Butler's House of Rest for sick and indigent prostitutes founded, as well as her Industrial Home, offering work to the destitute.

Butler elected first President of North of England Council for Promoting the Higher Education of Women. University Extension Scheme is inaugurated.

1868 22 January: death of John Grey.

Butler becomes Secretary of the Married Women's Property Committee. Butler's first publication, *The Education and Employment of Women*. Butler presents Memorial to Cambridge University seeking access for women to higher education examinations.

1869 Butler edits *Woman's Work and Woman's Culture*, a series of essays calling for access to all forms of education and employment for women. She also publishes a well-received biography of her father, *Memoir of John Grey of Dilston*.

Third Contagious Diseases Act is passed, extending 1866 Act to cover eighteen towns and increasing the radius from five to ten miles.

Detention period extended to nine months.

September: Josephine Butler asked by Elizabeth Wolstoneholme to lead opposition to the Contagious Diseases Acts. She waits three months before consulting her husband. Ladies' National Association for the Repeal of the Contagious Diseases Acts founded (LNA), with Butler at its head.

1870 March: LNA periodical, *The Shield* begins publication. Butler tours northern industrial towns. April: Butler tours Kent garrison towns.

LNA helps to defeat regulationist Sir Henry Storks in Colchester bye-election. *The Moral Reclaimability of Prostitutes* published.

1871 *The Constitution Violated*. Butler provides a constitutional justification for opposition to the Acts on the grounds of their assault on civil liberties. In *Sursum Corda* Butler addresses her own movement in more religious terms. 28 March: Butler gives evidence to Royal Commission on the working of the Acts.

1872 George Butler attempts to read paper opposing Contagious Diseases Acts to Church Congress at Nottingham but is shouted down.

1 March: Bruce Bill 'for the Prevention of Contagious Diseases and for the better protection of women' to repeal Acts. It seeks to raise age of consent to fourteen but also to extend the range of the Acts to whole of British Isles. It is withdrawn for lack of support on 15 July but causes divisions in the repeal movement.

1873 1,500 Anglican clergy sign petition for repeal of the Acts, Methodist Conference added its support the previous year, as did the General Assembly of the Free Church of Scotland.

1874 Sent to Europe to improve her health, Josephine Butler tours brothels and lock hospitals of Continental cities, and examines the workings of state regulated prostitution. She visits the St Lazare prison in Paris.

This tour lays the foundation for the international movement. James Stansfeld M. P. joins the campaign for repeal.

1875 19 March: inaugural meeting of the British, Continental and General Federation in Liverpool. 30 March: body of Mrs Jane Percy found drowned after she had protested against the accusation by the special police that she was a prostitute. She had written to the *Daily Telegraph* on 12 March. The Butlers take care of her young daughter. Josephine Butler has a breakdown. She publishes a pamphlet setting out her Continental experiences, *The Voice of One Crying in the Wilderness*, which is immediately translated into several European languages but not in English until 1913.

1876 *The Hour Before the Dawn: An Appeal to Men*. Butler attacks the double standard in sexual relations.

1878 *Catherine of Siena: A Biography*.

1880 Josephine Butler assists in the prosecution of the Belgian Chief of Police for the kidnapping and trafficking of young English girls into prostitution.

1882　George Butler retires from Liverpool College and is appointed by Gladstone to a canonry at Winchester, where Josephine becomes friends with Mary Sumner, founder of the Mothers' Union.

5 May: Josephine Butler gives evidence to a new select committee on the operation of the Acts.

1883　20 April: Repeal of the Second Contagious Diseases Acts.

Parliamentary opposition led by James Stansfeld. Butler leads a two day prayer meeting in support in the LNA London headquarters in Bishopsgate. Others are held all over Britain. Josephine Butler founds a new House of Rest in Canon Street, Winchester.

1885　Butler becomes involved in W. T. Stead's attempt to reveal trafficking in children by offering Rebecca Jarrett, a Salvation Army convert and ex-procuress, to help 'buy' a girl to take abroad. Stead publishes results as 'The Maiden Tribute of Modern Babylon' in *Pall Mall Gazette*, week beginning 6 July. The resulting furore leads to the passing of The Criminal Law Amendment Act in July, which raised the age of consent to sixteen years. Stead and Jarrett are tried for abduction, and convicted on 7 November.

1890　14 March: Death of George Butler. Josephine Butler visits Geneva and Neuchâtel, addressing a number of issues and causes pertaining to women and children.

1892　*Recollections of George Butler* also contains material about Josephine's spiritual experiences.

1893-94　Butler visits Rome to press for abolition of compulsory regulation. Although she catches malaria and fails to meet Leo XIII, her visit produces his public support in 1895.

1894　*The Lady of Shumen*, a series of Bible studies, taking a feminist approach.

1895　George Frederick Watts paints Butler's portrait for his series on people who had made the century.

1896　*Reminiscences of a Great Crusade*. Butler in Geneva to support (unsuccessful) referendum for abolition of regulation of prostitution.

1897 *Truth Before Everything* written to protest against the support of titled women for the regulation of prostitution in India. Butler resigns from 'World Superintendency' of World's Women's Christian Temperance Union, in a break with the 'social purity' movement as too punitive. *Prophets and Prophetesses* calls for the witness of women as well as men to address great social wrong and show the mind of God.

1900 *Native Races and the War*. Unlike most liberals, Butler supports the Boer War on the grounds that the Boers treated the Africans like slaves.

1906 30 December: after much pain from emphysema, an ulcerous stomach and cancer, Butler dies peacefully in her sleep at Wooler in Northumberland. She is buried at Kirknewton.

Bibliography: Works Cited
Works by Josephine Butler

'Address at Croydon, July 3, 1871' (London: Office of the National Association, 1871).

'An Appeal to the People of England on the Recognition and Superintendence of Prostitution by Governments' (Nottingham: Banks, 1870).

Catherine of Siena: A Biography (London: Dyer Brothers, 1878).

The Constitution Violated (Edinburgh: Edmonston and Douglas, 1871).

'The Dark Side of English Life. Illustrated by a Series of True Stories', *Methodist Protest*, Jan-May 1877.

The Hour Before the Dawn: An Appeal to Men (London: Trubner and Co., 1876).

Josephine Butler and others, *Legislative Restrictions on the Industry of Women* (London: Matthews, 1872).

Memoir of John Grey of Dilston (Edinburgh: Edmonston and Douglas, 1869).

The Moral Reclaimability of Prostitutes (London: Ladies National Association, 1870).

Our Faith Tested by the Irish Question (London: Fisher Unwin, 1887).

Personal Reminiscences of a Great Crusade (London: Horace Marshall, 1896) .

Prophets and Prophetesses: Some Thoughts for the Present Times (Newcastle-on-Tyne: Mawson, Swan and Morgan, 1898).

Recollections of George Butler (Bristol: J. W. Arrowsmith, 1892).

Social Purity: an Address (London: Morgan and Scott, 1879).

Sursum Corda (Liverpool: T. Brackell, 1871).

Truth Before Everything (Liverpool: Pewtree and Co., 1897).

Woman's Work and Woman's Culture (ed.) (London: Macmillan, 1869).

Other Works Cited

Adams, C. and M. Fortune (eds). *Violence against Women and Children. A Christian Theological Source Book* (New York: Continuum, 1995).

Ahmed, S. *The Cultural Politics of Emotion* (Edinburgh: Edinburgh University Press, 2004).

Anderson, A. *Tainted Souls and Painted Faces: The Rhetoric of Fallenness in Victorian Culture* (Cornell UP: Ithaca and London, 1993).

Anon. *The New Godiva: A Dialogue* (London: Fisher Unwin, 1885).

Aristotle, *The Metaphysics*. H. Lawson-Tancred (ed.) (Harmondsworth: Penguin, 1998).

Atwell, R. *Celebrating the Saints* (London: Canterbury Press, 1998).

Bales, K. *Understanding Global Slavery* (Berkeley CA, University of California Press, 2006).

Banton, M. *The Coloured Quarter* (London: Jonathan Cape, 1955).

Barry, K. *The Prostitution of Sexuality* (New York: New York University Press, 1995).

Bauman, Z. *Identity* (Cambridge: Polity Press 2004).

Believing in the Church: The Corporate Nature of Faith. The Doctrine Commission of the Church of England (London: SPCK, 1981).

Bell, D. *Liberation Theology After the End of History: The Refusal to Cease Suffering* (London and New York: Routledge, 2001).

Bell, E. Moberly. *Josephine Butler: Flame of Fire* (London: Constable 1962).

Bindel, J. and Kelly, L. *A Critical Examination of Response to Prostitution in Four Countries: Victoria, Australia; Ireland; the Netherlands; and Sweden*. (London: Child and Woman Abuse Studies Unit, London Metropolitan University London, 2003).

Bond Stockton, *K. God Between their Lips* (Stanford: Stanford University Press, 1994).

Boston, R. 'Americans United for Separation of Church and State', *The Guardian*, 11 March 2006..

Boyd, N. *Three Victorian Women who Changed their World* (London: Macmillan, 1982).

Brueggemann, W. *The Prophetic Imagination*, second edition (Minneapolis: Fortress Press, 2001).

Burridge, K. *New Heaven New Earth* (Oxford: Blackwell, 1969).

Butler, A. *Portrait of Josephine Butler* (London: Faber & Faber, 1954).

Byatt, A. *Passions of the Mind: Selected Writings* (London: Chatto & Windus 1992).

Carter, J. *Life and Works of Rev. T. T. Carter* (London: Longman, Green and Co., 1911)

-- *Essays on Penitentiaries by John Armstrong* (London: John Henry and James Parker, 1857).

Carter, T. *A Memoir of John Armstrong* (Oxford and London: John Henry and James Parker, 1857).

Colliers' Cyclopedia of Common and Social Information (London: P. F. Collier, 1882).

Daggers, J. and D. Neal (eds) *Sex, Gender and Religion: Josephine Butler Revisited* (New York: Peter Lang, 2006).

Davies, S. *Unbridled Spirits: Women of the English Revolution, 1640 1660* (London: Virago, 1999).

Dearmer, P. (ed.). *The English Hymnal* (London, Oxford University Press, 1906).

Dench, G. *The Maltese in London: a Study in the Erosion of Ethnic Consciousness* (London: Institute of Community Studies, 1975).

Downes, D. *The Delinquent Solution* (London: Routledge and Kegan Paul, 1966).

Easson, A. *Elizabeth Gaskell* (London: Routledge, 1979).

Eastman, M. and S. Latham (eds). *Urban Church: A Practitioner's Resource Book* (London: SPCK, 2004).

Ehrenreich, B. and A. Hochschild (eds). *Global Woman: Nannies, Maids and Sex Workers in the New Economy* (Cambridge: Granta, 2003).

Fishman, W. *East End 1888* (London: Duckworth, 1998).

Flegg, C. *Gathered Under Apostles: A Study of the Catholic Apostolic Church* (Oxford: Clarendon, 1992).

Flint, K. *Elizabeth Gaskell* (Plymouth: Northcott House, 1995).

Forman, C. *Spitalfields: a Battle for Land* (London: Hilary Shipman, 1989).

Forster, M. *Significant Sisters* (London: Secker and Warburg, 1984).

Fulford, T. (ed.) *Romanticism and Millenarianism* (New York and Basingstoke: Palgrave, 2002).

Gateley, E. 'A good Catholic girl', *The Tablet*, 3 July 1993, pp. 851-52.

Gitay, Y. (ed.) *Prophecy and Prophets* (Atlanta: Society of Biblical Literature, Scholars Press, 1997).

Goldsmith, S. *Unbuilding Jerusalem : Apocalypse and Romantic Representation* (Ithaca: Cornell University Press, 1993).

Gore, C. *The Incarnation of the Son of God* (London: John Murray 1891).

Grosz, E. *Sexual Subversions: Three French Feminists* (London and Sydney: Allen and Unwin, 1989).

Gutiérrez, S. *A Theology of Liberation: History, Politics and Salvation*, new edition, C. Rowlands (intro.) (London: SCM, 2001).

Hampson, D. (ed.) *Swallowing a Fishbone?* (London: SPCK, 1996).

Harries, R. 'Religion and Science – Old Enemies or New Friends', *in Modern Believing* 47, 1, January, 2006), pp. 22-27.

Harrison, J.F.C., *The Second Coming: Popular Millenarianism 1780-1850* (London: Routledge, 1979).

Hays, E. *Morning Star: A Biography of Lucy Stone* (New York: Octagon, 1978).

The Health Risks and Consequences of Trafficking in Women and Adolescents: Findings from a European Study (London: London School of Hygiene and Tropical Medicine, 2003).

Hewitt, C. *The Police and the Prostitute*, Alison Neilans Memorial Lecture (London: 1951).

Hollingshead, J. *Ragged London in 1861* (London: Smith and Elder, 1861)

Hollis, P. *Women in Public: A Woman's Movement 1850-1900* (London: Allen & Unwin, 1979).

Hørigård, C. and L. Fristad, *Backstreets: Prostitution, Money and Love,* K. Hanson, N. Sipe, and B. Wilson (eds) (University Park, Pa. : Pennsylvania State University Press, 1992).

Indices of Deprivation 2000. (London: DETR, September 2000).

James, S. 'Hookers in the House of the Lord', in J. Holland (ed), *Feminist Action* (London: Battleaxe Books, 1983), pp. 180-203.

Jeffreys, S. *The Idea of Prostitution* (Melbourne: Spinifex, 1997).

-- 'Challenging the Adult/Child distinction in theory and practice on prostitution'. *International Feminist Journal of Politics*. (November 2000). Online at http://mc2.vic. net.au/home/catwaust/web/myfiles/adultchild.htm.

Johnson, G. and L. Johnson (eds.). *Josephine E. Butler: An Autobiographical Memoir* (Bristol: J. W. Arrowsmith, 1909).

Jordan, J. *Josephine Butler* (London: John Murray, 2001).

--and I. Sharp (eds.). *Josephine Butler and the Prostitution Campaigns: Diseases of the Body Politic*, 5 vols. (London: Routledge, 2003).

Keane, F. *All of These People* (London: HarperCollins, 2005).

Knight, M. and E. Mason, *Nineteenth-Century Religion and Literature: An Introduction* (Oxford: Oxford University Press, 2006).

Kroeger, C. and J. Beck (eds). *Women, Abuse and the Bible. How Scripture can be Used to Hurt and to Heal* (Grand Rapids MC: Baker, 1999).

Lee, M. 'The globalisation of sexual slavery'. *San Francisco Bay Guardian*, 5 March 2001.

Leech, K. 'Human Casualties in a Crisis District', *East London Papers* 11, 1968, pp. 3-19.

-- *Pastoral Care and the Drug Scene* (London: SPCK, 1970).

Lewis, V. *Satan's Mistress : the Extraordinary Story of the 18th Century Fanatic Joanna Southcott and her Lifelong Battle with the Devil* (Shepperton: Nauticalia, 1997).

Loades, A. *Feminist Theology: Voices from the Past* (Cambridge: Polity Press, 2001).

Maitland, S. and W. Mulford *Virtuous Magic Women Saints and their Meanings* (London: Mowbray, 1998) .

Marcus, L. *Auto/biographical discourses: Criticism, theory, practice* (Manchester University Press, Manchester and New York, 1994).

McTernan, O. *Violence in God's Name* (London: Darton, Longman & Todd, 2003).

Martin, B. 'Whose soul is it anyway? Domestic tyranny and the suffocated soul' in R. Fenn and D. Capps (eds) *On Losing the Soul. Essays in the Social Psychology of Religion* (New York: State University of New York Press, 1994), pp. 69-96.

Mathers, H. 'The Evangelical Spirituality of a Victorian Feminist: Josephine Butler 1828-1906', *Journal of Ecclesiastical History*, 52, no. 2 (April, 2001), pp. 282-312.

Maze Marigold Project Research February 1998-August 1999 (London: YWCA, 1999).

Milbank, A. 'Josephine Butler: Christianity, Feminism and Social Action', in Obelkevich, O., L. Roper and R. Samuels (eds.), *Disciplines of Faith: Studies in Religion, Politics and Patriarchy* (London: Routledge and Kegan Paul, 1987), pp.147-59.

-- *Dante and the Victorians* (Manchester: Manchester University Press, 1998).

Michie, E. *Outside the Pale* (Ithaca and London: Cornell University Press, 1993).

Nagle, J. (ed.), *Whores and Other Feminists* (London: Routledge, 1997).

Newman, J. *Essay in Aid of a Grammar of Assent*, I. Ker (ed.) (Oxford: Clarendon Press 1985).

-- *Sermons, chiefly on the theory of religious belief, preached before the University of Oxford* (London: Rivington, 1844).

Nolland, L. *Josephine Butler: Victorian Feminist Christian, Studies in Evangelical History and Thought* (Carlisle: Paternoster, 2004).

Nord, D. *Walking the Victorian Streets: Women, Representation and the City* (Ithaca and London: Cornell University Press, 1995).

Obelkevich, O., L. Roper and R. Samuels (eds.). *Disciplines of Faith: Religion, Politics and Patriarchy* (London: Routledge and Kegan Paul, 1987).

O'Neill, M. *Prostitution and Feminism: Towards a Politics of Feeling* (Cambridge: Polity Press, 2001).

-- O'Neill, M. `Prostitute Women Now`, in Scambler, G. and A. Scambler (eds) *Rethinking Prostitution Purchasing Sex in the 1990's* (London: Routledge, 1997).

Paley, M. *Apocalypse and Millennium in English Romantic Poetry* (Oxford : Clarendon Press, 1999).

Pascal, B. *Pensées*, Louis Lafuma (ed.) (Paris: Editions du Seuil, 1962).

Petrie, J. *A Singular Iniquity: The Campaigns of Josephine Butler* (London: Macmillan, 1971).

Phetersen, G. *The Whore Stigma : Female Dishonour and Male Unworthiness. Report sponsored by the Dutch Ministry of Social Affairs and Employment* (The Hague: Emancipation Policy Co-ordination, 1986).

Phoenix, J. *Making Sense of Prostitution* (London: Macmillan, 1999).

Ramsey, E. 'Prostitution in the Commercial Road/Cable Street area'. ms. April, 1958.

-- 'The lust that lies in wait', *News of the World,* 12 June 1960.

Reardon, B. *Religious Thought in the Victorian Age* (Newton-le-Willows: Longman, 1980).

Report from the Royal Commission on the Administration and Operation of the Contagious Diseases Acts 1866-69 (1871), PP, 1871 (C.408-I), XIX.

Rich, A. 'Notes on Honour', in *On Lies, Secrets and Silences* (London: Virago, 1980)

Rickards, E. *Felicia Skene of Oxford: A Memoir* (London: John Murray, 1902).

Robson, A. and J. Robson (eds). *Sexual Equality. Writings by John Stuart Mill, Harriet Taylor Mill and Helen Taylor* (Toronto: University of Toronto Press, 1994).

Rolph, C. (ed). *Women of the Streets: a Sociological Study of the Common Prostitute* (London: British Social Biology Council / Secker and Warburg, 1955).

Sanders, T. *Sex Work A Risky Business* (Collumpton Devon: Willan Publishing, 2005).

Schlesinger, A. 'Forgetting Reinhold Niebuhr', *The New York Times*, September 18, 2005.

Segundo, J. *The Liberation of Theology*, John Drury (trans.) (London: Gill and Macmillan, 1977).

Shaeffer, E. *Kubla Khan and the Fall of Jerusalem: The Mythological School in Biblical Criticism and Secular Literature* (Cambridge: Cambridge University Press, 1975).

Skene, F. *Hidden Depths: A Story of a Cruel Wrong*. Shepherd Allen, W. (intro.) (London: Hodder and Stoughton, 1886).

--*The Ministry of Consolation: A Guide for Confession for the Use of Members of the Church of England* (London, 1854).

--*Penitentiaries and Reformatories* (1865) (Whitefish, Montana: Kessinger Publishers, 2004).

[Skidmore, P. (ed.)] *Report of the Working Party on Prostitution and Commercial Sex Work in E1* (London: Providence Row Charity and Toynbee Hall, 2003).

Smith, S. and J. Watson (eds.). *Women, Autobiography, Theory: A Reader* (Madison, WN and London: University of Wisconsin Press, 1998).

Sokoloff, B. *Edith and Stepney: the life of Edith Ramsey* (London: Stepney Books, 1987).

Spender, D. (ed.). *Feminist Theorists* (London: Women's Press, 1983).

Stanley, Liz, *The auto/biographical I: the Theory and Practice of Feminist Auto/biography* (Manchester and New York: Manchester University Press, 1992).

Stanton, E. Cady. *Eighty Years and More. Reminiscences 1815-1897* (Boston: Northwestern University Press [1898] 1993).

Starkey, P. 'Saints, Virgins and Family Members: Exemplary Biographies? Josephine Butler as Biographer', in J. Daggers and D. Neal (eds), *Sex, Gender and Religion: Josephine Butler Revisited* (New York: Peter Lang, 2006), pp. c. 149.

Stoddart, H. *Rings of Desire: Circus History and Representation* (Manchester and New York: Manchester University Press, 2000).

Summers, A. *Female Lives, Moral States* (Newbury: Threshold Press, 2000).

Szura, J. OSA, and D. Genska, OFM. 'Ministry with Persons in Female Heterosexual Prostitution with Emphasis on Ministry Education'. *New Theology Review* 4, 2, pp. 105-07.

Walkowitz, J. *Prostitution and Victorian Society: Women, Class and the State* (1980) (Cambridge University Press, 1994).

-- *City of Dreadful Night: Narratives of Sexual Danger in Late-Victorian London* (London: Virago, 1992).

Ward, G. *Cities of God* (London, Routledge 2000).

Warnock, M. 'Imagination – Aesthetic and Religious', *Theology*, LXXX, no. 111, (November 1980), pp. 403-09.

Weems, R. *Marriage, Sex and Violence in the Hebrew Prophets* (Minneapolis: Fortress, 1995).

Weil, S. *Waiting on God* (London: Collins, 1973).

Wheeler, M. *Death and the Future Life in Victorian Literature and Theology* (Cambridge: Cambridge University Press, 1990).

--*Heaven, Hell and the Victorians* (Cambridge: Cambridge University Press, 1994).

Williamson, J. *Father Joe* (London: Hodder and Stoughton, 1962).

--*Josephine Butler-The Forgotten Saint* (Leighton Buzzard: The Faith Press, 1977).

Wollstonecraft, M. *Political Writings*. J. Todd (ed.) (Oxford: Oxford University Press, 1994).

Wright, M. 'The Dialectics of Still Life: Murder, Women, and Maquiladoras', in Jean Comaroff and John L Comaroff (eds). *Millennial Capitalism and the Culture of Neoliberalism* (Durham, NC, Duke University Press, 2001), pp. 125-46.

Yeo, E. 'Protestant Feminists and Catholic Saints in Victorian Britain', in Yeo, E. (ed.), *Radical Femininity: Women's Self-Representation in the Public Sphere* (Manchester University Press, 1988).

Zindars-Swartz, P. and S. Zindars-Swartz. 'Apocalypticism in Modern Western Europe', in *The Continuum History of Apocalypticism*, B. McGinn, J. Collins and S. Stein (eds) (New York and London: Continuum, 2003).

Afterword

Claire Dawson

*C*laire Dawson managed the Edge Project in Derby throughout her ordination training, offering support to children and young people who have been sexually abused and exploited through prostitution. This extract is from her unpublished M.A. dissertation, 'Theological Perspectives on Child Prostitution' (University of Nottingham, 2004).

One day Emma came to the project with Elisha, her two week old baby daughter. Emma sat on the settee and cradled Elisha and gazed into her eyes. I have never seen so much love expressed between a mother and her daughter. I knew Emma's life was never going to be the same again. Her life had been redeemed in and through the birth of her daughter Elisha. Emma's life would no longer be driven by; which man should she sleep with tonight, or how was she going to get enough money to fund her mother's drug habit? There was someone now in her life who was utterly dependant upon her and she was not going to let her down. For once, in Emma's life, something miraculous had occurred, something very good indeed, something that would stay with her for the rest of her life.

I have now finished my work at the Edge Project and am waiting, preparing to be ordained. When I write about the young people I have a deep urge to go back to them and baptise all their babies. To seal their lives with the sign of the cross and to say, your lives have been redeemed, you are no longer slaves to sin and death and all that is evil in the world. You are children of God, children of the living God. See, look, you have passed from darkness to light, nothing can harm you now.

'They shall be mine, says the Lord of Hosts, my special possession [...] and I shall spare them as parents spare their children' (Malachi 3.17).